Also by Lester Thurow

D1188503

FORTUNE
FAVORS
THE BOLD

LESTER THUROW

FORTUNE
FAVORS
THE BOLD

WHAT WE MUST DO TO BUILD A NEW
AND LASTING GLOBAL PROSPERITY

HarperBusiness
An Imprint of HarperCollins*Publishers*

FIRST EDITION

Designed by Nicola Ferguson

Library of Congress Cataloging-in-Publication Data

Thurow, Lester C.
    Fortune favors the bold : what we must do to build a new and lasting global prosperity / Lester C. Thurow.— 1st ed.
      p. cm.
    Includes index.
    ISBN 0-06-052365-4
    1. International economic relations. 2. Globalization. I. Title.

HF359.T48 2003
337—dc21

2003051146

03 04 05 06 07   10 9 8 7 6 5 4 3 2 1

Acknowledgment

would like to thank a good team of MIT student research assistants who came from around the world. They are a tribute to the soft power of American Universities.

Ming-Hsin (Minson) Lu, Kritapas Seripassorn, Aylin Sasa,
Sarika Singh, Kathrym Auw, Jose Pacheco,
Sonia Monarrez, Basil Enwegbara, Jannette Papastaikoudi

Climb High, Climb Far,
Your Aim The Sky,
Your Goal The Star

Williams College Stone Gate

Our Future Is To Be Found
Not In The Stars
But In Understanding The Path
That We Trod

Contents

{ 1 }

A GLOBAL ECONOMIC TOWER OF BABEL

Globalization is much like the biblical Tower of Babel. The construction of a global economy has begun. Some are for it! Some are against it. Neither group knows exactly what "it" is.

This economic Tower of Babel is being built without a set of construction plans. The necessary architectural drawings aren't even in the process of being drafted. Governments aren't thinking about the appropriate designs, since the tower is being privately built. National governments would, in fact, rather not think about globalization because it diminishes their role and their powers to control economic events. The actual builders, private firms that are moving their economic activities around the world, don't think about the design and construction of the global economy since each is small relative to what is being built. For those who are true believers in the efficiency of private markets, there is no need to think about the institutions and rules of globalization. Whatever is necessary will simply evolve in the marketplace without private thought or government action. Markets will automatically set the necessary construction standards!

As in the biblical Tower of Babel those involved in constructing the global economy are speaking many different languages. Globalization means many different things to many different people. Arguments for and against it are often self-contradictory. Perhaps these different languages and the associated disputes will stop a global economy from being built—just as they stopped the biblical tower design to go to heaven from being built. If so, is that a good thing or a bad thing? Have we prevented ourselves from getting to an economic heaven? Or have we prevented ourselves from over-reaching, trying to play God, and ending up in what will surely be an economic hell?

Anxieties are high. The violent antiglobalization demonstrations that have occurred at both public (WTO, IMF, World Bank, Seattle, Goteborg, Bologna) and private (Davos) global meetings in the last few years have delivered that message. Although the number of actual demonstrators is few, I suspect that if every newspaper in the world tomorrow were to have the headline "Globalization Ends," far more than half of humanity would feel relieved. In global public opinion surveys less than 20 percent of the population thinks the world is doing well.[1]

What do the protestors dislike? What would they like to see happen? Beneath the noise and babble what is their real message? What are they trying to tell us about globalization? They predict disaster! But which of the predicted disasters are possible and which are impossible? For those that are possible, what are the real causes?

Real disasters are almost never caused by a single factor alone. Investigators start with a jumble of possible causes that have to be sorted out to find the sequence of individual causes that together produced a particular disaster. The same procedure has to be followed when trying to understand the predictions of disaster by those who are against globalization. The nature of the predicted disasters and their potential causes are all jumbled together. They have to be sorted out.

In the conflicting babble generated by the construction of our global economic tower, the problem is to distinguish noise from information—truth from fiction. The investigator begins by trying to separate out what is true and false in the different arguments. Only when truth has been separated from fiction is it possible to add up the pluses and the minuses to determine whether we should accept or reject globalization.

But there is a third choice. The third choice is to build a global economy that eliminates some of the minuses that have been found. Even if the initial summation indicates the benefits far exceed the minuses, the minuses can be further reduced. The global economy will partially evolve in response to foreseen and unforeseen uncontrollable forces, but in the end it is a human, not geological, construction and can be built to different specifications. Globalization can be shaped.

But to do so it is necessary to understand the dynamics of globalization so the forces of globalization can be used to change the course of globalization. There are actions to be taken that can enhance the positive effects of globalization and minimize its negative effects. These possibilities are outlined and discussed near the end of the book, since an in-depth understanding of the full range of the forces of globalization is necessary to evaluate the various possibilities. What seem like disconnected problems are often connected problems.

In separating the facts from the fiction in all the babble about globalization, it is important to understand that the economic Tower of Babel looks different depending upon where you stand. The rich and successful at the top of the tower see something quite different than do the poor just starting to climb the stairs at the bottom. Those standing far away, outside of the global economy, see a tower with very different contours than what are seen by those working inside the tower. Not surprisingly, the economically, militarily, and politically large and powerful fear the construction of the tower much less than do those who are small and weak.

It is not that one of these perspectives is right and the others are wrong. Each focuses on different elements of the tower. All reflect some aspects of the truth. No one can have all these perspectives simultaneously because no one can see the entire tower or the entire truth. That is why those who are rich and successful, large and powerful, and inside the building of the tower have to listen to the views of those who are poor, unsuccessful, small, powerless, and outside of the global economy. The first group cannot see what the second group sees, but the first group can listen to what the second group has to say.

This warning applies to no one more than Americans—the richest, most successful, largest, and most powerful players and the ultimate insiders in the construction of the global economy. In terms of military and economic power no nation has ever loomed larger in human history. Imperial Rome dominated a large region around the Mediterranean Sea. America dominates the globe. American views will be central in the shaping of globalization, but the structure of globalization is also one of the factors that will limit the arbitrary use of America's enormous power vis-à-vis the rest of the world. An America playing in a global economy is very different and much better from the perspective of the rest of the world than an America engaging in a contest for one-country bilateral national economic dominance. An America trading with the rest of the world, investing in the rest of the world, transferring technology to the rest of the world, and educating many from the rest of the world is far better for both those inside and outside of America than is an America that retreats into its traditional isolation.

This imbalance of economic and military power between the United States and the rest of the world has arisen because of decisions made in Japan and Europe.[2] Japan simply does not play the geopolitical military game. Kosovo is not its concern. It looks only at Asia and even there lets the United States deal with China and North Korea. The European Union has a population big enough and the economic resources large enough to create a modern military force equal to that of the United States. Yet with the end of the Cold War and any immediate military threat to itself, it has decided not to spend its economic resources on military activities. It is inwardly focused on the peaceful effort of building an integrated Europe. Large military budgets are seen as irrelevant to the success or failure of European integration because if there are military problems in Yugoslavia, the United States will be there. What happens in North Korea is of little interest to Europe and there is no willingness to be engaged in dealing with North Korea, since Europe is confident that America will keep such dangers under control and out of its neighborhood. America outspends the rest of NATO militarily by more than a 2 to 1 ratio. What looks sensible if one is heavily armed looks very different if one is only lightly armed.

Although sympathetic to those who died, the rest of the world did not experience 9/11 as a direct attack. Three thousand people died and 50,000 could easily have died as America's two largest buildings, in some ways the symbols of America itself, came crashing down. And if the truth be told, right under that layer of sympathy many of those in Europe and elsewhere felt that America had it coming. It was too arrogant, too big, too much of a bully, gave too much support to Israel, and needed to be taught a lesson. They hoped that the attack on the World Trade Center would make America a little more humble and a little more cautious.

This hope flows from a fundamental misreading of the American character. When attacked, Americans get aggressive. They strike back. The 9/11 attack simply changed American attitudes. Defense spending rose sharply, and attitudes about using military power changed even more sharply. One pays for a large modern army only if one intends to use it. The rest of the world has yet to recognize these realities. What happened in the Iraqi war merely underlines these vastly altered American attitudes.

The rest of the world cannot stop America from doing anything it really wants to do or force America to do anything it does not want to do. But the rest of the world can create an environment where it makes sense for Americans to work together with them to solve mutually recognized problems—Saddam Hussein in the case of Iraq. The French overplayed their hand in the UN Security Council. They could not stop the United States from invading Iraq, but had they been willing to support a firm deadline for military action if Iraq failed to totally disarm, they could have given inspections and the United Nations a chance to work. But they seemed to be more interested in controlling U.S. military power than in eliminating dangers in Iraq. They predictably failed in the effort to control American military power and in the process made it more difficult, if anything, for the rest of the world to control American military power in the future. In similar situations in the future the United Nations is not likely to be consulted.

There is a central political message to be learned. America cannot be controlled, but it can be engaged. Building a global economy is one way to engage America. And to some extent the rest of the world should see globalization in that light. For the rest of the world, understanding American views on globalization is central to being able to shape globalization in ways comfortable to themselves.

Because of their unique perspective, Americans fear globalization less than anyone else, and as a consequence they think about it less than anyone else. When Americans do think about globalization, they think of the global economy as an enlarged version of the American economy. They do so partly because this is precisely what much of the rest of the world says they fear about globalization.

Yet globalization is, in fact, changing America faster than any other society. Nowhere is production moving offshore more rapidly. Nowhere are more people's jobs being displaced by the rearrangements of global supply chains. No one's culture is changing more rapidly. Yet Americans hardly notice what is happening because their belief that the global economy will simply be an enlarged American economy is so strongly held. Specific political cries of economic pain are heard (the steel industry gets tariff protection), but there are no politically powerful general objections to the construction of a global economy that will in the end, in fact, ingest the American economy.

The global economy will not be an enlarged copy of the old pre-existing American economy. It will be something quite different. As a result, Americans have as much at stake in how the global economy is built as anyone else. It will change them as much as it will change anyone else. At the same time no one will have more influence than America as to how globalization is shaped.

GLOBAL OUTPUT

Before we can understand the different perspectives on globalization or how globalization can engage America, we must begin our investigations of the merits and demerits of globalization with a broad picture of the existing global economic landscape. How much output, or Gross Domestic Product (GDP), does the world produce and where is it located? In the past the global GDP was a statistical term without much organic meaning.* Few knew or cared what it was. Real economic activity occurred at the level of the nation-state. But increasingly a new global perspective is replacing our old national perspectives. The reasons are simple: Technology and economics are pushing us out of our old national economies and into a new global economy.

As with a pair of binoculars, the viewer has to look through two lenses to get a clear view. Using the first lens the viewer converts the GDP of each country in the world into dollars using market exchange rates. When added together the world produced $31,000 billion ($31 trillion) worth of output in 2000 at the start of the third millennium. Seventy-three percent of all these goods and services were produced in what might be called the core wealthy industrial countries. The United States accounted for 32 percent of

---

*Technically, the world has a Gross Product rather than a Gross Domestic Product (GDP), since the term "domestic" makes sense only in the context of discussing national economies.

the world's GDP, the European Union 25 percent, and Japan 16 percent. What might be called the peripheral wealthy industrial countries—developed countries such as Canada, Norway, Switzerland, Australia, and New Zealand and semideveloped countries such as Taiwan, South Korea, Singapore, and Israel where per capita incomes are above the level found in the poorest country within the European Union (Greece)—produced another 6 percent of world output. This leaves the developing world producing 21 percent of the world's total output. Even this percentage includes some oil-rich countries such as Kuwait or Brunei, but it is probably right to leave them in the developing world since they are rich but not developed.

To sum up, approximately 1 billion people in the developed world produce roughly 80 percent of the globe's output and 5 billion people in the developing world produced the remaining 20 percent.

Using the second lens in our economic binoculars, the viewer can aggregate the world's GDP using what economists call purchasing power parity (PPP) indexes to convert the output of different countries into a common measure of global output. Instead of using market exchange rates to convert national GDPs into a common currency, this method looks at the basket of goods and services purchased in any country and asks how many dollars would be required to buy that same basket of goods and services in America. Using PPP conversion indexes puts the world's GDP at $44 trillion in 2000. The world's PPP output of goods and services is bigger than the world's currency value output of goods and services, since the average internal purchasing prices of local goods and services in most developing countries are lower than those found for the same goods and services in the United States.

On a PPP measure of global output the core industrial countries produce 51 percent of world output—the United States 23 percent, the European Union 20 percent, and Japan 8 percent. The peripheral industrial countries produce another 5 percent of world output, and the developing world the remaining 44 percent. As measured using PPP, the developing world more than doubles in size. Instead of an 80–20 split there is a rough 55–45 split between the developed and the developing world.

Country rankings change substantially depending upon which measure is used. The two techniques for measuring the world's output give radically different results in Asia. Japan loses the most when shifting from currency values to PPP values and China gains the most. This happens because Japan's internal prices are far above those found in the United States, and China's internal prices are far below those found in the United States. As measured using currency values, Japan is four times as large as China (16% of world GDP versus 4%). As measured using PPP, China is 50 percent bigger than Japan (12% versus 8%).

Elsewhere there are also dramatic changes in relative size. As measured using currency values, China and Latin America are both about 4 percent of world GDP; as measured using PPP, China (12 %) is twice as big as Latin America (6 %). China's internal price levels are simply much lower than those found in Latin America, so when one corrects for purchasing power China gains a lot more output than Latin America.

It is not that one measure is right and the other is wrong. To see our economic world clearly, both lenses of the binoculars need to be used. Both measures of global output are correct. If one is looking at the size of potential markets for foreign goods and services (international purchasing power), financial might, global economic clout, or how much purchasing power the average tourist from a particular country has when going abroad, currency values give the right measure of economic output. If one is trying to determine welfare differences among individuals, families, or nations, PPP measures are the right indices to use.

Using PPP measures, the per capita income of the European Union is about 25 percent below that of the United States. Member states range from being 30 percent richer (Luxembourg) to being 47 percent poorer (Greece). In 2000 Japan's per capita GDP, using exchange rate conversions, is 17 percent above that of the

United States whereas its PPP per capita GDP is 24 percent below that of the United States. China's $850 per capita income in currency terms rises to $3,700 in PPP terms. This latter number is the right number to use when making welfare comparisons with America's $36,868 per capita GDP in 2000.

HOW BIG?

The geographical definition of any economy is given by the area across which business firms maximize profit—that is, they search to find the cheapest places to produce and they search to find the most profitable places to sell their goods and services. Supply chain management best illustrates the forces at work. What should be outsourced? What should remain in-house? Where in the world should either be made? Increasingly, answers to these questions dictate global operations. Supply chains for making components now encircle the world. Sales can be managed in any number of countries.

In this process some geographic areas are found to be cost effective and profitable for production and sales, some are profitable for one but not the other, and some areas are found wanting on both dimensions. They are simply not good places to do business and are left out of the global economy as private businesses deploy their activities.

As businesses scan the world to find the most profitable places to sell and produce, national economies are slowly dissolving to be replaced by a global economy. It is this reality that makes the world GDP and not national GDPs the relevant numbers to think about. It is this search criterion and not any specific economic measure— sales or profits earned abroad, world exports relative to world GDP (12% in 2000), or the size of foreign investments—that determines the existence of a global economy.

No single economic statistic reflects the extent of globalization because globalization comes in many forms. When Proctor &

Gamble produces and sells soaps or shampoos inside China and keeps the profits within China to finance its expansion plans, it is part of globalization although no money flows across national boundaries. Toyota's export of cars to Europe and the Japanese investors who buy American home mortgages are both aspects of globalization. So is a Mercedes takeover of Chrysler. A laptop computer assembled in Taiwan with Intel inside, a Microsoft operating system, a Japanese flat panel display, and Korean memory chips to the specifications of a large variety of multinational sellers is the prototype of globalization. Key punching American insurance forms in Jamaica, joint software design teams located in India and the United States, and American telephone call centers located in Ireland are part of global reality. So is a U.S. firm selling Latin American bananas to Europeans. Movies, TV programs, and music are all marketed globally. Internet interactions by their very technology are automatically global. Everyone can log on.

It is important to understand that the current wave of globalization was not started as a matter of public policy. Governments did not decide to start global sourcing and marketing. Governments did not encourage cross-border corporate mergers. Governments did not start electronic commerce. Governments did not create global financial markets. It is not a process where governments can start it, stop it, speed it up, slow it down, or pick and choose exactly where they want to participate.

A seismic shift in technology has either seduced or forced, depending upon your views, national business firms into becoming global business firms. With the new computer-telecommunications technologies, a profit-maximizing company must make its products wherever in the world they are cheapest to make and it must sell its products wherever in the world the greatest profits are to be earned. If the firm does not find the cheapest places to produce its products and the most profitable places to sell its products, others will. The firm that doesn't go global will be driven out of business by those that do. Corporate survival is at issue. From the point of view of businesses, improvements in communications have made

global sales and sourcing possible, highly profitable, and necessary
all at the same time.

As evaluated by the same valued-added calculations used to
measure national GDPs, twenty-nine of the hundred largest
economies in the world are now companies—and not countries.[3]
The largest company, Exxon, comes in at number 45 in the
world—about the same size as Pakistan.

Looking at American-headquartered global firms, three-
quarters of their production is inside the United States and one-
fourth is outside.[4] Trade between onshore and offshore affiliates of
America's global corporations accounted for 56 percent of America's imports and 35 percent of its exports in 2000.[5] Sixty-six percent of American firms' offshore production goes to citizens in the
countries where their offshore factories are located, 23 percent goes
to other foreign countries, and 11 percent comes back to the
United States. Half of the foreign production of American-
headquartered firms is in just six countries—the United Kingdom,
Canada, Germany, France, Japan, and Italy. In Ireland 17 percent of
the national GDP is produced in the facilities of "American" firms.
Conversely, America receives two-thirds of all the investments that
flow across national borders. If foreign investment and production
is the measure of globalization, it is the first world and not the third
that is being globalized.

What we used to call multinational firms are increasingly
becoming global firms. Among firms, what passes for national
identification depends upon history and where their corporate
headquarters happen to be located. But the latter is increasingly
becoming a matter determined more by local taxation than by economic functionality. The recent fuss about U.S. firms moving their
legal headquarters to Bermuda to get lower taxes is but one example. National identification means little when it comes to predict-
ing a firm's behavior. Place of origin or the nationality of the
passports held by the top managers makes less and less difference
when it comes to making real decisions. Ownership is often not
what it seems to be. Nokia is seen as a Finnish company, but more

of Nokia's shares are owned by Americans than by Finns. Is Honda a U.S. or a Japanese firm when it makes and sells more cars in the United States than it does in Japan?

PAST GLOBALIZATIONS

The world was a lot more globalized in 1900 than it is in 2003. Colonial empires then dominated the world. Almost 25 percent of the globe was ruled from London alone.[6] The French ruled Indochina and much of Africa. The Russian Empire spread across the Eurasian land mass. The Ottoman Empire still dominated the Middle East and some of the Balkans. Central Europe belonged to the Austro-Hungarian Empire. Germany (German Southwest Africa) and Japan (Korea, Taiwan) had their colonies. The United States was ruling Cuba and the Philippines. China was a quasi-colonial split up among the great powers. As opposed to today's almost two hundred independent countries, there were then only fifty independent countries and a large number of these were only quasi-independent. Latin American countries lived with the Monroe Doctrine and, while technically independent, were kept on a short leash by the United States.

Historically, "getting rich" was central to global empires and military expansion. The conquistadors went to North and South America seeking to get rich. Spain became the richest nation in Europe because of the gold and silver that flowed from its New World Empire. All of the previous global empires—the Roman, Mongol, Ottoman, Spanish, British, and French—were organized by governments and conquered by military force.

Traditional empires ended after World War II because of changes in technology and changes in attitudes. Conquering land and natural resources was no longer the route to "getting rich." Large land areas and the natural resources that went with them had ceased to be the technological drivers of economic success. This fundamental shift can be seen in the fact that the developed world did not invade Saudi Arabia in 1973 when it raised the price of oil. Militarily, it would have been easy to conquer Saudi Arabia. But invading Saudi Arabia wasn't even considered because the sources of future economic success were not going to be found in cheap oil. Higher oil prices were a temporary inconvenience but not a fundamental determinant of long-run economic success. One did not need colonies to be rich. Quite the reverse, colonies had become an economic burden—costing the mother country more than what the mother country could earn from them.

The sources of future economic success were to be found in developing new breakthrough technologies and having the social capabilities, culture, and mental attitudes to take advantage of these new technologies. Intellectual property rights have replaced mineral rights as the drivers of success. The soft power of cultural, educational, and technological dominance has replaced the hard power of colonial rule and geographic military expansion. In a very real sense intellectual conquest had replaced geographic conquest.

Ideologically, World War II changed attitudes on both sides of the colonial arrangement. The German drive for "lebensraum" in Europe and the Japanese drive for a "co-prosperity sphere" in Asia—their respective names for the large colonial empires they'd hoped to build if they won the war—discredited all colonialism, including the colonialism of the old British and French empires. World War II weakened the old colonial powers militarily and economically. Nonwhite colonial subjects saw their white colonial overlords being beaten by a nonwhite Asian power. They came to believe they could win wars of liberation. Without World War II there is no doubt that colonialism would have lasted much longer than it did.

It is important to remember, however, that there was not just one form of colonialization. The British Empire was very different from the Ottoman Empire. Even within the same empire there were different models. Canada and India were not treated alike. Algeria was treated as a province of France; French Indochina wasn't.

Globalization also comes in many forms, but the world jointly will have to choose the form of globalization it wants since globalization is a multilateral phenomenon. Countries will not be able to pick and choose which form of globalization they would like to join. There will be only one choice. But decisions as to the forms of globalization will be interactive. A country such as China may well end up having more impact on the rules for globalization than a country such as France.

Geographic perspectives have widened before. In the mid-19th century prior to electrification no one would have said, if asked, that they worked in the American economy. They would have said that they lived in America but worked in the Boston economy or the Chicago economy. These local-regional economies did some trade with each other, but there wasn't an American economy in any real sense. Today no one would say that they worked in the Boston or the Chicago economies. They live in Boston or Chicago but they work in America.

The technological revolution now underway is essentially extending this process. Fifty years from now few of us will be apt to say we work in the U.S. economy or the Japanese economy. We live in the United States or Japan, but we work in a global economy.

BUILDING TO DIFFERENT SPECIFICATIONS

Globalization is often portrayed as if it could be the beginnings of a new Dark Age. If one traces history from the peak of the Roman Empire to the bottom of the Dark Ages, standards of living went down 90 percent, cities essentially disappeared, and illiterate societies replaced what had been literate societies. Humans sometimes get on the wrong track. There have been major negative reversals in human history. But what happens to human societies is not determined in the stars. If globalization is a step in the wrong direction, the responsibility is ours. We will have made it so because we did not build the right global economy.

Economic predictions have often been wrong. In the late 1980s the end of the American century was widely predicted. Japan would dominate the 21st century. Yet the United States in the early 21st century is probably more economically dominant than it has ever been. This American turnaround did not "just happen." Americans took actions to make those predictions wrong.

Businesses responded to their obvious quality-control weaknesses in the 1980s by studying those who were then doing better—Japanese corporations. They were willing to adopt and adapt foreign practices. As just one small example, in 1987 some of America's biggest manufacturing firms—Ford, General Motors, Chrysler, Boeing, Alcoa, Johnson & Johnson, Digital Equipment, Eastman Kodak, Hewlett Packard, Motorola, Polaroid, and United Technologies—helped design and start MIT's Leaders in Manufacturing program. As dean of MIT's Sloan Management School at the time, I hired a Japanese professor, Professor Shiba, one of Japan's great experts on total quality management, to teach in the program. In his first class he threw all of his students out of the class on the grounds that they were sloppily dressed and those who dressed sloppily could not build high-quality products.

Americans learned to adopt and adapt. Total quality management and just-in-time inventories became the order of the day. Cars delivered with defects because they were built on a Friday became a historical anecdote. New-car buyers quit keeping lists of defects to be repaired on their first service visit to the dealer.

At the same time no one foresaw that the economic game was going to change from one of pushing mature technologies slowly forward (reducing the number of defects in DRAMs) to one of revolutionary technical change (inventing the microprocessor). Closing down the old and opening up the new was a game much more favorable to the American character than meticulously reducing the defect levels in DRAMs or automobiles. In the end Americans became much better at playing the game where they weren't very good (pushing mature technologies slowly forward) and did not lose their ability to play the game where they had always been very good—taking advantage of the opportunities opened up by the third industrial revolution and the new knowledge-based economy.

In contrast with the United States in the 1980s, Japan in the 1990s was unwilling to adopt and adapt what was working elsewhere to end its economic crisis. In Japan what used to work in the past cannot be abandoned even though it does not work in the present and is unlikely to work in the future.[7] The result of this failure to study what worked elsewhere and apply what it had learned to its own disasters was a decade of no growth. And there is no reason to believe that a decade from now what is known as the "lost decade" won't become known as the "two lost decades."

At the same time technology moved in a way that handicapped the Japanese. "Closing down the old" is a game the Japanese are horrible at playing (no one can be fired), and "opening up the new" is a game at which they are not much better. One has to be willing to tolerate a lot of failures to find out what will work when brand-new industries are being built. Tolerating failure is not a Japanese cultural characteristic. Because of widespread economic failures and the social stigma that goes with economic failure, Japan is the only country in the world where suicide deaths exceed traffic deaths.[8]

As geographic perspectives widen, new unexpected problems will arise. The past evolution from local to national economies teaches us, or should teach us, that problems that weren't problems often become problems if the context changes dramatically. There were many local financial crashes in 19th-century America. But they never brought the American economy down. There wasn't an American national economy to be brought down. A crisis in Chicago was not a crisis in Boston. But with the development of a national economy, the 1929 stock market crash and the 1930 banking crash became very different events. They did bring America to its knees in the Great Depression.

To survive, a different, stronger, and more resilient American economy with unemployment insurance, social security, securities regulation, and bank deposit insurance had to be built. But rebuilding in the aftermath of major economic disasters is a very tough task. It may, in fact, be impossible. The damage is so great that the existing system is simply abandoned.

Americans were lucky in the Great Depression. It could easily have been the end of capitalism. As the Great Depression dragged on with no end in sight, Americans began to elect communist local city governments in the late 1930s and were clearly losing their faith in capitalism. It is important to remember that word "Nazis" stood for national socialism and that the only capitalist country left standing at the end of World War II other than the United States was the United Kingdom, which would vote for a socialist labor government in 1945. If the Germans had negotiated a peace treaty with Great Britain after they had conquered Western Europe, if they had not invaded Russia, and if Japan had not attacked the United States at Pearl Harbor, the end of capitalism could easily have occurred sixty years ago.

Disasters such as the Great Depression are an important part of learning. The Great Depression forced Americans to learn how to do damage control (macroeconomic stimulus using monetary and fiscal policies) and deliver disaster relief (unemployment insurance). Americans learned the weak points in the system that could turn minor accidents into major disasters. Bank deposit insurance is central if minor financial crashes are not to spiral into major economic disasters. Because of what Americans learned in the Great Depression, the Savings and Loan crisis of the 1980s came and went with little impact on America's GDP despite the fact that 3,000 banks were closed.[9]

The Great Depression taught us much about containing recessions and about preventing them from becoming bigger, but it could not teach us how to completely avoid recessions. Thinking that we can do so is just as naïve as thinking that an understanding of geology will prevent earthquakes.

Most of what are called disasters are not random, never-to-be-seen-again, bizarre, negative events but events that regularly flow from the standard operating characteristics of our systems—only their timing and precise location are random and unpredictable. Hurricanes, volcanoes, and earthquakes are part of Mother Nature's geological system. It is absolutely certain that a giant earthquake, "the big one," will occur in California. The only question is when. But our organized responses both before the big one (construction techniques) and after the big one (emergency services) can mitigate the damage done by these geological forces. The same reality applies to economic disasters.

We could choose economic systems that do not have recessions and financial crashes. In the seventy years after World War I there were no recessions and no financial collapses under communism in the USSR. In the same period the United States has had four financial crashes, eleven recessions, and one Great Depression. The reasons for the difference are straightforward. In communism there are no financial markets to collapse. In central planning excess demand always exists, since the planners always want more than the producers can supply. Recessions are simply impossible. Yet we willingly choose the dangers of capitalism because we want the high standards of living that communism cannot deliver.

Economic history teaches us that we should use the lessons from small disasters to build a robust global economic system that can resist and weather the big crises that will undoubtedly happen at some unknown time in the future. We need to consider what could potentially blow up the global system and what could be done to build a more robust global system to withstand these possible events.

In learning how to build more robust systems and coping with disasters, good events teach us little. An airplane successfully flies from Boston to New York. Everything worked as it should have worked. There is little to learn. It is only by studying accidents that we can learn to build better air transportation systems. But it is also true that we have to get organized both to listen and to implement the recommendations that flow from that listening. Where we are willing to investigate, listen, and change our behavior, we get much better results than where we are unwilling to do these things.

In America airplanes are forty-five times safer than autos per mile traveled.[10] Some of that difference is due to centralized airline systems run by professionals rather than a decentralized system run by millions of owner-drivers, but a lot of it is due to the fact that America has an institution to systematically investigate the causes of each and every airplane accident (the National Transportation Safety Board, or NTSB) and an institution to require compliance with the safety recommendations that flow from these investigations (the Federal Aviation Administration, or FAA). Airlines are forced to operate as if the unexpected should be expected even if its timing cannot be predicted.

In contrast, auto accidents, even a small sample of auto accidents, are not scientifically investigated. There are no institutions to require the various actors (the manufacturers, the drivers, the builders of roads) to change their behavior. America does not have a systematic feedback loop designed to make its auto transportation system better. Congress occasionally imposes some ad hoc safety standards—seat belts, air bags, bumper crash standards—but no one systematically investigates, listens, and forces changes in behavior in auto transportation as they do in air transportation.

Although accidents are inherently part of any system of land or air transportation, these systems can be built to very different safety levels. Even within the United States there is more than a 3 to 1 difference in auto traffic fatality rates from the worst state (2.7 deaths per 100 million miles traveled in Mississippi) to the best state (0.8 deaths per 100 million miles traveled in Maine).[11] Deaths cannot be completely eliminated, but within limits societies choose how many deaths they are willing to tolerate. If Americans were all willing to travel by professionally driven buses, the traffic death rate would for all practical purposes be zero.[12] But Americans like their cars and are unwilling to incur the lower performance, convenience, and customization of safer bus systems. Americans choose auto systems knowing they have associated dangers but believing the benefits are worth the risks.

Similarly, within the limits given by technology humans can build the global economic system they want. As with autos, most humans have chosen the riskier mode of economic travel, global capitalism, with its instabilities and inequalities, because they like the performance and comfort of the system. National socialism has far fewer ups and downs, but it also generates much lower and slower rising standards of living.

When very infrequent, bigger than normal, or completely unexpected accidents happen, there is a lot of initial interest and comment; but without an institutionally organized response nothing happens. From this perspective it is going to be interesting to watch what happens from the scientific investigation into why the two World Trade Center towers collapsed after being hit. Will the information be used to build better buildings, more resistant to both terrorism and more normal events like fires? Or will America collect the information and then do little to change its standard operating procedures?[13] The odds favor the latter outcome. We don't have the institutions to force us to implement what we will learn. Building standards are set by thousands of local governments with no central coordination.

Often we refuse to study disasters because we think doing so is too pessimistic. Such events won't happen again. Such events are just too horrible to contemplate. These attitudes explain why we delayed so long (more than a year) in setting up a commission to investigate the World Trade Center disaster.

Or, to avoid having to deal with changing the existing system and our own responsibilities for building those systems, we seek to find devils to blame. From this perspective the California electrical power crisis in 2001 wasn't the inevitable product of a flawed system that Californians themselves created. It was produced by the machinations of evil forces who deliberately created shortages to raise prices.[14] "Thirty billion was extorted from the state," according to Governor Davis of California.[15] By blaming evil people

Californians did not have to blame themselves or, more important, to undertake the difficult tasks of changing the system. They just had to punish the evil people. There are often evil people connected with economic disasters, but when evil people cause a lot of damage there is also something wrong with the system. It should have been designed to stop or limit the destruction caused by evil people.

OPTING OUT

The world could certainly turn its back on globalization. There are historical examples of societies deliberately deciding not to use the technologies available to them. Before Columbus discovered America, China had demonstrated its technical ability to sail the world's oceans (an armada with ships four times as large as those of Columbus had landed 28,000 soldiers on the east coast of Africa), but the emperor decided that these technical abilities threatened domestic tranquility. When the ships returned, they were ordered burned, the logs destroyed, and no one was to sail outside the sight lines of the coast of China. Technical retrogression set in (gun powder was also known but left unused for military purposes), and instead of discovering and conquering the globe, much smaller European countries discovered China and turned it into a quasi-colony.

No one forces countries to participate in global supply chains and to allow multinational firms to invest in their countries. No one has to have a McDonald's. But those who participate become richer at a much faster pace than they would have had they not participated. They get the advantages of specialization, economies of scale, technology transfer, foreign direct investment, market access, and specialized management skills that come only with participation. But in return they have to offer the factors global businesses demand—education, infrastructure, personal safety. If they don't, they are simply left out and left behind.

Although theoretically the new technologies that permit a

global economy could be ignored, today's revolutions in communications technologies are not apt to remain unused by everyone. They are too profitable. Some subset of people will use them. The world is not 15th-century China with an emperor to stop us from using these new technologies. Some form of globalization involving some fraction of the globe will evolve in the marketplace. Some countries will accept globalization and others will reject it—or more often be rejected by it because they do no meet the entry standards. Everyone will be on the globe but not in the global economy.

The nonparticipants do not have to worry about the disappearance of their national economies. They have a far bigger worry. Their decision not to participate may effectively be a decision to remain poor. Many would argue that the successful isolated national economy is already an extinct species.

Realistically, most developed countries probably do not have the choice of opting out. Too many citizen-voter-workers depend upon the global economy for their livelihoods for their governments even to think about forcing their companies to opt out. Their corporations have committed themselves to the global economy, restructured themselves to fit that global economy, and could not easily return to serving solely national markets even if they wished to do so. If governments attempted to force their corporations to return, most would simply migrate their corporate headquarters to countries participating in globalization. As participants in the global economy, the developed world has already passed the point of no return. If citizens of these countries don't like what they see, their only choice is to think about a different set of construction plans for building the global economy in which they will live.

All governments are generally hesitant about globalization, since it reduces their powers of control. More events are global events outside of their control. This applies to the largest and the smallest of economies alike.

But it should also be remembered that globalization is not just for countries. Individuals can participate as individuals. And millions do. As they move to the developed world from the developing world (Mexico to the United States; North Africa and Turkey to Europe), they raise their incomes substantially. For them as individuals globalization is a golden opportunity.

Ultimately the real issue is not "go" or "no go." There is a third choice—namely, to deliberately design and build a global economy that is different from the global economy that will evolve by itself. Accept, reject, shape to another design—these are the global choices. Whether globalization is a force for human betterment depends upon what kind of global economy we build. It is not determined in the stars but in the path that we tread and the systems that we build.

{2}

A GLOBAL SUPERSTRUCTURE RESTING ON A CAPITALISTIC SUBSTRUCTURE BUILT WITH NEW TECHNOLOGIES

The world is in the midst of three simultaneous revolutions.

First, a set of new technologies has emerged to produce what will come to be called the third industrial revolution. The world is moving from an industrial era based upon natural resources into a knowledge-based era based upon skills, education, and research and development.

Second, the new communication technologies that are emerging in this third industrial revolution make it possible to create a global economy—and perhaps they mandate its construction. Businesses located anywhere can manage activities everywhere. National economies are slowly dissolving to be replaced by a global economy.

Third, much of the world is throwing away its communist or

socialist inheritance and moving toward capitalism. Communism has been abandoned as unworkable (China), imploded (the USSR), or been overthrown (Eastern Europe). In Western Europe socialism is in retreat with widespread privatization and deregulation. Communist or socialist political parties have had to change their names to get elected. Even that most capitalistic of countries, the United States, is more capitalistic than it was two decades ago. Transportation, communications, electrical power, and finance have all been substantially deregulated.

Each of these revolutions is changing the economic world in which we live. Many of the effects ascribed to globalization spring from the other two or from interactions among globalization and the other two. A global superstructure is being built on a capitalistic substructure using new technologies.

Navigating through these three revolutions requires the mental attitudes of an explorer. Above all explorers are bold. They embark on journeys without knowing exactly where they are going, what will work, and how they will get there. They go "where no man has gone before." They initiate voyages of exploration knowing that many of their voyages will almost certainly end in failure. Yet they are willing to set sail.

But successful explorers have a second important attitude. They are willing to listen. They seek the best possible knowledge on how the systems they are about to explore work. They don't sit back waiting for accidents to happen. They study the failures and successes of others to improve their chances of success. They are willing to adopt and adapt whatever has worked elsewhere. If they experience failure, they learn from it and set sail again. Failures exist to teach them how to succeed. They remain bold.

Consider the great geographic explorers of the 14th, 15th, and 16th centuries—Christopher Columbus, Vasco da Gama, Ferdinand Magellan, Amerigo Vespucci, Henry Hudson, Sir Francis Drake. We marvel at what they did, but there is one embarrassing question that is not asked. Why didn't people sail across the Atlantic and Pacific oceans five hundred years earlier? We know they could have. The Vikings actually did it in A.D. 850. They had all the necessary technologies, but they sat there not using them.

Earlier Europeans did not refuse to sail because they believed the world was flat and they would sail off its edge. Educated Europeans had known the shape of the world since the days of the ancient Greeks. The Latin poet Ovid in the year 7 in his book the *Metamorphoses* talks about the world being a spinning sphere with five zones—two polar, two temperate, and one tropical. What stopped Europeans from sailing into the unknown was a fear of the unknown—a belief in sea monsters: It is too dangerous; we will be eaten.

How does one scientifically prove there are no sea monsters? There could have been sea monsters. It was a logical possibility. No one, and no scientific investigation, can ever prove a negative. To prove there are no sea monsters one has to be willing to undertake voyages of exploration. The first explorer to successfully cross the Atlantic or Pacific Ocean heaves a sigh of relief. He's lucky. He wasn't eaten. After fifty successful voyages, everyone knows there probably aren't any sea monsters. And after a thousand successful voyages everyone knows sea monsters do not exist.

The people willing to make the first voyages, those who take the risk that there really are sea monsters, are the ones who conquer the world, get rich, and put their names in the history books. They are the bold. Those who follow after the voyages are known to be safe are just that—followers. They live comfortable but unexciting lives. Those who never learn to sail because of their fears remain poor. Historically, they become the colonies of those who were bold enough to sail into the unknown.

The moral of the tale is simple. Those who want to win cannot sit on the sidelines. They must be proactive. Others will act if they don't and they will be enveloped by the resulting events. They may lose if they participate, but they will certainly lose if they do not participate. Fortune favors the bold—even if some of the bold are numbered among the losers.

The importance of being bold is seen in our economic as well as our geographic history. Economic historians tell us that the differences in per capita income between the wealthiest country in the world and the poorest country in the world were small to non-existent in 1700.[1] In every country in the world 98 to 99 percent of the workforce was employed in farming. All used the same technologies—horses, oxen, human power, animal manure, and seeds gathered from the previous year's crops. Some areas of the world had better soils and climates for agriculture, but the good areas were simply much more densely populated than the bad areas. Half of the world's GDP was inside India and China because half of the world's population was inside India and China.[2]

Then the first industrial revolution arrived. With the invention and perfection of the steam engine during the 18th century, an agricultural era 8,000 years long comes to an end. The industrial era begins in Great Britain between 1760 and 1780.[3] To this day there are historical arguments as to why Great Britain was the first to use these new technologies.[4] One probably needed local coal deposits to get started, but lots of countries had coal. The British certainly didn't have a better scientific understanding of steam. Perhaps it was their willingness to be economic explorers. They were bolder.

Some countries made the leap from agriculture to industry and others did not. Individuals and countries that moved with these new technological forces became rich. Very quickly the new British industrialists were wealthier than the landed dukes—a group that had been Britain's wealthiest for hundreds of years. Those who did not participate remained where they were and gradually became poorer relative to those who were getting rich.

One did not need to invent the industrial game to be successful, but one needed to be willing to learn to play it. The United States and Germany joined the first industrial revolution in the 1830s and 1840s. Japan didn't get started until the 1870s. Some countries never learned to play the industrial game.

Today arguments focus on why some countries lag behind. Is it their policies, their institutions, their natural environment, or perhaps their attitudes? They aren't willing to be explorers. They cannot get organized. They aren't bold enough to take the risks.

In the late 19th century a second industrial revolution based upon one key invention (electrification) and one key German idea (systematic investments in industrial research and development based upon academic science) again disrupted the economic system. Systematic industrial research and development speeded up the pace of technical change and changed its nature. Those who would be economic leaders had to invest in industrial research and development. For the first time, a large educated workforce became central to economic success. Germany and the United States made the investments; Britain did not. America's catch-up with the per capita income of Great Britain prior to World War I is attributed to a much better educated labor force and the higher productivity that goes with an educated workforce.[5] Britain was still listed among the rich, but it lost its position as the technological and economic leader of the world. It fell from having the world's highest per capita income in 1880 to being tied for the 16th and 17th places in the world tables in 2002.

Again some countries leapt into this second industrial revolution and others did not. Those who did not make the leap remain where they were with per capita incomes similar to those that existed during feudal times. Starting from equality in 1700, three hundred years later in the year 2000 the gap in per capita GDP between the world's richest country and the world's poorest country is approximately 140 to 1.[6] Great inequality has replaced equality. But billions of people are also living better than the kings and queens of just a few centuries earlier.

Looking backward, one can easily chart the major disruptions. The impacts of the steam engine, electrification, and systematic science are clearly seen even if their impacts could not have been anticipated. The steam engine is a good example. Its biggest economic impact was in transportation and manufacturing, although it was developed as a device to solve an energy problem. Wood supplies and the coal deposits lying above the water table had both been exhausted in Europe, and water had to be pumped out of coal mines if food was to be cooked and homes heated. The steam engine was designed to solve a slowly festering energy problem, but it became the biggest transformational technology since the invention of agriculture 8,000 years earlier. Humankind had learned how to harness mechanical power.

THE THIRD INDUSTRIAL REVOLUTION

Looking forward, it is often very difficult to see major technical disruptions even when they are already underway. We now live in a period of time historians of the future will call the third industrial revolution. Leaps forward and interactions between six key technologies (microelectronics, computers, telecommunications, man-made materials, robotics, and biotechnology) are once again sending the economy moving off in new directions. Collectively, these technologies and their interactions are producing a knowledge-based economy that is systematically changing how we conduct our economic and social lives.[7]

A whole series of major transformations is now visible. Developments in new materials are making the long-known fuel cell into a practical device that will lead us from a hydrocarbon energy economy into a hydrogen energy economy. But it is clear that biotechnology will come to hold the place steam and electricity held in the earlier revolutions. Humans have for the first time gained the ability to change their own genetic code. They can make themselves into something different. They now control their own evolution. It is not hard to imagine that this ability to change ourselves genetically will come to be seen as the central inflection point in all of human history—more profound than the initial shift from hunter-gatherer societies to agricultural societies or the invention of writing and reading.

Bill Gates stands as the symbol of this new era. For all of human history the richest person in the world has owned natural resources—land, gold, oil. But Bill Gates owns no land, no gold, and no oil. Owning neither factories nor equipment, he is not a capitalist in the old-fashioned sense. He has become the richest person in the world by controlling a knowledge process. As such he marks our fundamental shift to a knowledge-based economy. For the first time in human history it is possible to be fabulously rich by controlling knowledge.

All technological revolutions are frightening. No one knows where they will lead and what the world will look like when they are completed. Looking at the history of economic success and failure, there is a simple message: To undertake geographic, intellectual, or economic voyages of exploration one needs individuals willing to take risks, but one also needs societies willing to tolerate risk and finance the voyages of exploration. In the age of geographic exploration individuals were bold enough to sail into the unknown, but they were economically supported by their countries—the king and queen of Spain in the case of Columbus. In our age of knowledge exploration, societies similarly have to be willing to finance voyages into the scientific, rather than geographic, unknown. Fearful societies are not rich societies. They won't make the bold voyages of exploration they need to make.

Technological revolutions are hard to date. Once seen, signs of their development can be found much farther back in time. Looking back, observers often wonder how those alive at the time could have missed understanding that a revolution was underway. The double helix was discovered in the mid-1950s and the first courses in biotechnology, then called biophysics, were taught at MIT in the late 1950s. The dating of revolutions is in many ways arbitrary, but what counts for our purposes is when those who were alive at the time came to see that something very different was happening around them. In the case of the third industrial revolution this self-knowledge was hard to find before the 1990s but arose at an accelerating rate during the 1990s.

The Internet was first used in the late 1960s as a means of military communications, but it emerged in its civilian incarnation in the mid-1990s. Suddenly the power of computing (something that had been developing since World War II) was widely available, widely useful, and most important, widely visible. There was now a reason, other than word processing, to own a personal computer. New activities such as downloading music became possible. Old activities such as retailing could be done in new ways. Those first to figure out what was happening in this revolution would grow rich. No one knows what won't work. Everything might work. It is the lip of a new era. New industries and new terms such as "dot.com" came into existence.

Anyone wishing to be successful in this third industrial revolution must develop the mentality of an explorer. They must actively embrace the unknown and learn from their experiences. Like previous geographic explorers they will discover that their economic world is bigger than they thought. New previously unknown technological continents exist and great economic rivers flow through them. The results of these newly discovered realities will change their economic diets just as the sugar cane, potatoes, corn, and tobacco of the new world changed the diet of the old world.

A new economic world will have augmented their old economic world just as five hundred years ago a new geographic world augmented an old geographic world.

The geographic model we should attempt to replicate in our intellectual voyages is that of Sir Francis Drake. He made seven voyages with six essentially ending in failure. In one he never got farther than the Azores. But his willingness to keep sailing and his one successful voyage made him the richest man in England, made him a knight for his services to his country, and put him in the history books forever. May we be so lucky and do likewise.

But it isn't just luck. Successful explorers study accidents to learn about preventing future accidents, to better predict when disasters will occur, to improve crisis management, to have higher survival rates, to understand how to clean up post-disaster messes quickly and efficiently, and to make what they build more disaster proof. Successful explorers study the path, nature, and momentum of the existing economic system because it lets them understand how the new forces that are hitting the existing system will affect its future trajectory. Most of all, explorers have fun. Let no one doubt that the intellectual explorations of the new global knowledge-based economy can be as exciting as the discovery of the nature of our physical globe was five hundred years ago. The traits needed to be a geographic, intellectual, technological, or economic explorer are all rather similar.

But the explorers or those who follow them also have to be builders. When technologies change, and they are changing, economies must change. The first industrial revolution, the steam engine, and the second industrial revolution, electrification, destroyed feudalism. The third is just as profoundly destroying our old national industrial economies.

GLOBALIZATION

Searching the globe to find the cheapest places to make your products and the more profitable places to sell your products is made possible by the new communication technologies that flow from the third industrial revolution. As a result, the effects of the third industrial revolution and the effects of globalization get hopelessly confused. Globalization is an effect and not a cause in a big picture sense. Being willing to participate in globalization is one of the ways countries can use the new technologies to get rich. But the third industrial revolution is also a derivative revolution because it is also a cause that produces a subsequent set of effects.

For business firms the decision to expand from being national to being global is just one of several new dimensions upon which they must make strategic decisions. The new technologies are blowing up their old business models, and they must develop new business models if they wish to remain profitable. This is as true for those firms that think of themselves as being in the old economy as for those business firms that tout their participation in the new economy. Strategic consultants tell both sets of companies that they can grow, merge, or sell out to become big global players doing everything everywhere (a Goldman Sachs in finance) or become small, fast-on-their-feet niche players who are the world's greatest experts in some narrow area of interest (prime example: Long Term Capital Management with its sixteen partners—a mixture of Nobel Prize winners, a former vice chairman of the Federal Reserve Board, and the most successful traders on Wall Street—and a trillion dollars in loans). But the midsize national bank or insurance company is becoming extinct.

For countries the distinction between those willing to leap and those unwilling to leap into this new global economic game is not a first world, third world distinction. Some of the countries currently making the leap into a knowledge-based global economy are in the third world. China is the best example. China, with its 1.3 billion people, would not be growing as rapidly as it is if it could not take advantage of global markets to make components for the wealthy industrial world. It attracts by far the most foreign direct investment among developing countries. Its exports are soaring. It is a winner precisely because it participates in globalization. And because it is a winner, we will look at China in detail in a later chapter.

Sub-Saharan Africa is the prime example of a region that does not participate in globalization. It receives less than 2 percent of the world foreign direct investment and accounts for less than 2 percent of the world's exports. Sub-Saharan Africa is the only part of the world with per capita incomes below where they were in 1965 and continuing to fall. It is a loser because it does not participate in globalization. And because it is a loser, we will look at Sub-Saharan Africa in detail in a later chapter.

The division between those willing to leap and those unwilling to leap into this third industrial revolution is not a division limited to the third world. Many of those struggling to leap into the global knowledge-based economy now emerging are in the first world. As the lead participant in the third industrial revolution, America widened the income gap between itself and much of the rest of the industrial world in the 1990s. In 1991 France's per capita GDP was only $1,000 below that of the United States; Germany and Italy were $2,000 down, and the United Kingdom was $5,000 lower. Ten years later in 2001 the United Kingdom's per capita GDP was $11,000 below that of the United States, Germany was $12,000 down, France was $13,000 lower, and Italy faced a $16,000 gap.[8] Western Europe's GDP per capita is now lower relative to that of the United States than any time since the 1960s.[9] Even the income gap between the United States and its closest and most similar neighbor, Canada, is up sharply—from $2,000 to $15,000.

In the midst of technological revolutions rich countries that wish to remain rich must be technological leaders in some area of endeavor. Canada falls behind because it isn't making the necessary investments in research and development.[10] Rich countries that wish to remain rich during an economic revolution must be able to build the new big companies of the future. Five out of the twenty-five largest firms in the world are new American companies founded after 1960 that did not grow big by mergers. One does not find a new start-from-scratch European firm until one reaches number 73 (S&P) and it is the only new European firm in the world's top one hundred firms.[11] Europe is falling behind because it doesn't build the new big firms of the future.

As was true with the first two industrial revolutions, some countries will make this third leap and some won't. The existing 140 to 1 gap between the world's richest country and the world's poorest country will undoubtedly grow bigger if current trends are simply extrapolated forward. What happens to some more general index of world inequality depends upon who jumps and who does not jump. China, for example, is so big that if one uses a general global measure of income inequality for either individuals or countries, the world is currently becoming more equal if China is included in the statistics and less equal if China is left out of the statistics.[12]

Participating in globalization differs enormously across countries. Using a variety of measures such as political engagement in international organizations, use of international technologies such as the Internet, personal contacts through travel or telephone calls, and economic integration in terms of trade or investment, Singapore was the most globalized country in the world in 2000. At the bottom were the countries that were not globalized at all. Although India was not in the latter category, there was a 23 to 1 gap between Singapore's index and that of India.[13] The United States ranked number 11 in this globalization index.

In the 1990s those countries participating in globalizing were growing at more than 5 percent per year, whereas those not globalizing had falling per capita GDPs.[14] As one goes up the index of globalization, there is a strong correlation with both higher wages and better management of the environment.[15] But which is cause and which is effect? Does good performance lead to globalization, or does globalization lead to good performance?

Whether you say that globalization is a "cause" of rising income inequality among countries is a matter of semantics. It is clearly not a cause in the sense that globalization can be accused of making the world's poor countries poorer. Globalization does not crush countries. It ignores them. The poor are those left out of globalization.

Countries can veto globalization. They can refuse to provide the educated work forces and infrastructure necessary to participate. They can impose tariffs or quotas to reduce or eliminate international trade. They can place restrictions on foreign investment. But opting out of globalization probably means opting out of the only existing process of economic development. It may effectively be a decision to remain or become poor.

But participation is not a decision that countries alone get to make. Business firms can effectively veto any country's entry into the global economy. Business firms, not countries, decide whether a country has the right criteria to participate when they decide where they should locate their activities. Countries have to provide the ingredients global firms want. No one is interested in producing the goods and services of tomorrow in a country with an illiterate workforce, without a modern electronic infrastructure, and in a context of social chaos—crime, corruption, and no social services. Since companies have many places where they could locate their offshore production facilities, countries have to learn how to sell themselves to global firms as good places to do business. Selling themselves to companies is not something that comes naturally to many countries in either the first or the third world.

Globalization also creates a forward momentum of its own. Large numbers of people scan the world when they consider where to take their annual vacation or get their educations. Foreign travel and study change mental attitudes. There is a growing elite that think of themselves as citizens of the world. The television set brings events in the rest of the world directly into our homes with the same immediacy as national events. We play with global toys as children—the Japanese Pokémon, the Danish Lego blocks. Globalization affects our sexual practices: AIDS starts in Africa and spreads to the rest of the world. National boundaries come to have less meaning psychologically and physically as millions of people legally and illegally move across those national boundaries.

Conversely, if everyone is basically forced to play the same global, capitalistic, third industrial revolution economic game, national differences mean less and less when it comes to economic systems. Governmental freedom to conduct different expenditure policies effectively shrinks as countries have to compete to attract foreign direct investment with similar levels of taxation. As a result, governments can offer their citizens less and less that is different from what is being offered by neighboring governments. Not surprisingly, this leads to less interest in maintaining separate national economies. The construction of the European Union is only the most dramatic illustration of the phenomenon. Countries with long historic existences are gradually phasing themselves out of existence—and there is a long waiting line of countries wanting to join.

The illusion that national governments can simply choose to

participate or not participate in today's globalization flows from the fact that choice was an important element in earlier forms of post–World War II globalization. Facing a confrontation with communism, the United States set out to integrate its military allies economically after the war. The GATT (General Agreement on Tariffs and Trade) trading rounds, starting in Geneva in 1947, set out to dismantle tariffs and quotas and to create a more integrated noncommunistic global economy. Although the United States was not in Europe and is not a member of what is now the European Union, it was the European Economic Community's biggest supporter in the 1950s. The "United States of Europe" was a phrase commonly used on both sides of the Atlantic. In the American view European prosperity would keep large communist parties in France and Italy from gaining control of their countries at the ballot box. On the opposite side of the world Japan would be a prosperous unsinkable aircraft carrier in northeast Asia. Holding out the possibility of joining this global economic alliance would keep third world countries from being seduced by socialism and communism.

The USSR set out to do much the same. The European Economic Community in Western Europe and Comecon in Eastern Europe were both expressions of the same mindset. The two superpowers felt they had to more tightly tie their military partners together economically. Global capitalism would be matched off against global communism. A country could decide to join the capitalistic block, the communist block, or remain in the nonaligned world.

THE END OF SOCIALISM

To a great extent ideology (the Cold War) brought globalization into existence in the 1950s, and then the demise of ideology (communism) strongly pushed it forward in the 1990s. As long as communism was believed to be a viable economic system, there were limits to global capitalism whatever the technological imperatives. Capitalism could not go completely global because much of the globe was beyond its reach. Forty percent of humanity lived under communism.

But the limits were even tighter than those imposed by the existence of communist countries. Much of the third world was attracted by communism and ideologically stood on the sidelines (the nonaligned world) between communism and capitalism. Third world countries operated economic systems that were mixes of capitalism and communism, but typically their beliefs in the efficacy of socialism put them much closer to communism than they were to capitalism. India is the prime example.

Within the wealthy developed world, socialism was also a counterpoint to capitalism. Europe had strong communist and socialist political parties. Government ownership of the means of production was widespread. These beliefs resisted the spread of free market capitalism and the globalization that was increasingly being built into it.

But that is now all history. China by choice in the late 1970s and the Soviet Union by default in the early 1990s decided to abandon communism and move toward capitalism. Their failures and decisions discredited socialism everywhere. In Western Europe communist or socialistic parties could no longer claim to represent an alternative to capitalism. These parties collapsed or changed their names. No one could stand up and say that they were against capitalism because to do that one had to have a viable alternative system to recommend and there were no viable alternatives to support.

Japan's economic failures in the 1990s also played a role in the spread of American-style global capitalism. The Japanese government was not ideologically attached to socialism, but the economy was tightly controlled by the government through a system of administrative guidance. It wasn't central planning, but it wasn't free markets either.

Japan's economy was built as a powerful nationalistic export economy. It bought as little as possible from the rest of the world. Foreign investment in Japan was discouraged. The Japanese pioneered supply chain management, but their supply chains lay entirely within Japan in their association of affiliated Japanese companies, the kereitsu. To this day Japan gets almost no foreign investment.

Whatever Japan was, it wasn't an example of globalization.

In the 1970s and 1980s as Japanese firms in industry after industry were taking market shares away from their American and European competitors, Japan was seen as the model of the future. When the Japanese model collapsed in the 1990s and it became clear that the Japanese way was not the wave of the future, the only model left standing was the American model. Some feared and hated it; some loved and wanted to copy it. But all the other viable choices had melted away.

Although capitalism is a powerful economic engine, free markets are not easy to start. They demand a whole range of social supports they cannot provide for themselves if they are to work. Legal systems must be designed and enforced. Property rights, physical and intellectual, are central. Everyone has to know who owns what and who has a right to sell what.

In the formerly communist societies in Eastern Europe, the failure to decide who owns what and to then enforce those decisions lies behind much of the corruption and a lot of the economic failure. If physical property rights are not clear, anyone who sells anything is selling something to which they do not have a clear legal title. Technically they are all thieves. The only question is: are they big thieves (selling a boatload of oil they do not own) or little thieves (selling a chicken they do not own)?

Physical infrastructure must be provided. Without using the government right of eminent domain (compulsory sales of private property when needed for infrastructure development), no country can build a high quality system of physical infrastructure—transportation, electrification, and communications. Since many of these infrastructure systems are natural monopolies, some level of government control is unavoidable if they are to operate well after they are built.

Social infrastructure is just as important. Modern capitalism needs an educated workforce. Although theoretically education could be financed privately, no country has gotten an educated workforce by relying on private education. The reasons are those clearly seen more than a century and a half ago when mass, universal, paid-for-by-the-state compulsory education was invented in the United States. Illiterate parents with an anti-education culture cannot be allowed to hand illiteracy down to their children. The link has to be broken between parental income and a child's education.

Even educated parents underinvest in education—often for sound economic reasons. The payoffs occur many years in the future. Using standard discounted net present values, dollars earned after graduation twelve years or sixteen years into the future have very little current value relative to the investments that must be made now. The benefits also accrue to someone (the child) other than the persons (the parents) who must lower their current standard of living to finance educational investments. And we often exaggerate how willing parents are to do this. The rapid growth in student loans to finance higher education for children from high income families reflects this reality. The benefits of having everyone educated pays off big time to societies where risks can be averaged but need not be smart personal investments, since the risks that investments will not pay off for any one individual are often high.

As seen in the transition from communism to capitalism, the shift from planned markets to free markets can easily end up in chaos. This happens because free markets in some ways are very close to chaos—but they are not chaos. The yelling and shouting that accompanies trading on the floor of the New York Stock Exchange is a good example. It looks much like chaos, but it is in reality a highly organized dance. But if you get the organization even slightly wrong, markets often ends up in real chaos.

Think of the market California created for the sale of electricity. It was created in a society with a lot of market experience, yet it still ended up producing chaos. The reasons are easy to understand. In the movement to free markets many of those who were successful in the previous system, whatever it is, are going to lose their sources of wealth. Not surprisingly, they try to rig the new free markets to prevent their losses. Often their rigging stops the market from working.

This was the source of much of the problem in the deregulation of the electricity market in California. The old utilities thought their existing nuclear power plants would become worthless (stranded costs), and they wanted the markets rigged so the consumer and not their shareholders would pay for these stranded costs. Using political pressures, they succeed in achieving their desires. Retail prices would be frozen, although wholesale prices were expected to fall. This difference between falling wholesale buying prices and constant retail selling prices would pay for the stranded costs. But when contrary to everyone's expectations wholesale prices went up, the previous rigging of the system caused it to implode. Flexible wholesale prices were above, not below, the fixed retail prices that could be charged. Buying high and selling low, the utilities quickly went into bankruptcy and the state of California had to take control of its power system to keep the electricity flowing.

In the transition to market economies, often a country's GDP has to go down in the short run to go up in the long run, and in frustration at this reality the transition is aborted before it has any chance of succeeding. This phenomenon was very visible in the USSR. Communism had to be dismantled before capitalism could be built. In the dismantlement, declines in production led to falling incomes and the transition to capitalism was halted before capitalistic production ever got started. No one wanted to suffer the downs that were necessary to eventually go up. But stopping halfway between communism and capitalism doesn't work. The capitalistic economy doesn't get the price signals it needs to make efficient decisions, and the centrally planned economy is no longer able to give the orders that once made it work.

The worldwide shift to capitalism is happening because capitalism is built on assumptions about human nature and technology that seem to correspond with the realities of human attitudes and modern technology. All the alternatives to capitalism assume that the prime human motive is, or should be, to help others. Capitalism, in contrast, assumes that the prime human motivation is greed, helping oneself. Individuals want to have more, and if possible, they want to get rich.

Ethically speaking, the motivational assumptions of socialism are better than those embodied in capitalism. Helping others is nobler than helping oneself. Unfortunately, the primacy of helping others just doesn't seem to correspond with human reality.

Socialism, communism, cooperatives, and kibbutzim have all been tried. Some have worked for short periods with an initial cadre of motivated self-sacrificing individuals, but none have been able to work over the long run. These other systems don't generate the same economic energy, the same self-sacrifice, and the same willingness to take risks—the factors that lie behind capitalism's success. Some countries have moved farther and faster than others in reducing the remains of socialism within their economies, but everyone is moving in the same direction. Nowhere is socialism expanding.

HONEST INTELLIGENCE

Building a global superstructure on a capitalistic substructure using new technologies is a complex construction. Understanding what is happening is not easy. What to the casual observer look like effects being caused by globalization can easily be effects caused by new technologies, by the shift to capitalism, or by interactions among the three. Understanding what must be done is even harder.

New economic forces are impacting our economic lives, but their impacts depend upon a complicated interaction with the path, trajectory, and momentum of the existing economic system. The whole is not just the sum of the parts or even more than the sum of the parts. A new and very different global economy is being created. But it is not some proportional mixture of the new and the old—it shares more with the metamorphosis of a caterpillar into a butterfly.

Normally, wisdom is extracted from experience. But in the current context wisdom cannot be extracted from experience. The economic game is changing too fast. Consensus, common wisdom reflecting past experiences, is often wrong. Individuals, firms, and nations need to understand the new global game if they are to get an edge. But since this is a new era, no one knows exactly what "getting an edge" means in practice or how the edge should actually be gotten. But we do know that those who catch this wave will have a tremendous advantage. We also know that those who don't catch the wave are going to fall behind just as those who did not catch the waves created by industrialization and the steam engine and by systematic science and electrification fell behind.

To sail into the unknown without learning everything there is to be known is not to be bold. It is to be foolish. Every scrap of possible knowledge has to be acquired before setting sail. Smart choices cannot be made without the best possible intelligence. Getting that necessary intelligence isn't going to just happen. A process has to be put in place for generating and managing knowledge.

Each of us has to participate in that process, but something more is needed. As we have seen in the case of auto and aviation accident investigations, either the investigations don't happen or what is learned from them is not implemented unless there are institutions and people held responsible for learning what can be learned and using it to improve future performance. Someone has to be responsible for acquiring and using the knowledge that is to be had. Put simply, someone has to be responsible for being knowledgeable about knowledge management.

A Superstructure Built with New Technologies

If a help wanted advertisement were being written, it mig,
read: "Wanted: a Chief Knowledge Officer (CKO), someone
knowledgeable about technology, economics, sociology, politics,
and global affairs who can lead investigations that will allow individuals, firms, and nations to better understand the path they will
tread in the 21st century and to let them better shape that path to
their liking. For those wishing to apply a more detailed job
description is available upon request—see chapter 9."

{3}

THE VIEW FROM THE
TOP OF THE GLOBAL TOWER

Skyscrapers were built in New York City first because it has few earthquakes and bedrock lies close to the surface of the earth. Modern skyscrapers are now built almost everywhere, since construction engineers have learned how to build tall buildings in places where bedrock cannot be found and where earthquakes are frequent. Often the skyscrapers sit on Teflon pads that allow the buildings to move rather than break when the earth itself starts to move.

The global economy skyscraper has to be similarly built to withstand economic earthquakes—financial crashes and recessions—if it is to remain standing. These economic earthquakes flow from the unstable capitalistic substructure upon which globalization rests. In capitalism there is no economic bedrock to be found and economic earthquakes are frequent.

The earthquakes that matter are the ones that hit the top of the tower where the wealthiest economies reside. The ups and downs of the global economy depend upon events in the biggest economies, those of the United States, Europe, and Japan. The reasons relate to both economics and mathematics.

Financial crises and recessions in the third world are globally marginal events. Successful countries in the third world depend upon exports sold in the first world, and if these exports are growing rapidly, no serious downturn can occur in the third world. But the third world also represents only one-fifth of global output. Big ups and downs in that one-fifth of global output don't matter much to total global output.

Mathematically, if Japan had continued growing in the 1990s at its 1980s rate of 5 percent per year, the world's GDP would be $2.3 trillion or about 7 percent bigger than it actually was in 2002. China claims to have grown at a 9.7 percent rate in the 1990s, but even so it added only $750 billion to the global economy. What was lost in Japan's failure was three times as big as what was gained in China's success. If the United States grows at 5 percent, it adds 1.6 percentage points to the world's growth rate. If China grows at 5 percent per year, it adds 0.2 percentage points to the world's growth rate.

Within the big three, the United States and Japan have been actors while Europe has been a reactor over the last two decades. As a result, it is to Japan and the United States that the analyst must look to understand the globe's current and future economic performance.

In the 1980s Japan threatened to competitively roll over the rest of the world. But it did not happen. The 1990s opened with a Japanese financial crash. Japan's crisis did not begin with foreign capital flight or with a balance-of-payments crisis. Japan did not need to borrow funds from the international community because Japan itself held the world's largest stockpile of foreign exchange reserves. The Japanese crisis had nothing to do with globalization. The crisis began an abrupt correction of a grossly overvalued stock market and grossly inflated land values. Japan's inability to deal with these crashes produced ten years of little or no economic growth—what the Japanese now call their "lost decade." What everyone believed could not happen—a major lengthy contraction in a wealthy developed economy, essentially another Great Depression—happened.

Japan had quit growing and became brakes on the global economic train. More important, Japan had caught capitalism's worst disease, deflation. The deflationary disease has spread to East Asia (price indexes are now falling everywhere in East Asia) and, as we will see later, threatens to spread to Europe and America.

America is the global economic locomotive. Only America employs countercyclical fiscal and monetary policies to combat recessions. Europe and Japan are content simply to let the American economic locomotive move them and the rest of the world's economic train forward. And when the American locomotive stops, Europe and Japan sit passively waiting for the American locomotive to restart.

In the 1990s America looked as threatening as Japan had in the 1980s. America was the first to implement the new technologies of the third industrial revolution, and the world was forced to react to this leadership. America boomed for most of the 1990s, but its dot.com stock market crashed in the spring of 2000, its economy went into a recession in 2001, and there was a wider stock market crash in 2002. By early 2003 the Nasdaq had fallen 80 percent and the New York Stock Exchange 45 percent. Hundreds of firms were delisted from the stock exchanges as their shares fell below $1 and stayed there. In the heart of high-tech America, Silicon Valley, eight hundred businesses went out of business, per capita incomes declined, and rents fell 40 percent.[1] For the American family $7,000 billion in stock market wealth disappeared.[2]

This American crisis did not start with capital flight or a balance-of-payments problem. Like the Japanese crisis, it was home grown. But in an integrated world economy, an American recession has enormous ramifications for the rest of the world. The American stock market crash and recession spread to Europe and to the export-led economies on the Pacific Rim such as Taiwan and

Singapore. Economically, the rest of the world rides the American bucking bronco.

With European unification at the beginning of the 1990s, it looked like Europe would create a formidable competitive presence, but it did not happen. The Europeans were passive participants in the big economic events of the 1980s and 1990s.

AN UNSTABLE CAPITALISTIC SUBSTRUCTURE

Recessions and financial collapses flow from the capitalistic substructure upon which the global superstructure is being built. It is important to understand that capitalism's failures are caused by the same genetic structure that causes capitalism's successes. The crises of capitalism aren't accidental. They are genetic. To stop the bad would be to stop the good. As a result, globalization has to be built to withstand capitalism's economic instability. The failures cannot be eliminated.

The history of capitalism is littered with hundreds of financial crashes and economic recessions. Professor Kindleberger in his classic book *Manias, Panics and Crashes* counted twenty-eight major ones in the 19th century alone.[3] The names of the really big meltdowns ring down through history: tulip mania in Holland in the 1600s, the South Sea Bubble in Britain and the Louisiana Bubble in France in the 1700s, and the Great Depression in the United States in the 1930s.

Past infections do not provide future immunity. The normal historical pattern in capitalism is to cycle between periods of stability and instability. Memories of the Great Depression make people cautious and lead governments to impose tough regulations that crack down on speculative behavior. As a result, after World War II in the 1950s and 1960s there were no financial crashes. By the 1970s those with actual memories of the Great Depression were retiring from businesses and government. Those who followed came to believe it "could not happen again."

Not surprisingly, financial crashes started to appear in the 1970s and accelerated into the 1980s and the 1990s. In America the process started with the effective bankruptcy of the country's largest city, New York, in the mid-1970s. A short time later a government bailout was needed for one of America's largest corporations, the Chrysler Corporation. The Savings and Loan crisis erupted in the mid-1980s. The stock market fell 25 percent in October 1987. This crash was rated by some economists as the sharpest in the last century because it occurred in just three days.[4] It was followed by a sharp fall in property prices that then rolled around much of the rest of the industrial world. A $12 billion investment in Canary Wharf in London ended up being purchased for $0.5 billion; Parisian apartments fell 50 percent in price.

Capitalism's successes and its instabilities are both traced to three fundamental human attitudes—greed, optimism, and the herd mentality.

Why would anyone work one hundred hours a week, save most of their money as opposed to taking a long vacation in Bora Bora, and then risk it all on setting up a new business where there is a 95 percent probability of failure? The answer is simple: "I want to get rich." Greed is what makes people work hard, cut back on their consumption, and risk everything starting new businesses. Greed leads to economic growth and higher standards of living.

But greed also causes financial crashes. Tulip mania in Holland in the 1620s is usually considered to be the first capitalistic financial crash. The growing of tulips was new to Holland, the craze of planting tulip bulbs having just arrived from Turkey. No one knew which business models would work. Anything seemed possible. At the peak of tulip mania one of those nice six-story row houses along the canals sold for four black tulip bulbs. Everyone then, as now, knew that this price was crazy. In the long run the price of a tulip bulb cannot be significantly higher than the cost of growing a tulip bulb.

But there had been an earlier day when eight black tulip bulbs bought a house. That was also crazy. But investors who get out of the market when the price is 8 to 1 miss an opportunity to sell out at 4 to 1 and double their money. Such opportunities are irresistible. They are a chance to get rich. They don't come every day. Everyone knows that those prices cannot last, but they all believe that they will get out before the end comes—and that they must trade today.

Who did not know in the late 1990s on the left, rational, side of their brain that dot.com companies with no profits and little sales could not be worth tens of billions of dollars? We all knew that. But it was a chance to get rich. Our critical faculties were suspended because we all saw people getting very rich with little or no effort. After reading about all those new billionaires, we felt stupid if we weren't participating. As in the case of tulips almost four hundred years ago, none of us could resist.

It is a simple law of economic gravity that when prices reach silly levels, they will eventually come down—usually very fast. Sophisticated insiders and naïve outsiders both get caught in the quick downturns. Very few of the dot.com billionaires, in fact, cashed out.[5] They believed their own hype.

Optimism is the second characteristic necessary to make capitalism work. Those running firms must believe that their firms are going to succeed. If they didn't believe this, they would not risk their money and their careers. Suppose every firm in an industry is asked what their market share will be next year. When the reported numbers are added, will they add up to less or more than 100 percent? Of course they will be more than 100 percent. They should add up to more than 100 percent. Something would be wrong if they didn't. If our analyst is looking at industries where significant investments must be made in upfront infrastructure and productive capacity to have a larger market share, then the economy is automatically going to have cycles of overinvestment—and the recessions necessary to work off these overinvestments.

The herd mentality is the third factor lying behind the instability of capitalism. Suppose an antelope sees a lion. It should run! Suppose an antelope sees the grass move. It should run!

Suppose an antelope sees other antelope running. It should run! The antelope that stops to investigate whether there is or is not a lion and whether the lion is or is not hungry is the one that gets eaten. If there is no lion, the antelope can always come back at a later time and eat the grass. Running is both good fun and great exercise.

The same applies to financial markets. Before the March–April 2000 meltdown the dot.coms could do no wrong. Firms with no profits and few sales were worth tens of billions. After April they could do no right. Two marketing firms tracked Christmas 2000 sales. During the selling season eight months after the dot.com crash one of those tracking firms reported that dot.com sales were up 54 percent and the other 85 percent.[6] The same marketing firms reported that sales at brick-and-mortar stores went up 0.1 and 0.2 percent. Yet the financial headlines were "Dot.com Failures" and "E-tail Welcomes Ho-Hum Season."[7] Their sales were expected to go up 150 percent. When sales did not rise by that amount they were considered failures, despite the fact that they were doing far better than conventional stores.

By the end of 2000 the financial herd was in panic and running away from electronic retailing despite announcements that electronic airline ticket sales had for the first time accounted for more than 50 percent of airline ticket sales, that Amazon was selling 10 percent of the books in America, and that 16 percent of financial services were being provided electronically.[8] Electronic retailing was seen as a subjective failure even when it was becoming an objective success.

During the dot.com boom a small number of mutual fund managers refused to buy the dot.coms on the grounds they were overvalued.[9] What happened to these fund managers? All were fired because they could not keep up with the market averages. The fired mutual fund managers have been proven to be right. The dot.coms were not worth those high prices. Have any of the fired managers been rehired as mutual fund managers? The answer is no.

The message is simple. It always pays to run with the herd even when you believe the herd is wrong.

Warren Buffet, the nation's wealthiest and perhaps its shrewdest pure investor, also refused to buy the dot.coms. He called them a "chain letter."[10] He was ultimately right, but his fund, Berkshire Hathaway, fell far behind the market averages—down more than 20 percent in 1999 while everyone else's funds were up more than 17 percent.[11] He was too wealthy, owned too many shares in his own company, and had been too successful in the past to be fired, but he was heavily criticized in the financial press as an out-of-it, over-the-hill, behind-the-times investor. Here is just a sampling of the headlines:

"Warren Buffet yesterday's man"[12]

"Buffet confesses blunder"[13]

"This might be the year that the rest of us got smarter than Warren Buffett"[14]

"It is time for the Sage of Omaha to retire"[15]

"Guru today, gone tomorrow. There is something sad, almost embarrassing, about witnessing a fading star who refuses to retire gracefully"[16]

Anyone else would have been fired. In his annual March 2000 company meeting Buffet essentially had to make a capitalistic public confession of error very similar to those made under duress in China's cultural revolution: "The numbers show just how poor our 1999 performance was. . . . [My] report card showed four Fs and a D. . . . It is no sure thing that we will regain our stride."[17]

Understanding the genetic structure of capitalism (greed, optimism, the herd mentality) tells us that any global economy has to be built to minimize the economic shocks that will inevitably occur, and it has to be built to minimize the damage done by these minimized shocks. No one is going to be able to build a completely stable global superstructure on an unstable capitalistic substructure. But a global superstructure can be built that will withstand the economic earthquakes that will occur.

The Great Depression happened in America because Americans had not built a shockproof national economic structure. Japan's lost decade occurred because it had not built a shockproof national economic structure. Neither had to happen.

AMERICA: A SOURCE OF ECONOMIC INSTABILITY; AN ESSENTIAL LOCOMOTIVE FOR GLOBAL SUCCESS

Leaving aside the transition from wartime to peacetime in 1945, America entered its tenth recession since World War II in 2001. What had come to be called the new economy was not recession proof. The nine preceding recessions lasted from sixteen months at the worst to six months at the best, and the declines in GDP ranged from 0.5 percent down at the best to 3.6 percent down at the worst. The 2001 recession produced a 0.6 percent decline in GDP and lasted nine months. Growth resumed in late 2001. In 2002 the economy expanded at a 2.4 percent rate.

The 2001 recession felt worse than the statistics seem to indicate, since manufacturing entered an extended recession that would prove to be its worst since World War II. Profits of the five hundred largest global firms were cut in half between 2000 and 2001.[18] But America did not face the "1,000 year flood" (John Chambers' phrase at Cisco) or the "perfect storm" (a phrase often used on the Pacific Rim). The 2001 recession was a perfectly normal, everyday garden variety recession that on average occurs every five years in America. The only unusual thing about the 2001 recession was that it had been ten years since the last recession.

Of the ten recessions since World War II, seven have had a common cause and an easy cure.[19] The Federal Reserve Board would raise interest rates to slow the economy and stop inflation. Rates would get too high, and housing and auto sales (the two big items bought on credit) would plunge. The economy would stop. But since the economy had been stopped by raising interest rates, it could quickly be restarted by lowering interest rates. The Fed would push interest rates down and housing and auto sales would quickly rebound. As a result, most American recessions have been short with a sharp recovery, what economists call V recessions—quick down, quick up.

What the Japanese had in the 1990s, a decade without growth, is an L recession—go down and stay down. America's Great Depression was an L.

Three of America's recessions, and the 2001 recession is one of those, had different causes. These causes led to a different timing pattern—what economists call a U recession—go down, stay down for a while, and then slowly recover.

The second recession of the ten postwar recessions (1953–1954) was induced by sharp cutbacks in military spending after the Korean War that were not offset by tax cuts or increases in other forms of government spending. The sixth recession, in 1973–1975, was caused by the first OPEC oil shock. Fiscal authorities did not understand that a huge increase in oil prices is the equivalent of a huge tax increase—just paid to the king of Saudi Arabia rather than to the U.S. government. Consumer incomes available to be spent on other products fall precipitously. To avoid such a recession the oil tax increase must be offset with a local tax reduction.

The third of these U recessions, the 2001 recession, flowed from a complicated interaction between the recessionary genes of capitalism and the shift in technologies that were part of the third industrial revolution.

EVERYTHING IS GOING TO WORK; NOTHING IS GOING TO WORK

New firms in any new industry effectively participate in a lottery. No one knows what will work. Many new business models have to be tried. Most won't work. Most of the new firms experimenting with these new business models will go broke; a few will be very successful. Most investors will lose their money; a few will get rich. It has happened over and over again historically.

Consider the auto industry: More than 2,000 auto manufacturing firms were set up prior to 1929. Every bicycle maker like Henry Ford went into the business of making cars. By the late 1950s only three firms were left—Ford, General Motors, and Chrysler. An investor lucky enough or wise enough to have invested in those three became fabulously rich in the 1950s even though there would be a stock market crash in 1929 and a Great Depression in the 1930s. But investors in all those other firms lost their money.

Economists know why the three who survived, survived. Ford invented the business model for making cars—assembly lines, component manufacturing, and supply chain management. Sloan at General Motors invented the business model for selling cars— annual model changes, colors, understanding that the car is an extension of the owner's personality—so buyers don't treat them as refrigerators and buy a new one once every twenty-five years. Chrysler consolidated a few of the most successful firms among the also-rans and has, as a result, always been an also-ran, finally losing its independence and becoming a German company in 1998.

But anyone looking forward in the midst of an industrial revolution will find it very hard to identify successful business models. Suppose it is 1983 at the beginning of the PC revolution. You are Moses and go up Mount Sinai to talk to God about the personal computer business. He tells you that in 2001 the world will sell 140 million personal computers. Given this inside information, which stock would you have bought? Probably you would have bought Commodore Computer. It was then the leading maker of PCs, growing rapidly with a 33 percent market share. Yet in 1994 it went out of business.[20] You could not have bought the stock of the big winner, Microsoft, since it was not a public company in 1983.

As any new industry develops, it will go from an overoptimistic, overhyped period where everything is going to work to an overpessimistic, underhyped period when nothing is going to work. There is a gold rush mentality. Everyone is going to get rich. The place is full of gold. Or—there is no gold. Move on! The truth is always in between. A few things are going to work; most are going to fail. But it is very hard to know which are the few successful business models that will work.

The rhythm of these shifts in sentiments leads to financial crashes as certain as their timing is uncertain. The 2001 recession began with the dot.com stock market crash in March and April of 2000. Electronic retailing was going from the "everything is going to work and we are all going to get rich" period to the "nothing is going to work and everyone is going to go broke" phase of development. Following the initial dot.com crash, the declines spread to the technology sector and then to everyone else in 2002. For the first time since the Great Depression stock markets fell for three consecutive years. Only the four years' decline at the onset of the Great Depression had been worse. A deep, prolonged bear market had arrived.

As in all financial crashes the question is not why the stock markets crashed but how values could ever have been so high in the first place. Dot.coms with no profits and few sales had been worth billions. Given such inflated market values, the markets were going to fall. The only question was when. Given a big stock market crash, a recession is sure to follow. It did.

ASSIGNING BLAME

Looking for someone to blame, investors accused the Federal Reserve Board of not tightening monetary policies earlier to force stock prices down. In the words of the financial press, Alan Greenspan's failure to prevent the boom and bust "turned his luster from gold to nickel."[21] But preventing this cycle is simply impossible even when the Federal Reserve Board, in the words of Alan Greenspan, saw "irrational exuberance" in America's financial markets in 1996—four years before the markets actually peaked and crashed. To stop stock prices from rising in the midst of a bubble would have required very high interest rates—rates so high they would have thrown the rest of the economy into a sharp recession. Any Federal Reserve Board that attempted to follow this policy would have been removed—and should have been removed. The cure would have been far worse than the disease. Margin requirements (the cash required to buy a share of stock) should probably have been raised, but there is no reason to believe this would have stopped the bubble from occurring.[22]

Many others, like Greenspan, saw dot.com stock prices as a bubble and acted on their beliefs. They sold short the stocks of the electronic retailers in 1998 and 1999, expecting their stock market prices to go down. They were right in the long run, but without the right timing they all ended up losing money. By the time the actual crash arrived, there were few left brave enough and wealthy enough to still be shorting a bull market.

One can ask why financial analysts, accountants, bond rating agencies, the business press, and economists are so bad at foreseeing crashes. Looking back, it is all foreseeable. The signs are visible. Looking forward, it is all visible—but also invisible. Everyone wants to believe the boom can continue. This desire blocks out clear signs that the boom has gotten out of hand.

There are no rewards to those who foresee doom and gloom before it appears. No one is willing to pay for "don't buy" bad news from stock market analysts in the middle of a boom. The business press is no different. People don't want to read doom-and-gloom articles in the middle of a boom. It is costly to dig beneath the surface optimism. The press looks silly when the boom doesn't end quickly.

There are always a few analysts who are negative and get it right, but there are also always a few analysts who are negative about every stock—good or bad—at all points in time.[23] When the naysayers are proven right, they will be heralded as great forecasters. They aren't. Consistently predict bad things long enough and eventually you will be right.

Bond rating agencies are profit making firms that do not want to incur the costs of digging out information unavailable in company reports. They foresaw nothing at Enron until a few days before its bankruptcy.[24] Analysts who did see something wrong were not believed. Sophisticated big banks like Citicorp made large loans to Enron.[25] Banks make money by lending money, not by not lending money. All of the incentives within the bank lead to the belief that big borrowers can repay and encourages lending officers not to look too deeply at the details. The big mutual funds continued to increase their holdings of Enron until the end.[26] It wasn't just the little guy who got squeezed.

Although economic models are good when it comes to fundamental forces and pressures, no economic model can predict the precise timing of events. Forecasting downturns and then having them not happen is the road to oblivion. The forecaster looks silly and loses clients as a result.

TELECOMS

When stock prices crashed in the dot.com sector in March and April of 2000, everyone started to re-evaluate other sectors. The precise causes of 2001's recession are found in the re-evaluation of telecommunications investments. In the first three quarters of 2000, business investment in plant and equipment, mostly in telecommunications broadly defined (Internet, servers, routers, fiber optics, communications software, etc.), was rising $31 billion per quarter. In the fourth quarter of 2000, business investment went down $9 billion and then fell $31 billion per quarter in each of the next four quarters of 2001. Again, almost all of the decline was located in telecommunication equipment investment. Given these big ups and downs in telecom investment, the 2001 recession is no mystery.

The downturn in telecom investment is easily understood. More than $70 billion too much had been invested in fiber optics alone.[27] In America, 95 to 98 percent of the fiber optics buried in the ground wasn't being used.[28] Excess capacity was everywhere in the telecommunications industry.

How investment could have gone up so much in the first place is also not a mystery. Remember the universal causes of booms and busts outlined earlier—greed, optimism, and the herd mentality. Never have they been so clearly at work as in telecommunications.

The telecom industry must build infrastructure ahead of demand. With the Internet and cellular telephone both experiencing exploding demand, the telecommunications companies were predicted to grow rapidly. Being *optimistic,* every firm assumed its market share was going to go up. To take advantage of this opportunity to win, they all needed massive investments in infrastructure.

Someone was going to be the Henry Ford of the new telecommunications industry. Those who invested the most and had the most infrastructure would have the best chance to be the eventual winners of the telecom wars. Their managers and owners would get rich—*greed.*

Everyone believed this to be true and rushed in—*the herd mentality.* Five third generation (3G) telecommunications licenses were auctioned off for $35 billion in Great Britain. Think of it—five pieces of paper that only give one the right to invest a lot more money in infrastructure sold for $35 billion.[29] The UK results were not an anomaly. In Germany six companies bid $46 billion.[30] If we aggregate across Europe, the winning bids totaled $150 billion.

The market value of each of the winning companies actually went down in the aftermath of the auctions, since the market believed the bidders had overpaid in what economists know as the "curse of the winning bid." The winner of an auction, by definition, believes the item is worth more than everyone else in the world believes it to be worth. Unless the winner has inside information others do not have, there is no reason to believe the winner is right and everyone else is wrong. The reverse is probably true. It is highly likely that the winner has overpaid.

But each of the winning European firms believed that those who owned the 3G telecommunications network would be the ultimate winners of the telecom wars regardless of the market's short-run judgments about overpaying. They also knew that if they did not get a 3G license, the firm would not be able to build a 3G telephone network and would essentially be forced to exit the telephone industry. Their stock prices would fall to zero if this happened. They had to obtain a license even if this meant knowingly overbidding—and many did know they were bidding too much.

If those European third generation telecom licenses were auctioned off again today, they would probably have no value. Many people, perhaps most people, think the world will wait for fourth generation telecommunications technology and skip the third generation. The licenses may even have a negative value, since technically they are an obligation to build a third generation network no one now wants to build.

After the dot.com crash in 2000 the financial herd was rushing away from technology stocks and firms were being severely punished for having too much debt. Because of their big investments, telecom companies had big debts. Telecom stock market values fell rapidly. WorldCom's stock market value went from $180 billion to $7 billion in just a few months.

Since this recession was caused by an autonomous decline in business investment and not induced by high interest rates, the economic patterns of the 2001 recession were different from those of the previous seven "inflation fighting" recessions. Housing and auto sales were actually increasing during 2001. They did so because the economy was not being squeezed by interest rates. Precisely the opposite: The Federal Reserve Board started to lower interest rates in December 2000 and repeatedly cut them in 2001. Housing and auto sales could not rebound, since they had not been slumping. And as a result, America had a U and not a V recession.

DOUBLE DIP RECESSION

As in the Sherlock Holmes mystery *Silver Blaze*, the key to understanding the 2000–2003 period is the dog that did not bark. From

1992 to 2001 the savings rate of the average American household went down from 9 percent to 2 percent, actually reaching less than 1 percent in the fourth quarter of 2001. The American family took on enormous amounts of consumer debt. Household debt went up from 89 percent to 117 percent of disposable income.[31]

Seemingly, Americans quit saving for their future. But Americans did not really stop caring about their children's education and their own retirement. The stock market was roaring upward, and they were getting rich without saving out of their annual incomes. Stock market gains would allow them to provide for their future and to raise their consumption levels simultaneously. Economists call this the "wealth effect." Wealth, not just income, affects consumption. On average, economists have found that a dollar of extra wealth seems to lead to about five cents of extra annual consumption.

But by the summer of 2002 American families had lost $7,000 billion worth of wealth.[32] Rational economic analysis would say that a negative wealth effect should kick in. With savings near zero, having maxed out their credit card borrowings, and being much poorer, American families should have had no choice but to lower their consumption and start saving again. Thus the recession of 2001 would be a "double dip" recession.[33] The first downturn would be caused by the fall in business investment, and the second downturn would be caused by a fall in consumption. But it did not happen. Had it happened, the 2001 recession would not have been so short or so mild.

The "why" is partly understandable and partly mysterious. Alan Greenspan and the Federal Reserve Board were aggressively lowering interest rates in 2001. These cuts were not designed to turn business investment around. Everyone knew that was impossible because of the huge amounts of excess capacity. The cuts were designed instead to stop the second stage of the double dip recession. For 90 percent of American families the value of their home is at least three times as important as the value of their stock market portfolios.[34] Median households have four times as much equity in their home as they do in the stock market.[35] What Americans can pay for a house depends on the size of the monthly mortgage payment, and if lower interest rates lead to a lower monthly payment, Americans can afford to pay more for their homes. Put simply, lower interest rates lead to higher housing prices.

The Fed's strategy worked. Despite the recession and the stock market crash, housing prices went up in America. The stock market's negative wealth effect was offset by the housing market's positive wealth effect. Higher home values meant that family wealth was going up, not down, for most families.

Lower interest rates also provided a source of cash for spending on items other than housing. Families could refinance their existing mortgages, cut their monthly payments, and use the money they had been spending on their mortgages to buy other items. When they refinanced, many families also took some of their home equity out in larger mortgages and used the money to buy other items such as automobiles. Lower energy prices and a warm 2001–2002 winter provided a third flow of cash. The money that did not need to be spent on heating could also be used to buy other items.

Together these factors prevented a double dip recession in 2002. But perhaps the simpler answer is that American consumers never cut their consumption as long as other options exist. There are no credit card limits. One simply gets another credit card. Everyone who has ever bet that the American consumer would retrench has always lost the bet.

SCANDALS

Given a financial bubble and a big slowdown, financial scandals were sure to follow. Every capitalistic boom ends in a scandal. At the end of a boom the pressures to keep the good times going just a little longer are enormous. Everyone has to meet the numbers (revenues and profits should rise at the rate the analysts expect), and the pressure to do so cascades up and down the corporate pyramid.

At Enron a last minute sham transaction for $60 million in December 1999 allowed the company to meet its numbers—to raise earnings per share from 24 cents to 31 cents. As a result of meeting those numbers, by the end of the week the value of the stock had risen 27 percent.[36]

People get fired up and down the corporate ladder if they don't meet the numbers. Adjusting the numbers is better than getting fired. Small adjustments to the numbers gradually become large adjustments to the numbers. WorldCom ended up with more than $7 billion of accounting irregularities as it raised earnings and profits by misclassifying operating expenses as revenue and by moving reserved funds set aside to cover bad debts into the normal revenue stream.

No one wants to look too closely at the numbers and be the one who announces that the good times are over. That is not the route to corporate promotions and personal success. No one wants to give up their dream of getting fabulously rich. All kid themselves into believing the good times are about to return. It is just a temporary downturn. If so, jiggling the numbers a little this quarter will be forgotten when the good times do return. Good times will, in fact, convert those false numbers into true numbers. Some of the booming revenues and profits of the next quarter can be backdated into this quarter to make this quarter's reported numbers real.

Highly predictable but not precisely identifiable scandals break out. American charges in 1997 that the Asian crisis was caused by "crony capitalism" were always the height of chutzpah. Americans ignored their own history. Crony capitalism exists everywhere. It cannot be completely stamped out. Examine the end of any financial boom in American history and one finds scandals. The scandals in the boom preceding the Great Depression led to the formation of the SEC (Securities and Exchange Commission) and most of the accounting and financial regulations Americans now live with. Anyone, including President Bush, who treats the current round of corporate accounting scandals as if they were abnormal in American capitalism has a very short memory. In Texas less than two de-cades ago almost every bank went broke during the Savings and Loan crisis because of loans that were dubious the day they were made. People bought small savings banks to make loans to them-selves. Hundreds of business people went to jail.

It is interesting to speculate whether the collapse of Enron would have been given the same extensive press coverage if it had collapsed in the middle of a stock market boom rather than in the middle of a stock market crash. I suspect that coverage would have been much less extensive. It is just human to want to believe the American family lost all that money on the stock market, not because it was silly enough to get sucked into a stock market bub-ble, but because evil people were doing fraudulent accounting.

Blaming the analysts is easier then blaming oneself. Merrill Lynch analysts were recommending stocks they knew were "a piece of junk."

Yet on the left, rational, side of our brains we all knew that companies with no profits could not be worth tens of billions of dollars. Individuals invested not because they were duped but because on the right, emotional, side of their brains they wanted to believe they could easily get rich. Each of us has a 401(k) that has become a 201(k). There are two ways to look at this much emptier pension plan: I was silly and let myself be sucked into a bubble or I was cheated. Either way I have lost lots of money, but it is far easier to live with the second belief.

Making today's devils out of yesterday's heroes is well under-way. A recent book on the dot.com crash, *Dot.Con: The Greatest Story Ever Sold,* opens with the sentence, "Ever get the feeling you've been cheated?"[37] When the stock market value of the telecommunications company WorldCom goes from $180 billion to $7 billion, the CEO founder is for the first time described in the *Financial Times* as a possible crook who unethically borrowed $400 million from the company he headed.[38] The *Financial Times* knew about those loans much earlier.

Scandals also depend upon perception. Think about Jack Welch's generous, completely legal pension benefits: Manhattan apartment furnished with food, wine, cook, and staff; use of company aircraft, cars, and office; and personal financial planning services.[39] Suppose these perks had been revealed in a year in which General Electric stock prices had gone up 40 percent rather than down 40 percent.[40] His pension benefits would have occasioned little or no notice. Perhaps they were a little generous and above the norm, but everyone would have said he deserved it. The benefits were seen as scandalous precisely because General Electric stock price was plummeting.

There are always insiders who see the end coming and sell their shares before the general public has the same information. In an exposé the *Financial Times* found that executives with companies that had gone broke made $3.3 billion in salaries and stock sales immediately before their companies went broke.[41] First place in the race to receive the most in a losing performance goes to an executive of Global Crossing with $512 billion in share sales and salaries. Twenty-fifth place was held by another executive of Global Crossing with a mere $38 million.

Scandals are completely normal events. The Enrons and World-Coms are not abnormalities. At the same time, the system is sound. What is meant by "sound" is that the system picks itself up and moves on with little aggregate economic damage. But that sound system is also populated with people who easily slip into unethical and perhaps criminal behavior under the pressure of economic events.

Anyone who thinks changing the rules governing the accounting profession will permanently fix the problem of scandals following in the wake of an economic boom is incredibly naïve. Accounting is based on a fundamental conflict of interest. No one pulls the trigger on those who hire them, those who can fire them, and those who determine how much they get paid. If one wanted completely honest accounting, the federal government would have to set up and pay a financial police force that would randomly audit a firm's books based on legally defined accounting rules. This is not about to happen. And it also wouldn't completely stop scandals. People would find areas where the rules do not apply, or are vague, and they'd engage in creative fraud.

Similarly, anyone who believes that putting up a Chinese wall between investment bankers and stock market analysts will stop stocks from being overhyped in the analysts' reports is equally naïve. The same fundamental conflict of interest exists. The analyst's reports will inevitably be biased in favor of whoever paid for them. Preventing investment bankers from talking with analysts (in a Wall Street settlement the head of Citigroup agreed not to talk to his own analysts) or stopping cross payments from one financial firm's investment bankers to another financial firm's analysts to get good reviews is not going to change this reality.[42] People do what they think their boss wants them to do. They would be stupid if they did not do so. And although the public did not know about the direct cross payments for favorable reports, we all knew, or should have known, that the analysts' reports were being hyped during the boom of the 1990s. That is the nature of the capitalistic beast during a bubble.

New sets of rules to prevent financial scandals from reoccurring are like French generals building the Maginot line after World War I. If the Maginot line had been in place before World War I, it would have stopped Germany's frontal attacks across the border. But it did nothing to stop the actual German blitzkrieg through Belgium in World War II. Tomorrow's scandals will be new scandals in different places. They will not be prevented by today's new rules.

Post crisis changes in the organization and regulation of the savings and loan industry prevent that particular 1980s scandal from reoccurring, but they did nothing to stop 2002's accounting scandals. New rules should be adopted to prevent today's scandals from reoccurring tomorrow, but let no one think those new rules will prevent the next set of scandals.

There are two ways to deal with the endemic scandals of capitalism. The first and right answer is to put up a big sign warning the little investors that the game is rigged and that they don't play on a level playing field with the big investors and the insiders. Capitalism is a positive sum casino where the house—the big guys—take a cut. Governments should act to keep the house's cut under control and to punish the big guys when their cut gets out of control, but no government can guarantee the little guy an equal chance of winning.

The second and wrong answer is to pretend rules can be written to prevent future financial scandals and to give the little guy an equal chance. This is ultimately the biggest fraud of all. No set of rules can guarantee complete fairness and transparency. To pretend they can is to set the government up as the ultimate liar in the system.

If Warren Buffet, America's biggest individual investor, wants to have lunch with the CEO of General Motors to discuss GM's prospects, it will be arranged. The average investor, in contrast, won't even have his phone call answered. Paul Allen, a big investment banker who specializes in media investments, sponsors a summer media mogul conference in Idaho to share generalized inside information about media firms. The average investor won't be invited.

"Buyer beware" (caveat emptor) lies at the heart of all capitalistic transactions, and those who argue they can stop this from being true with new rules and regulations are the ultimate con artists in the system.

SKATING ON THIN ICE

America's recovery from 2001's recession, a 2.4 percent annual growth rate in 2002, wasn't great, but it wasn't bad either. Yet there was a feeling that things were worse than they seemed. Output was up, but employment fell. With unemployment rising, it did not feel like a recovery. There was also a feeling that the second dip of a double dip recession was just around the corner even though it was hard to find a consumer who was actually spending less. And when the 2002 Christmas season had the smallest year-to-year increase in sales in a long time, those feelings of a vague impending disaster were intensified. And in the final quarter of 2002 growth did slow sharply.

Somehow it all felt like America was skating on thin ice. Although the phrase "skating on thin ice" is commonly used in American English, few know the real feeling of skating on thin ice. The ice starts to creak and groan. As the ice cracks, small explosions, like pistol shots, ring out. The ice under your feet may suddenly look as if it were a window shattering after being hit by a stone. Undulating waves start to move through the ice. What was previously solid becomes plastic.

The fear induced by skating on thin ice is far worse than actually falling through the ice. A sudden unexpected fall through the ice will cause a surge in adrenaline that powers you out of ice water so quickly you hardly know you have been in the water. Wet clothes and cold weather make for an uncomfortable situation, but they engender no fear. That is why the phrase "skating on thin ice" and not "falling through the ice" is used in idiomatic English.

The "skating on thin ice" metaphor applies to America's current economic experiences. America suddenly and unexpected fell through the economic ice with a stock market crash in 2000 and a recession in 2001. It did not feel that bad. The recession was over almost before Americans knew it had begun. Throughout the period of negative growth in 2001 many analysts were arguing that America wasn't really in a recession.

For the average person much of the feeling of skating on thin ice flowed from the jobless nature of the 2002 recovery. Despite the mildness of the 2001 recession (a peak-to-trough decline in the GDP of only 0.6 percent) and positive growth rates in 2002 and 2003, hiring was in its worst slump in twenty years.[43] Help wanted advertisements reached a forty-year low. In durable goods manufacturing one out every nine jobs disappeared. The feeling that America was skating on thin ice remained in 2003 even though the predicted growth rate was still above 2 percent as spring turned to summer.

One million workers finding no work dropped out of the labor force. By dropping out they made measured unemployment look much better than it really was. But those 1 million unemployed people really do exist, want jobs, and have friends and relatives who know they want jobs and are really unemployed.

When analyzing recoveries, it is important to understand that there are two definitions of a recovery. To economists a recovery is simply a return to sustained positive growth rates. A growth rate of 0.1 percent is a recovery if it continues quarter after quarter. But that is not what business people mean by a recovery. They see no difference between a negative 0.1 percent decline in GDP and a positive 0.1 percent rise in GDP. When they talk about a recovery, they are thinking about a growth rate high enough to make expansion, and not downsizing, the prime road to more profitability. The 2002–2003 recovery is an economist's recovery but not a businessmen's recovery since the growth rate is positive but not high enough to end downsizings.

For ordinary workers a recovery means jobs are easier to get. To generate jobs an economy's rate of growth of output has to be higher than its rate of growth of productivity. To find the number of jobs lost, measured in hours of work, the rate of growth of productivity is subtracted from the rate of growth of output. In 2001 the recession reduced the economy's growth rate to 0.3 percent while productivity was growing at a 1.1 percent rate. As a result, the American economy lost 0.8 percent of its jobs—measured in hours of work—in 2001.

In 2002 productivity growth accelerated to 4.8 percent—the best performance in fifty years. This means, however, that output must then grow at more than 4.8 percent if employment is to rise. In 2002 it didn't. The GDP grew only 2.4 percent. And if one subtracts 4.8 percent from 2.4 percent, one is left with a 2.4 percent loss of jobs. In the recovery year of 2002, three times as many jobs were lost as in the recession year of 2001. Despite positive economic growth in 2003 the loss of jobs continues. In May 2003 non-farm employment was one million jobs below where it had been a year earlier in May of 2002. With that loss of jobs the feeling of skating on thin ice is very real and not surprising.

Higher productivity growth due to the introduction of new technologies is good news in the long run even if troublesome in the short run. Jobs are down but output per capita is up. But some of the acceleration in American productivity growth comes from another source. Any economy has a distribution of firms operating at different levels of productivity. Some are very efficient and some are relatively inefficient. If globalization causes the inefficient to move offshore to get lower wages and costs, average productivity rises. Getting rid of the worst performers raises the average performance of those who remain. Output per hour of work is up, but fewer Americans work. To make this source of productivity gain into a national gain, macroeconomic policies have to ensure that jobs are being created in the middle and top of the productivity distribution faster than they are being destroyed at the bottom. In 2002 this was not happening.

Some of the feeling of skating on thin ice also goes back to the possibility of that double dip recession. It has not yet happened, but left-brain logic tells us that it must happen. Americans cannot lose that much stock market wealth without something bad happening to consumption.

In the spring of 2003 the dollar had fallen almost 30 percent from its peak vis-à-vis the Euro. Was this a harbinger of wider things to come? Left-brain (rational) logic tells us that the dollar should fall. America has a big trade deficit, and with its stock market performance why would foreigners want to move the hundreds of billions of dollars into the United States that are necessary to keep the dollar from plunging (see chapter 4)? When it comes to the value of the dollar, it certainly feels as if America is skating on thin ice.

Everyone would like the thick ice of a vigorous recovery. But for a vigorous recovery to occur something has to recover sharply. There are only seven possibilities, since these seven items together constitute the GDP: personal consumption, business investment, residential investment, changes in inventories, net exports, state and local government spending, and federal government spending.

Two are clearly not going to lead the recovery. Business investment led the economy down, and there is just too much excess capacity for business investment to lead the economy up. If net exports (exports minus imports) were to lead the recovery, the rest of the world would have to be booming. It isn't. Quite the contrary, the rest of the world sits waiting for an American boom to carry them forward.

Given consumers with very low savings rates, with record credit card debts relative to disposable income, and with losses of $7,000 billion in stock market wealth, it is difficult to see a consumer boom leading the economy forward. The funds just aren't there. The sharp slowdown in Christmas spending in 2002 drove this point home. The American consumer prevented any big decline in the GDP in the aftermath of the stock market's collapse, but the consumer isn't going to lead the economy vigorously upward.

The Fed's cuts in interest rates have led to a boom in home building, but residential investment isn't a recovery vehicle for the entire economy. One cannot add a boom to a boom, and it is difficult to drive the economy forward by stimulating a sector that is only 4 percent of the GDP. Housing investment kept us from falling into a sharp recession, but it is not the fuel needed for a vigorous recovery.

Inventory investment by definition cannot create an environment of long-term growth. Inventories adjust to sales expectations. They don't drive sales forward.

State and local government spending is going to be pushing the economy down. State and local governments run budget systems where this year's expenditures are basically determined by last year's tax revenue. Because state and local government tax collections boomed in 2000, state and local spending rose sharply in 2001 despite the recession. But because of the recession, tax collections fell sharply in 2001. For one year, accumulated "rainy day" funds could fill much of the gap and postpone the need to raise taxes or cut spending, but by 2003 nineteen states were contemplating substantial tax increases and thirty-eight were talking about cutting their budgets by a total of $50 billion.[44] Not all those tax increases and expenditure cuts will happen—but many of them will. To the extent that they do occur, they will force the GDP down.

There used to be a federal program of countercyclical revenue sharing with state and local governments to prevent recessions from feeding upon themselves in this manner, but the program was not renewed in the 1990s in the belief that recessions were a thing of the past. The Democrats proposed the adoption of a countercyclical revenue sharing plan in their 2003 stimulus package, but it was not in the package proposed by President Bush.

As a result, if there is to be a vigorous economic recovery, the launch vehicle will have to be federal government taxes and expenditures. There are no other possibilities.

President Bush's current fiscal package is enough to give America a recovery in the economist sense, but it seems unlikely to be enough to give America a recovery in the business sense. A stronger recovery will need stronger federal government fiscal policies. This requires bigger deficits in the short run combined with the expectations of budget surpluses in the long run. If those long-run budget surpluses are not expected, long-term interest rates rise in expectation of future capital shortages and squeeze out current spending such as home building, thereby offsetting the stimulating effects of larger short-run budget deficits.

Although a better institutional system for managing fiscal policies to counteract booms and busts can be designed (see chapter 8), America is going to remain a powerful but erratic locomotive for the global economy. Downturns are in the genes of capitalism, and America is the most capitalistic of the globe's economies. With

America as the sole locomotive, the global economy will slow or plunge into a recession when America slows or plunges into a recession.

JAPAN: A BRAKE OF ENORMOUS PROPORTIONS
A DISEASE CARRIER OF GREAT RISK

Japan should make any country both humble and cautious. There exists a set of circumstances that, if hit, can instantly turn the biggest successes into the biggest failures. The circumstances differ from country to country, but they undoubtedly exist for all countries. For the United States it was the Great Depression, ended by World War II ten years after it had begun. When or if it would have ended without World War II is not at all obvious.

Japan came into the 1990s as the first world's best economic performer in the 1960s, 1970s, and 1980s. The country was an economic organism genetically well suited to its circumstances. In the 1980s after it was already rich, Japan averaged a 5 percent real growth rate—far higher than the U.S. growth rate of just 2 percent. Most observers believed the era of American economic dominance was coming to an end. A period of Japanese economic dominance was about to begin.

The Japanese crisis started in 1990–1991with an initial plunge in stock market prices from 39,000 to 13,000 on the Nikkei index. Measured in constant prices, the Japanese stock market crash was actually a bigger percentage fall than that which occurred between 1929 and 1932 in the United States. Property prices relentlessly followed the stock market down. After some ups and downs during the 1990s, stocks again dived in the aftermath of the U.S. dot.com crash, ending up under 7,900 in the spring of 2003—an aggregate fall of 80 percent. By 2003, property prices were down 84 percent from their peaks in Japan's six biggest cities and relentlessly continued to fall.[45] For all of Japan, land prices fell 6.4 percent in 2002— the twelfth consecutive year of decline.

The reductions in Japanese stock and land prices were not surprising. Stock market price-earnings multiples exceeded 100 before the crash. In capitalism stock prices sooner or later have to be justified by earnings. In Japan they weren't—and stock prices fell. In capitalism land values sooner or later have to be justified by rents. Is what can be done on the land productive enough to support the prices at which properties are bought and sold? When the property value of the emperor's palace in central Tokyo, evaluated at the prices at which private land was selling around the palace, exceeds the total value of the entire state of California, as it did, something is fundamentally wrong.[46] And everyone knows it. The GDP of California cannot be produced on a land area the size of the emperor's palace in Tokyo. The Japanese invested in real estate projects that every sensible person knew were going to lose money on they day they were planned. But building mistakes did not matter, since rising land values would cover them up.

The end of the bubble economy led to a decade of little growth in Japan. Measured GDP was lower in 2002 than it had been in 1991. After correcting for deflation real output was up—1 percent higher than it had been in 1995 and 3 percent higher than it had been in 1991—but only slightly. By 2003 Japan's crisis had lasted longer than the Great Depression. And there is no light at the end of the tunnel. In 2002 a single Japanese bank, Mitzuho Bank, managed to lose $16.5 billion dollars.[47] If anything, the problems seem to be getting worse as Japan starts its second decade with little growth.

No one believed that 2002's real growth rate of 2 percent signaled that the era of stagnation was over. Nominal GDP fell in 2002, and much of the higher real growth rate that was reported came from changes in measurement techniques. At the onset of 2003 fourteen Japanese economic forecasting firms all agreed the nominal GDP would fall in 2003. The average predicted decline was 1.3 percent (real GDP was expected to rise 0.3 percent).[48] And right on schedule Japan reported a zero growth rate for the first quarter of 2003.

Everyone can learn from the Japanese mistakes. Japan provides a textbook of what not to do. Its bad economic policies led to what is called in Japan the lost decade and what might be called the Great Stagnation were we using the terminology of the 1930s.

I am sometimes asked what my biggest mistake has been as a professional economist. What did I get most wrong? There is an easy answer. In the early 1990s I wrote a book, *Head to Head,* about the coming economic battles among Japan, Europe, and the United States for global economic supremacy. The Japanese stock market had already crashed and land values were plunging. I mentioned these events but moved on without much comment because I assumed that Japan, like the United States in the Savings and Loan crisis that had just occurred, would smoothly pick up the pieces and move on. I could not have been more wrong.

No one inside or outside of Japan knew that Japan had an unknown genetic weakness. Unknown genetic weaknesses pop up when organisms face circumstances they have never before seen. Japan had never had a large financial crash. Japan had never had to put its people and its institutions through bankruptcy. When these circumstances arose, Japan could not do what needed to be done.

In 1990 Japan held a position of strength. Twelve of the world's fifteen largest financial institutions were Japanese, and six of the top ten industrial firms were Japanese. After a decade of no growth, none of the world's top fifteen banks were Japanese and only one of the ten biggest industrial firms, Toyota, was Japanese.[49] On the list of the world's 500 most valuable firms over the course of the 1990s, the number of Japanese firms fell from 149 to 50 whereas the number of American firms was rising from 151 to 238.[50] Parity with U.S. industrial strength was replaced by an almost 5 to 1 deficiency.

And as the crisis continues, it prevents Japan from playing any significant leadership role in the third industrial revolution. Companies on the edge of bankruptcy just don't have the funds to invest in high-risk new activities. Management time and energy is focused on coping with the legacies of the past rather than building the products and services of the future. One can find a few interesting third revolution companies—DoCoMo, the wireless telecommunications company is one—but there aren't many. More important, along with their diminished economic expectations the Japanese came to have a diminished view of themselves— a middling country of declining importance in world affairs unable to play a significant role in the world of ideas.[51]

NOT COPING

What is surprising is not the Japanese meltdown—sooner or later everyone experiences a meltdown—but the Japanese inability to clean up the resultant mess. Messes can be cleaned up. One of the benefits of having had a long history of financial crashes is that everyone knows what must be done to restore normalcy and quickly bring economic systems back into operation. New solutions don't have to be invented. All the potential options have been explored. That is the good news! The bad news is that what must be done involves some painful economic restructuring.

Technically, Japan understands what must be done but is unwilling to make the painful short-run adjustments necessary to reestablish long-run growth. In some sense the Japanese have been too good at sharing pain. There is a sense of crisis on the financial pages, but there is no sense of crisis on the streets in everyday life. Despite a decade of no growth, unemployment hovers slightly above 5 percent and is below the levels found in the United States or Europe. For the 95 percent who do work, cash wages are 10 percent above those in the United States. Without an obvious crisis, everyone is willing to talk about fundamental change, but no one is willing to make fundamental changes. No one can be a leader if someone else is not willing to be a follower.

What must be done is much like the advice given to those who need to pull a thornbush from the earth to make room for a flower garden. The bush must be grabbed ruthlessly and pulled quickly with great strength. There will be an initial jolt of pain, but it will rapidly pass. Given a strong grip, the bush can then be easily pulled from the ground to clear the area for more productive plants. After pulling the bush up, one wipes off the blood from one's hands and moves on to other activities. The wounds from the thorns are not deep and heal quickly.

But if one tries to grab a thornbush timidly, the pain is worse than if one grabs it vigorously, and one's grip is not strong enough to pull the bush from the earth. More grabs are necessary, and each grab leads to more wounds and more pain. The wounds never have a chance to heal. The ground is never cleared for a new burst of productive growth. The unproductive thornbush just grows bigger, stronger, and harder to remove the longer the timidity lasts.

Solutions start with an honest third party dividing the existing assets of the banking system into good assets and bad assets. For banks and firms with solid balance sheets (assets exceed liabilities), government-backed lending tides them over the period when credit markets are frozen, when they cannot roll over their existing short-term loans, when suppliers refuse to offer the normal credit terms, or when nervous depositors want their money back.

For those whose balance sheets are under water (liabilities exceed assets), some government agency takes charge. What had to be done in Japan was almost exactly what the United States did in the aftermath of its Savings and Loan crisis five years earlier. Bankrupt firms and banks are closed. Large amounts of government money are needed to pay off the banks' depositors. With government insured deposits, the bank depositors legally have to be repaid. Some government agency (in the United States called the Resolution Trust and in Japan called the Resolution and Collection Corporation) takes charge of the bad loans. It tries to minimize its own losses and recoup as much of the depositors' money as possible by quickly selling the collateralized assets it has acquired to the highest bidders.

In Japan it was estimated that $800 to $1,700 billion would be needed to repay depositors.[52] At the height of the U.S Savings and

Loan crisis the American Resolution Trust was expected to need $924 billion.[53] In the end it needed "only" $550 billion. No one knows the exact sums needed in a crisis until the mess has been cleaned up. Some of the money paid to depositors can then be recovered by selling the collateral that was taken over along with the bad loans. The exact net amounts needed in the crisis cannot be determined until all the banks with negative net equity have been shut down and the collateral backing their bad loans has been auctioned off. In the U.S. crisis what the Resolution Trust had to pay depositors ended up being $196 billion larger than what it collected from asset sales.

The taxpayer has to be willing to pick up the losses, whatever they are. There is no other option if the depositors are to be repaid and bad debts are to be cleaned off the books. Depositors have to be repaid if a financial crash is not to turn into a Great Depression. Bad debts must be erased if growth is to resume. Capitalism simply does not work when assets have to carry debts whose value is greater than the market value of the assets themselves. In this case the interest and principle payments owed exceed the intrinsic productivity of the assets, and no managers, whatever their skills, can solve this mathematical problem.

Since asset prices have fallen sharply, debts (negative assets) have to have a corresponding fall in value if growth is to resume. The process for writing down debts and getting them back in line with the value of other assets is called bankruptcy. It is important to remember that nothing real disappears in bankruptcy. All the land, homes, factories, machines, and office buildings involved in bankruptcy continue to exist. They produce the same amount of GDP. They just have different owners. Smaller amounts of equity replace larger amounts of debt. It is also important to remember that in capitalism every asset is a good asset at some price. A money-losing Japanese-owned hotel in Hawaii became a money-making hotel when it was sold for 15 percent of the value of its debts. With its old debt structure, it could never have become a profitable hotel.

Banks with liabilities greater than their assets are allowed to fail and go out of business. Three thousand banks were forcibly shut down in the Savings and Loan crisis, their good loans sold to other banks, their bad loans taken over by the Resolution Trust. Some of those closed down were very large banks—even Citibank (the nation's largest) came very close to being shut down. In the shutdowns only the depositors were made whole. Shareholders lost their money. Managers did not get golden parachutes.

Firms that cannot repay their loans are either sold or shut down, with their assets auctioned off to the highest bidder. Individuals who cannot repay are forced into bankruptcy, and the assets they used as collateral to secure their now nonperforming loans are added to those to be auctioned off as quickly as possible.

Technically, "bad debts" are those where the regular repayments of interest and principle are not being made. In Japan many of the debts that need to be reduced are technically "good debts." Consider a young couple buying a $1 million house in Tokyo in 1989 with $100,000 down and $900,000 borrowed after signing a two-generation mortgage. Today that house is worth $200,000 and slowly falling in value. Although this couple has negative net equity of $700,000 and are drowning in debt, they are regularly making their monthly mortgage payments. Since they are making their monthly payments, their debts are technically good debts. Forty percent of Japanese families have mortgages substantially above the value of their current home and are in this category.

But monetary and fiscal policies don't work if these good debts are still being serviced. Zero interest rates aren't going to persuade this couple to consume. The last thing they need is more debt, whatever the interest rate. A tax cut isn't going to persuade this couple to consume. It just allows them to pay down their debts a little faster.

In the United States couples in similar positions during the Savings and Loan crisis gave the keys back to the bank and walked away to start life over—essentially a hassle-free bankruptcy. But this is impossible in Japan. In Japan mortgages are obligations against the lifetime incomes of the borrowers and the lifetime income of their children. There is no escape. Yet if the Japanese economy is to resume growing, these families have to resume spending. They can do so only if there is some way out from under their debt burdens. The road out does not have to be called bankruptcy, but in effect it has to be a forgiveness of past lending.

But Japan could not do what had to be done. Its genetic weakness would not allow it to shut down the banks that could not repay their depositors and the firms that could not repay their loans. In the Japanese labor market, where workers are hired only upon graduation from high school or college, how would older laid-off workers find new employment? Japan could not politically and socially force individuals into bankruptcy. To do so would be to brand the individuals as moral failures. In Japan getting reemployed in a good job after having worked for a bankrupt firm is impossible. Bankruptcy is taken as sign of a permanent personal character flaw. "Moral failures" don't get hired.

Although similarly named, the Japanese Resolution and Collection Corporation did not do what the Resolution Trust did in the United States. The Japanese corporation became a government agency for collecting the money private banks could not collect from borrowers rather than an agency for auctioning off collateralized assets taken in bankruptcy hearings.[54] As a result, it became an agency for prolonging the crises rather than an agency for allowing individuals and firms to start over without their overhanging debts.

Assets taken in bankruptcies need to be quickly sold to the highest bidder, no matter how low the bid. At one point America's Resolution Trust held title to 1.5 million properties. For a short time it tried to manage these assets until they would be "worth more." But it predictably failed. No one can manage such a diverse portfolio of assets back to economic health. The assets have no common denominator other than the fact that the previous owner has gone broke.

Quick auctions have the added advantage of setting a floor for asset prices. When lots of properties are auctioned off all at once, auction prices are by definition minimum prices. Prices can only go up in the future. But even more important, with the sale of these assets, an equity-based economy replaces a debt-based economy.

Bringing in new equity owners often means letting outsiders buy. At the onset of the Savings and Loan crisis in America, every bank in Texas was owned by a Texan. When it was over, no bank in Texas was owned by a Texan. Many of the liquidated banks in America were sold to foreign banks. New ownership is essential to restructuring. Insiders are drowning in debt. Only outsiders have equity. Inside managers have also been tainted by the previous failure. Only outsiders have the untainted management talent that can turn failure into success.

Japan does not want to auction off assets taken as collateral in bankruptcies precisely because it fears foreigners might buy them. Worries about foreign owners should have been the least of Japan's problems. Eighteen percent of the U.S. GDP and 24 percent of the German GDP are produced by foreign firms. In Japan, in contrast, the corresponding percentage is less than 1 percent.

Instead of forcing firms into bankruptcy, the Japanese government bought corporate shares in the stock market. The ploy did not work. The problem is not abnormally low share prices. The problem is interest payments that cannot be generated by the productivity of assets that owe those large debts. Government share acquisitions simply let private investors get out of the market with smaller losses. The taxpayer effectively takes the losses the shareholders would otherwise have had to take.

The same holds true with respect to government land purchases. These purchases don't solve the real problem. The issue is not the price of land but the debts owed that the intrinsic productivity of the land cannot cover. Land prices cannot be held higher than rents dictate. Stopping land prices from falling makes the banks and real estate companies temporarily look better. They do not have to write down their portfolio of assets quite so much. But it is like applying cosmetics to a seriously infected wound. The cosmetics hide the damage, but they do not cure the infection. Lower-priced land consistent with underlying productivity is necessary if there is to be a recovery.

Delay is the enemy of success. If governments refuse to shut down bankrupt banks and firms, the problems simply get bigger. For firms, unpaid interest is accumulated and added into principle. What the firms owe grows larger and larger, yet the firms are less and less able to repay. Since the banks must pay interest to their depositors greater than the interest they are collecting from their nonperforming loans, the bank's cash reserves get smaller and smaller. The ultimate amount the taxpayer must pay to bail out insured bank depositors grows larger and larger. In the words of Shakespeare, "If it were done, when 'tis done, then 'twere well it were done quickly."

To clean up after a financial crash taxpayer-voters have to be asked for huge amounts of money. There is no option. It is necessary to restart the economic system. To be persuaded of this distasteful truth, taxpayer-voters have to feel they have not been abused. They need to believe that those who created the problems did not get wealthy and then leave average Mr. or Mrs. Taxpayer to pay the bills.

In the United States four things were necessary to make the takeover of bad debts of the banking system politically acceptable to the taxpayer.

First, all shareholders lost all of their equity before any public funds were used. Shareholders were never rescued. As the risk takers in capitalism, they have to pay for failure. They get the profits and, therefore, they must take the losses.

Second, in any failing institution all members of the top management team were fired without golden parachutes. No effort was made to determine whether top management was, or was not, directly responsible for the failure. As the decision makers they should have prevented such disasters, and as the decision makers they are ultimately responsible for failure regardless of the detailed actual causes.

Third, where criminal actions have occurred, such as insider trading, those involved are thrown in jail. Those who got rich in the preceding bubble must not be seen as the beneficiaries of the government bailout. In the Savings and Loan crisis, America's then most famous businessman, Mike Milken, and hundreds of other business people went to jail.

Fourth, when politicians were criminally involved, in the American crisis, they were also thrown in jail. When involved, but not criminally implicated, they were removed from office. Twenty congressional representatives lost their jobs (four were thrown in jail), and five U.S. senators, known as the "Keating Five," lost their jobs (Mr. Keating went to jail).[55]

In Japan no one believes anyone will be punished, since no one has been punished more than a decade later. With great fanfare officials in the Ministry of Finance are arrested, but they are never charged, never tried, and certainly never sent to jail. The same happens to business leaders. If those responsible are not held accountable, why should taxpayer-voters give the government their money?

Preventing speculative bubbles is impossible. Stopping bubbles from bursting once they have appeared is also impossible. But cleaning up the resulting mess is possible. Governments are to be judged based on their ability to do so. Japan's government failed the test when it came. In the process it lost its own credibility.

Government credibility is important in speeding up the effects of good policies. Business people believe what they hear and act on the basis of the announced policies without waiting to see if the policies will, in fact, be adopted (they assume they will be) and without waiting to see the effects of those policies in the marketplace (they assumed they will work). In Japan talk about restructuring abounds. Nothing occurs. What the Japanese government promises, no one now believes.

BAD MONETARY AND FISCAL POLICIES

Japanese monetary policies have been timid and ineffective, and they are now exhausted with interest rates near zero. Very sharp large reductions at the beginning of the crisis would have had very different effects than many small cuts spread out over a long period of time. Japan is effectively caught in what Lord Keynes during the Great Depression called a "liquidity trap." Money interest rates are close to zero, but with falling prices real interest rates can be high.

Fiscal policies have been worse. Fiscal stimulus packages don't work if an economy is drowning in debts. What is a small tax cut going to do for a family deeply in debt? It does not lead to extra spending. The normal multiplier effects disappear. Those who get employed because of new government spending programs similarly use their higher incomes to pay down debts rather than investing in new projects or in buying new goods or services.

The fiscal stimulus should have come in one big installment after debts had been written down. That is a lesson that should have been learned from America's failures to escape from the Great Depression in the 1930s—and the ease with which it escaped once the huge expenditures necessary to finance World War II had begun. Japan's fiscal stimulus dribbled out and never gave the economy the big jolt it needed. Timid fiscal stimulus packages came and went without major effects. After each of these small tax cuts came a weak recovery in the GDP rate of growth, which would then peter out within a short period.

Recessions are a good time to spend money on needed infrastructure. Land values are falling. Idle construction capacity is available. Infrastructure spending also does not swell government deficits when the economy returns to full utilization, since the projects will have been completed by then. But if antirecessionary spending is to be done on infrastructure projects, those projects have to be ready to go—they have to be picked and designed, land acquired, permits given, and contracts sent out for bid—before the downturn has begun. Otherwise, they take too long to get underway. Because Japan believed its downturn would be short and it would have taken too much time to do what was needed in its major urban areas, Japan built unneeded projects in rural areas simply because they could be gotten underway quickly. What was built wasn't needed; what was needed wasn't built.

There are things to be done. The Japanese are poor people living in a rich country, since they have many fewer square meters of housing space than do people much poorer than they. Countries with much higher population densities, such as Holland, have much more residential space per person. There are no excuses for letting this problem fester unsolved. Yet Japan has not made the changes in tax, shade, and earthquake laws that might lead to a housing boom.

If the term "government" means an institution that can take actions to put a recovery in place, then Japan does not have a government. It talks, it debates, it promises, but it does not act.

The political reasons why Japan cannot do what is necessary are as simple as they are hard to solve. Japan is a consensus society with a narrow establishment at the top. When problems occur because of outside forces (defeat at the end of World War II, for example), consensus societies have huge economic advantages. They are great at uniting people and directing their energy toward common solutions. But they have huge weaknesses in turbulent times when their problems are internally generated. One cannot rally insiders against insiders. It is simply impossible to get a consensus that a firm should go broke and out of business in a society where the managers and owners of those firms are part of the group seeking a consensus. How do you throw people into bankruptcy or jail when they are your sons, your social peers, your college classmates, or your in-laws?

Consensus simply does not work if the job is cleaning up the mess at the end of a speculative bubble. To do what must be done, consensus has to be at least temporarily abandoned. The existing system has proven it cannot do what has to be done. Giving it more time will simply make the problems worse. An economic czar with the power to close down those who are hopelessly bankrupt and sell off their assets to the highest bidder has to be appointed. America's Resolution Trust had one. Japan's Financial Supervision Agency does not have one.

DEFLATION

The failure to clean up its financial mess has left Japan with capitalism's most feared disease—deflation. Capitalism can live with inflation, even substantial levels of inflation. Many countries, China for one, have grown rapidly with inflation rates as high as 10 to 15 percent. In the late 19th century America grew in a deflationary environment, but the economy was still mainly an agricultural economy where falling transportation costs led to falling food costs in family budgets that were still dominated by food costs. In the last century, however, no capitalistic industrial society has been able to grow in an environment of deflation and falling prices. Systematic deflation almost guarantees negative GDP growth. Once started, deflation is extremely difficult to stop.

Japan's producer price index (the prices business firms pay to buy the goods and services they need) started falling in 1991. Consumer prices followed suit in 1998. Neither the producers nor consumers price indexes are falling rapidly. In a decade producer prices have fallen 10 percent, consumer prices are currently falling at about 2 percent per year, and the GDP deflator (the broadest measure of inflation) is falling at about 1 percent per year. But all of these indexes include government and private services where prices are stable or even rising. Prices for goods manufactured and sold in Japan are falling at 5 to 6 percent per year, and in some sectors the declines are much larger. The declines have become persistent and seem to be both spreading and accelerating.

There are reasons why capitalism does not work in a deflationary environment. Since the value of money is going up while the value of other assets is going down, the riskless option of holding cash, doing nothing, becomes the smartest investment. A dollar held today buys more tomorrow. One does not rush out to buy whatever one wants since it will be cheaper next year. Whenever possible postpone purchases. But if everyone is postponing consumption, how is growth to occur?

In a deflationary environment debt is to be avoided at all costs, since debts have to be repaid in dollars of greater value than those originally borrowed. If prices fall 10 percent, a $100 debt effectively becomes a real $110 debt a year later. The economically smart never borrow, and they repay old debts as quickly as possible. But if debt reduction is the central priority, no one is investing in the new things that cause growth.

Since interest rates paid to lenders cannot be negative (potential lenders would simply hold cash and refuse to lend if they were), borrowers end up paying very high real rates of interest. With a 10 percent rate of deflation, a 1 percent interest rate effectively becomes an 11 percent real interest rate. One percent has to be paid to the lender and the real value of the existing debt goes up 10 percent. With these very high interest rates new investments have to be very profitable if they are to be undertaken. As a result in deflationary environments monetary policies cease to work and central bank activities become almost irrelevant. Japan pushed interest rates very close to zero (0.25) with very little effect.

Since getting costs down is the name of the game in a deflationary world, firms have no choice but to lower the wages of their employees. If they don't, the real wages of their employees will effectively be rising (prices are falling) and they will be pricing themselves out of the market. The winners are those who can push wages down faster than the rate of deflation. Pushing wages down is hard since achieving a 3 percent real wage reduction in a 10 percent deflationary environment requires a 13 percent reduction in money wages. But the harder firms push, the faster prices fall. Workers resist overtly (strikes) and covertly (sabotage) to such large reductions in their paychecks. In America's Great Depression, money wages fell but real wages rose because prices were falling faster than wages even though unemployment approached 30 percent. The same is now happening in Hong Kong. Prices are down 13 percent, yet the government is finding it difficult to reduce civil servant wages by 6 percent.[56] When real wages are rising as sales prices fall, firms lose money and have to retrench or go out of business.

Governments find that tax revenue falls since incomes and profits are down. Their costs of buying goods and services from the private economy are also down, but other public obligations, such as monthly Social Security checks to the elderly or employee wages are politically difficult to reduce. This leads governments to cut spending on the goods and services they buy from the private economy to avoid having to make more painful cuts in public benefits where they will be directly blamed by the voters.

PROSPECTS

Japan is caught in a deflationary death spiral. A decade of no growth is behind it, and a decade of no growth seems to lie in front of it. Industrial production is at a fourteen-year low.[57] In 2002 there were again a few positive quarters, but there was no reason to believe that this upturn would be more long lasting than those of the 1990s. And in early 2003 the run of positive quarters did end.

Japan is a strong economy embedded in a weak economic structure. It has a bright, well-educated, hardworking labor force. Its companies are leaders in technology, productivity, and marketing. Yet its economy is sinking, and as time passes more and more of its powerful companies are reporting that they are losing money. Japan simply cannot bring its strengths to bear until it has cleared away the rubble of the mess at the end of its economic bubble.

Recessions and meltdowns are intrinsic to capitalism. They are built into its genetic code. They have occurred at many times and in many places in the past, and they will occur at many times and in many places in the future. Any economic entity that hopes to achieve long-run success has to be able to deal with both problems. The Japanese system will have to be rebuilt so it can deal with recessions and financial meltdowns. That rebuilding is important to the rest of the world, since achieving a prosperous global economy will be difficult if the third biggest economy on the globe remains a failure.

In Japan economic stagnation looms over its future as far as anyone can see. But the causes of that stagnation are not found in the economy. They are found in an unsolved political crisis—an inability to act when action is required. The required actions are not marginal. Most of what is recommended and required could be put under the classification "change your culture." Easy to say, but how is it done?

EUROPE: SITTING ON ITS HANDS

The tale of the 2001–2002 European recession and slowdown is a tale of Central Bank incompetence. Central banks can prevent recessions only if they start lowering interest rates aggressively well before a recession begins. That is usually impossible, since normally no one can predict that a recession is on the horizon with enough certainty to take action. But this time Europe had a lot of warning, since they could see the recession developing in the United States six to nine months earlier.

In the early fall of 2000, the European Central Bank predicted the EURO countries could grow by 3.6 percent in 2001.[58] Late in 2000 when the Federal Reserve Board had already started lowering U.S. interest rates, the European bank's prediction for 2001 were reduced to 3.2 percent. The U.S. recession, so they announced, would not have much impact on Europe because European countries export only a small fraction of their GDPs to the United States. Six months later, with the year 2001 almost half over, their forecast was reduced to 2.5 percent; and six months after that, with the year almost entirely over, their forecast was again reduced to 1.5 percent.[59] In fact, in 2001 Europe's actual growth rate was 1.0 percent, with major countries like Germany and Italy ending the year on a negative note with declining GDPs.

Peak-to-trough stock market crashes in Europe were bigger in percentage terms than those in the United States.[60] German and French stock markets were down twice as much.[61] Unemployment levels were twice those of the United States, and long-term unemployment (unemployed for more than 12 months) was seven times as high.[62] In 2002 Europe grew only one-third as fast as the United States. And at the onset of 2003 growth stopped in the Euro zone with Germany, Italy, and the Netherlands reporting negative growth. With two negative quarters in a row Germany was in a double dip recession and threatening to pull all of Europe into a double dip recession.

What the European Central Bank forgot was that the same factor causing the recession in the United States, overinvestment in telecommunications, was present in an even starker form in Europe and would, if anything, cause an even bigger recession in Europe. American firms overinvested in equipment, something that will eventually be used, but European firms overinvested in pieces of paper—those 3G licenses—that have no real value.

Even when it was clear that Europe was falling into a recession more severe than that in the United States, the European bank did not follow the Federal Reserve Board's pattern of aggressive interest rate reductions. While Alan Greenspan was lowering interest rates twelve times, the European Central Bank was sitting on its hands lowering interest rates only three times.

The only explanation for this behavior, other than stupidity, is that the European Central Bank is a new institution and it felt it had to prove it was tougher than the Bundesbank (the old German central bank) to gain credibility. "Tougher" in central bank language means holding interest higher longer to more vigorously fight inflation. Even as the 2001 recession developed, the European Central Bank talked about the dangers of an outbreak of inflation (hoof-and-mouth disease had led to an increase in meat prices). Their real worries should have been the deflation visible on the horizon and a weak recovery from the 2001 recession.

Central bankers should be protected from political influences, but they should not be protected from incompetence. If there is ever to be a case where the central bankers of a region should be fired for economic incompetence, this is it. The European Central Bank's predictions were horrible; their actions were worse. No case for dismissal will ever be clearer.

The Europeans have also entangled themselves in a "stability pact" that prevents their use of fiscal policies. Since deficits in 2003 cannot exceed 3 percent of GDP, tax cuts are ruled out. The stability pact also requires the elimination of budget deficits by 2005. In theory taxes will have to be raised or spending cut in the midst of a very weak recovery. In contrast, between 2000 and 2003 the United States had a 4 percent of GDP fiscal stimulus.[63] The federal budget went from a surplus of $236 billion in 2000 to a deficit of $165 billion in 2002.

A European slowdown has clearly arrived, yet there is no plan for getting out of it. In its annual 2001–2002 report entitled "For Steadiness—Against Actionism" the German Council of Economic Experts recommended doing nothing and relying on a U.S. recovery to carry Germany and Europe back up with it.[64] This was their advice even if the European economy should prove to be worse than expected in 2002. In their 2002–2003 report the German economic experts came to the conclusion that Germany's inadequate performance was due to structural and not cyclical causes.[65] Most of their suggested twenty structural policies were designed to reduce German wages or fringe benefits and to make it easier to fire unneeded workers. Even if true, just as one should be able to walk and chew gum at the same time, so countercyclical fiscal and monetary policies can be adopted at the same time as structural policies.

GLOBAL LOCOMOTIVES

In 2003 Japan, Europe, and the United States were simultaneously suffering from slow or zero growth. With all three of the major developed regions, sometimes called the triad, simultaneously stuck, restarting the world economy is much harder than if just one of the regions were in a recession. Just as geese fly with much less individual effort by flying together in their V formation, so the world economy performs much better if the big three are economically flying together.

If Japan and Europe were willing to become independent locomotives, the global economic train would have a smoother ride. The inevitable starts and stops of their independent locomotives would not occur at the same time as those in America, and they would keep the global train moving during the periods when the American engine is shut down. When one or another of their engines is shut down, the American engine would be working. The global economy would clearly be better off with three locomotives rather than one, but the other two non-American locomotives have yet to be built. They do not now exist. Technically, constructing these two locomotives would not be difficult. The real problem is a change in mindsets. Europe and Japan would have to want to be locomotives rather than being content to be cabooses.

FIRST WORLD INEQUALITY

While globalization, capitalism and new technologies may be accelerating the growth in wealth of those who live at the top of the global tower, there are losers among the winners. Despite overall improvements some individuals and families are falling behind economically in either absolute or relative terms. It is a simple statement of fact that income inequalities are rising. Although globalization is often charged with being the sole cause of this reality, it is but one of several factors pushing first world economies toward more inequality. Unfortunately, all three of our simultaneous revolutions are increasing the gap between the middle class and the upper class. Somewhat surprisingly, and in contrast, the poor are keeping up with the middle class.

Start with the shift to capitalism. Distributions of income are simply wider in capitalism than they are in communism or socialism. It is an old, but true, story. At the onset of capitalism, observed increases in inequality led the 19th-century British economist Spencer to invent the term "survival of the fittest" capitalism that was later borrowed by Darwin for his theories of biological evolution. Spencer foresaw a variant of capitalism so harsh that he expected the "economically unfit" literally to die from starvation and become "extinct." As new technologies were introduced, the need for previously skilled, well-paid workers, such as glass blowers, would disappear. Wages would fall. Seeing the same reality, British workers now known as the Luddites attempted to stop the spread of capitalism by literally throwing wrenches into the physical machines of capitalism. Visibly rising immiserization led Marx to invent communism.

Part of capitalism's greater inequality is due to the fact that socialist economies ideologically believed in equality and to some extent they also actually practiced it. In government-owned firms, wage distributions are far narrower than in privately owned firms. In America the highest-paid top one hundred CEOs receive wages 1,000 times that of the average worker.[66] CEOs aren't paid the same huge salaries in government enterprises. The secretary of defense is paid less than many CEOs of very small companies.

But most of the difference in inequality between the two systems is due to the fact that socialist economies do not have capitalistic owners of the means of production. Societies that permit the accumulation of private productive capital are inherently much more unequal than those (socialism) that do not permit private capital to be accumulated, even if the two systems pay exactly the same wages. In the United States the top 10 percent of all households have average incomes 16 times as high as those of the bottom 20 percent, but their wealth is 106 times as high.[67] Capitalistic wealth is much more unequally distributed than capitalistic wages.

Bill Gates' riches flow not from his high wages but from the fact that he and his charitable foundation own 25 percent of Microsoft. Successful entrepreneurs lead to an unequal distribution of income and wealth. Finland uncomfortably lives with this reality. The egalitarian distributions of income and wealth Finland viewed with pride in the past are gone—blown up by the success of Nokia. Finland now has a new class of millionaires.

In capitalism the new big firms of the future have to be built on the efforts of people setting up new small firms today. At the beginning no one knows what will work. To get a few big success stories, millions of start-ups are necessary. The rewards for those who win are very large, but few win. Capitalism is effectively a lottery that needs a lot of players to generate a very small number of very big winners. Individuals who wish to get rich buy a lottery ticket by being willing to work long hours, by sacrificing current consumption to finance investment, and by being willing to risk all they have to set up those millions of new businesses. Most don't win the economic lottery. They sacrifice their leisure, their consumption, and perhaps their futures without any reward. The few who do win and build the big new firms of the future get fabulously rich. Four of the ten wealthiest people in America are Waltons, the inheritors of the Wal-Mart fortune.

Capitalistic inequality grows over time, since economics is to some extent a relay race where those who get ahead stay ahead. Dominant leading positions are handed down not just from one generation to another but from one business deal to another. The first billion is by far the hardest to make. Once rich, families diversify their assets and don't easily return to the middle class. Losing a great fortune is just as hard as making a great fortune. The landed aristocracy in Britain, established centuries ago, still provides Britain with some of its wealthiest individuals. Leaving the queen aside, three of the wealthiest thirteen come from the landed aristocracy and many of the rest represent old wealth.[68] The initial generation of Duponts and Rockefellers made their fortunes a long time ago, but many of today's generation of those families are still very rich. The Waltons will be on America's list of the wealthiest for a long time to come. The myth about shirt sleeves to shirt sleeves in three generations is simply that—a myth.

Earnings inequality is built-in to capitalism. Profit maximization is a strong motive for efficiency (something seldom found among socialistic firms), but it also calls for discarding those individuals capitalism does not need (the old, the sick, the unemployed) and minimizing the wages it pays to its workforce. Firms are supposed to engage in offshore production to force wages down at home.

Economic uncertainty is very high in capitalism. Workers, not just entrepreneurs, have to be willing to take risks. Few jobs last a lifetime. Other economic systems such as feudalism offer more security. In feudalism the village makes sure that no one starves, since everyone is part of some family or clan. In communist China the fact that everyone was fed and housed regardless of their economic position was known as the "iron rice bowl."

For those not used to capitalism, individual behavior patterns have to change if inequality is not to rise under capitalism. The behavior pattern of rural villages (stick close to friends and relatives) doesn't work in capitalism. In capitalism, if their incomes are not to fall, workers must be willing to move from regions and industries that are declining to regions and industries that are growing. Attachments to families and friends cannot be too strong.

There is a large random, good and bad luck element to the distribution of income in capitalism. In biblical terms it rains on the just and unjust alike; manna from heaven falls on the just and unjust alike. In earthly terms some individuals win the economic lottery;

others get hit with the equivalent of economic hurricanes. Capitalism does not generate a fair distribution of wages with everyone being paid exactly what they "deserve." If one looks at the distribution of wages within homogeneous categories that have been corrected for education, experience, occupation, industry, age, and every other individual characteristic that can be measured, there are still enormous differences in wages within these supposedly homogeneous groups of workers. In fact, within-group wage distributions are almost as unequal as national wage distributions.

And this randomness is growing. It explains more than half of the increase in wage inequality from 1979 to 2000 for both men and women.[69] Why this should be occurring is a mystery.

Economic success and rising inequality are not antithetical in capitalism. They often go together for both the firm and the nation. The last half of the 19th century was a period of rapid American economic catch-up with Great Britain, but it was also a period of rapidly rising inequality. The second industrial revolution (electrification) then, like the third industrial revolution now, was creating many economic opportunities to get rich, but not everyone was able to take advantage of them.

Inequality has many dimensions from which it can be viewed, and any major change in the economic system has to increase inequality on some of these dimensions and decrease inequality on others. The shift to a knowledge-based economy along with equal opportunity and affirmative actions programs, for example, have pushed the wages of median full-time female workers from 56 percent to 78 percent those of men. Growing knowledge-based service industries pay women relatively more while the shrinking goods manufacturing sector provides fewer high wage male jobs.

At the same time, absent remedial actions, there is no doubt that the knowledge-based economy is going to magnify the skill gaps that exist across countries and among individuals. Skills are becoming more important. Raw labor is becoming less important. What is a poorly educated person going to do fifty years from now? This process has already started. Since the early 1970s the real earnings of the top 10 percent of full-time male workers age 18–64 has risen 30 percent, whereas the earnings of the median worker (fiftieth percentile) has fallen 8 percent.[70] The income gap between the two has more than doubled. Overall, the top 10 percent of the male workforce has gone from having a little less than 32 percent of total income to having a little more than 41 percent of total income, with two-thirds of that approximately 10 percentage point gain going to the top 1 percent of the population.[71] In America, inequality is back to where it was at the beginning of the Great Depression. Viewed over a period of thirty years, the changes are dramatic, but the changes in any one year were small—the gap between the top 10 percent and the median grew at $860 per year, to be precise.

Globalization augments the effects of shifting to capitalism and of shifting to a knowledge-based economy. When capitalists widen their horizons and scan the world for the cheapest places to make their products and the most profitable places to sell their products, they see a new, very different set of global opportunities. In response to this new set of opportunities, they redistribute their economic activities across national boundaries.

What they want to do is simply described. Profit maximizing firms move activities from low profit to high profit locations. Moving activities to raise profits is what globalization is all about. No one would move if doing so did not raise profits. As they search for higher rates of return on their investments, firms will move their activities from high wage countries (lowering wages in these countries) to low wage countries (raising wages in these countries) until skill-adjusted wages have been equalized. They quit moving their activities when capital earns the same returns at every location. When this happens, those with the same skills will be receiving the same wages. No individuals get a wage premium because they happen to live in a rich country, and no one is assigned an economic handicap because they happen to live in a poor country.

Economists call this process factor price equalization. Perfect factor price equalization does not exist (exactly equal wages for the same skills do not exist even within the United States), but factor price equalization pushes wages closer together than they previously were. Technically, factor price equalization is the index by which the extent of globalization should be measured. If wages and returns to capital are not becoming more equal, a global economy is not, in fact, being created.

Relative to what had been true in rich countries, such as the United States, factor price equalization calls for a rise in average returns to capital and a fall in average wages. The reasons are those of supply and demand. A global economy has less capital per worker than the U.S. economy has. Capital becomes scarcer and gets a higher economic premium. Globally, labor becomes relatively more abundant when poor economies are added to rich economies and wages fall. What the theory predicts is seen in the data. In America's statistics, over the last two decades the returns to capital and the share of national income going to capital are up and the wages of labor and the share of national income going to labor are down.[72]

Factor price equalization does not occur in isolation but is coupled with the development of a knowledge-based economy. Knowledge-based firms demand many fewer relatively unskilled production workers and many more skilled designers, engineers, technical sales reps, and managers. Design, marketing, finance, and research rise in importance while production declines in importance. Workers with skills are simultaneously laborers and capitalists. They have human capital. This shift in demand plus the investments that are necessary to create skilled workers make skilled workers the scarcest factor of all.

A skill-using shift is clearly seen in the data for male wages in the United States. In the 1950s and 1960s the wages for college graduates were falling relative to those of high school graduates. The reasons were simple. The supply of college graduates was growing faster than the demand for college graduates. The supply of those who were only high school graduates was shrinking faster than the demand for high school graduates. This pattern reversed itself in the 1970s, 1980s, and 1990s. High school graduates' wages started falling relative to those of college graduates. In the last twenty-five years a university degree has gone from raising college graduates' wages 50 percent above those of high school graduates to raising their wages 75 percent higher. The edge gotten from an advanced degree (master's or Ph.D.) has doubled from an 80 percent wage premium to a 160 percent premium.[73]

Ireland is a good example of factor price equalization. Twenty years ago the wages of engineers were much lower than those in the rest of Europe. As global firms moved capital into Ireland, they bid up the price of engineers. Engineering wages are no longer below those in the rest of Europe. In the process Ireland moved from being a country at the bottom of the European income tables to being a country in the top half of those tables, but it also ended up with a more unequal distribution of wages. Wages went up less for unskilled workers than for skilled workers.

Recently there has been a lot of discussion about factor price equalization between third world wages and the wages of the very unskilled in the United States. The effects, if they exist, have been small. If the third world wages were impacting American wages, they should be impacting the wages of the least-skilled Americans. But the wages of high school dropouts have been catching up with those of high school graduates, and the wages of the bottom 10 percent of the workforce have been catching up with those of the middle of the work force. Among males the gap between the tenth percentile and fiftieth percentile worker is 10 percent smaller than it was 15 years ago. Among females the gap is 5 percent smaller. [74]

Inequality has been rising, but the gap is growing between the middle and the top, not between the bottom and the middle. For both men and women the gap between the ninetieth percentile worker and the fiftieth percentile worker has grown about 25 percent in the last 15 years

In America the biggest effects of factor price equalization occurred back in the 1970s. The effects were produced by Germany and Japan, not by poor third world countries. The big impacts were felt not by the unskilled but by medium-skilled male high school graduates.

At the end of the 1960s the rebuilding from World War II was complete. German and Japanese firms were prepared for the first time to compete with their U.S. counterparts. The 1970s started with Japan's manufacturing wages just 32 percent of those in the United States and Germany's wages just 50 percent of those in the United States. Since the productivity gaps in industries such as autos, machine tools, and steel were far smaller than these wage gaps, Germany and Japan had lower production costs than their U.S. counterparts—industries that hired a lot of male high school graduates and paid them high union wages. As German and Japanese firms profitably exported their products to the United States and gained market share, high wage jobs were lost in these industries in the United States. Those thrown into unemployment went to work in other industries, mostly services, at much lower wages. As a result, wages for American male high school graduates fell sharply and are still about 10 percent below where they were in 1973 in real terms. In contrast, German and Japanese manufacturing wages rose as their industries expanded. By the end of the 1970s Japanese wages had risen to 100 percent and German wages to 109 percent of those in the United States.[75]

Factor price equalization does not say the world must become more unequal. In conjunction with the third industrial revolution, it says that income inequalities will rise unless education gaps shrink. But even without globalization this would be true because of the new skill using technologies.

Other factors magnify the effects. In a knowledge-based economy more people work in the service sector and fewer work in manufacturing, mining, construction, and agriculture. This would be happening with or without globalization, but the movement of manufacturing activities to other parts of the world accelerates the trend in wealthy developed countries. From 1990 to 2002 the service sector generated 23 million of the 22 million net new jobs in America. Mining, construction, and manufacturing lost 1 million jobs.[76] As a result, measures of national inequality are dominated by conditions in the service sector.

Here social systems make a huge difference. In countries such as Japan or continental Europe, where because of laws or union power the service sector pays wages similar to those in manufacturing, national inequality has not grown substantially. In countries such as the United States, where average cash wages in services are about one-third less than those in manufacturing and where fringe benefit packages (pensions, health care, vacations) are either much smaller or do not exist at all, the shift to services has resulted in a sharp increase in inequality. This is magnified by the fact that wages within the service sector are also much more unequal than wages within the manufacturing sector. The gaps between the investment banker and the dishwasher are bigger than the gaps between the CEO and the lowest-paid manufacturing worker.

Since globalization makes some workers better off and other workers worse off, it is important to remember that those who become worse off have every right to attempt to stop globalization politically. That is what democracy is all about. Everyone is not supposed to be a philosopher-king worrying only about what makes his nation richer or the world a better place. Those who lose have the political right to stop globalization. But it is also important to understand that this democratic right leads to global inequality. Nowhere is this more clearly seen than in the protection and subsidies offered to first world farmers. These subsidies lower urban-rural income gaps in the first world and raise income gaps between the first and third worlds.

Agriculture is the largest employer in the third world and is a sector that could competitively export many of its products to the first world were it given a chance. Yet agriculture is the developed world's most protected sector and becoming more protected. More than half of the European Union's budget is spent on farmers. In 2002 the Bush administration and Congress added large amounts of money to the $80 billion per year already going to American farmers. Because of these subsidies and the restrictions on agricultural imports, agriculture is the one place where globalization is in retreat.

First world farming is now a very small industry. Less than 3 million out of 140 million American workers are employed in agriculture. Most are part-time workers. Sixty percent of farm operators work off the farm, and 40 percent work more than two hundred days per year off-farm.[77] In 2000, gross farm income was $246 billion and net farm income only $46 billion—out of a GDP approaching $10,000 billion. If farming were to disappear, its disappearance would not be seen in GDP statistics. Relative to urbanites, the average American farmer has less income but more wealth. On the big commercial farms that produce most of the nation's crops, farm incomes are above urban incomes.

Given agriculture's small size and the wealth of its commercial farmers, protecting farmers does not make economic sense. But it makes political sense. Politically, farming is grossly overrepresented in the United States and in every other developed country. Farm votes simply count for more than urban votes. In America this overrepresentation occurs in the U.S. Senate. America now has twenty-five states whose combined population is less than that of California. Those twenty-five states have fifty senators to look after the welfare of American farmers. California has two senators to look after an equal number of mostly urbanites. This is not what the founding fathers intended when they established the U.S. Senate. In 1776 there was a 4 to 1 difference between the largest and smallest state. Today that difference is more than 75 to 1.

Urbanites, the vast majority in every developed country, also do not seem to object when large sums of public money are spent subsidizing farmers. The reasons may have to do with desires for picture postcard rural areas or primitive beliefs about the need for national food self-sufficiency, but whatever the reasons, there is little urban opposition to farm subsidies in any part of the developed world.

The effects of protecting first world agriculture are just as easy to describe. Subsidized first world farmers produce more output than they would if prices were lower. Markets for third world agricultural exports to first world countries shrink or disappear entirely. When first world consumers cannot eat all that is produced by first world farmers at high subsidized prices, the first world's excess agricultural production is dumped onto world markets. Global agricultural prices then fall. Third world farmers are paid less. With smaller markets and lower prices the rural poor in the third world get poorer.

Since third world farmers are the poorest of the poor, global inequality rises. The World Bank estimates that first world agricultural protection reduces GDPs in third world countries by $32 billion. This loss amounts to a lot of money per farmer when you are a Chinese farmer with average cash sales of $90 per year.

Although easy to understand politically, subsidizing first world agriculture does not promote global welfare.

Whatever the effects on average wages at different skill levels, the shift to capitalism, the third industrial revolution, and globalization are together creating a feeling of economic insecurity for everyone. The feelings are not imaginary. Jobs are less secure. The lifetime job is much less a reality than it used to be. Wages are more volatile. Wages are not going to rise smoothly over a working lifetime and peak right before retirement. For male college-educated workers the peak earnings that used to occur between 45 and 55 years of age now occur between 35 and 45 years of age. Experience is less valuable; having the latest skills is more valuable. Older workers face falling wages.

The normal political response to both rising income inequality and more economic insecurity would be larger government programs to reduce market inequalities and insecurities. But at precisely the time stronger social welfare programs are needed, the egalitarian policies of the social welfare state are in retreat. Globalization is often blamed, but the real reasons lie elsewhere.

Those who run Europe have discovered that there are real incentive limits on redistribution. Individuals won't work hard if the income gap between those who work and those who do not work is too small—if too much of the income of those who do work is taken in taxes and given to those who do not work. In Sweden a state requirement that the sick must be paid their normal wages led—no great surprise—to the Swedes being "sicker" and more absent from work than anyone else in the developed world, especially on Fridays and Mondays.

In both Europe and the United States manufacturing employment is shrinking. In America those who lose their jobs in manufacturing find jobs in services. This does not happen in Europe. High European social welfare benefits mean that workers won't take American-style low wage service jobs. Why should they? French unemployment benefits are higher than average wages in America's service sector. Forced to pay high wages, service companies either don't expand or use capital-intensive production technologies that do not provide very many jobs. Europeans complain about high unemployment (over 10 percent), but they do not want to change the social welfare benefits that produce that high unemployment rate. But by forcing service wages to equal those in manufacturing, the Europeans have stopped inequality from growing.

Put simply, Americans accept inequality and get employment. Europeans resist inequality and get unemployment. While the United States was creating 22 million net new jobs in the 1990s, Europe was creating no net new jobs. As a consequence, unemployment rates are twice those of the United States and long-term unemployment (over 12 months) is almost seven times as high. Thus far continental Europeans have decided to protect their job security and tolerate high unemployment, but they don't like the fact that this choice is forced upon them.

International organizations such as the OECD repeatedly chastise Europe for not "deregulating its labor markets" and letting wages fall. They correctly point out that the high payroll taxes necessary to finance a generous social welfare state are not globally viable. Businesses won't expand in Europe as long as its total wages (cash, fringe benefits, and employment taxes) are out of line with the rest of the world. Businesses will simply move to countries where they do not have to pay high payroll taxes. And it is happening. More and more European firms seeking to expand, expand outside of Europe to avoid paying European social welfare charges.

The economic problem is not tax collections in the aggregate but the payroll tax in particular—the tax generally used to finance social welfare benefits and a tax that is now often a country's largest tax. If payroll taxes get too high, firms simply move to countries where they pay lower payroll taxes or else they get run out of business by firms that operate in countries with lower payroll taxes.

In Europe cash wages are substantially lower than those in the United States. But if one includes payroll taxes and looks at total employment costs, a different picture emerges. Total labor costs are higher in Europe even though productivity is lower. Whereas the United States' total employment costs are 20 percent higher than its cash wages, France's total employment costs are 45 percent higher than its cash wages.[78] As a result, European firms such as Mercedes and BMW can cut their costs dramatically by moving production to the United States.

In the jargon of economists, globalization has made the demand curve for labor more elastic (flatter in the traditional supply-and-demand diagrams).[79] Because of global competition higher payroll taxes on earnings cannot be passed on to the consumer in the form of higher purchase prices as they used to be. If payroll taxes rise, either cash wages have to be reduced or jobs disappear. Existing firms either move abroad or foreign-based firms gain local market share. As a result, using the current tax collection system, it is becoming harder and harder to collect the extra tax revenue necessary to finance ever-growing social welfare benefits.

The need for cutbacks in the social welfare state do not flow from globalization. Incentive issues spring from the internal dynamics of the social welfare state and have nothing to do with globalization. The budgetary issues of the social welfare state spring mostly from the aging of the population and rising costs of health care and also have nothing to do with globalization. Yet when European governments propose cutbacks for incentive reasons or because of demography or health costs, they almost always blame the need for reforms on globalization. Not surprisingly, politicians find it far easier to blame globalization and the need for competitiveness for the cutbacks in social welfare benefits they are "forced" to make than to defend cutbacks as self-imposed measures necessary to restore incentives or fiscal stability.

Firms do the same. They often tell laid-off workers that globalization is the source of their misery when other factors, such as bad management, are the real source of the problems.[80] Blame the foreigners is the operative rule in both the public and private sectors.

While social welfare benefits can be as generous as the taxpayer-voters want them to be in a global economy, globalization does require changes in the financing of the social welfare state. It must be financed with a value-added tax (a sophisticated national sales tax) and not payroll or corporate income taxes. Since value-added taxes are applied to imports as well as to local production, they do not raise the costs of local production relative to that of imports. Since value-added taxes can be legally rebated on exports under the rules of international trade, they do not raise the costs of exports relative to that of foreign products.

There are even two big side benefits to making the change from payroll taxes to value-added taxes. Although the value-added tax is regressive (as a proportion of their income, middle income consumers pay more than high income consumer with higher savings rates), it is more progressive than the payroll tax (not applied to capital income at all and often not to all of earnings). As a result, the entire tax system becomes more progressive with less taxes on low wage earners when value-added taxes are raised and payroll taxes are reduced. Wealthy retirees also end up having to pay some of society's retirement benefits when they make their purchases rather than leaving all the costs to poorer wage earners. Tax burdens on workers go down with a shift from payroll to value-added taxes.

Whenever anyone says that globalization requires cutbacks in social welfare benefits, they are simply wrong. Governments may choose to cut back on social welfare benefits for numerous reasons, but the cutbacks are not due to globalization. Governments could shift to value-added taxes to finance social welfare benefits, but this means raising taxes on individuals who are also voters rather than collecting more payroll taxes from corporations, which are not voters.

When it comes to preventing inequality, what must be done is as clear as how to do it is murky. If skills are becoming more valuable and the handicap of being unskilled is becoming larger, then those without skills have to be given more skills. Skill levels must be raised among those who do not have them. Education is the name of the game. Unfortunately, improvements in education are much talked about and little done.

Often inequality is described as if it were a disease of our economic system. Its existence is to be deplored. But it isn't a disease. It is one of the system's basic characteristics. It doesn't automatically disappear as countries grow richer. Deliberate measures have to be taken to reduce it. The reasons for taking those measures are political and moral, not economic. Capitalistic economies can easily adjust to more unequal distributions of purchasing power. Middle-class stores find themselves with smaller markets (Sears) or go out of business (Gimbels). Upscale stores (Bloomingdale's) and downscale stores (Wal-Mart) boom. America, it must be remembered, simultaneously operated a market economy marked by both capitalism and slavery for more than two centuries.

Inequality has always existed, but for most of human history it was viewed as normal and unchangeable ("the poor are always with us")—as an almost geological condition. One accepted it like one accepts the weather. There is no evidence that the ancient Egyptians, the Greeks, the Romans, or those living during feudal times worried about economic inequality or spent any of their time dreaming up ways to reduce it. They worried about famines and starvation, but they did not worry about the income gaps between their emperors and the average citizen or between the richest quintile of their citizens and the poorest quintile of their citizens.

Economic inequality became a social or political issue only after the first industrial revolution. This happened for four reasons.

First, as we have seen, before the invention of the steam engine in 1700 economic historians believed there were no significant per capita income gaps between the richest and the poorest countries in the world. No one worries about problems that do not exist.

Second, when most economic output is made in factories and does not dependent upon differences in the climate, rainfall, and land fertility, it becomes obvious that humans can, if they wish, control the distribution of economic output just as they control the level of their output.

Third, before the first industrial revolution there were differences in how much people had to eat, how big their bedrooms were, and how many servants they had to help them, but all these factors were inherently self-limiting. It doesn't take too much food until one is full. Having a bigger bedroom doesn't really make much difference to perceived standards of living if one is asleep. If one is warm, that is really all that counts. There weren't really too many things that a servant could do for a medieval lord that weren't rather easily done for one's self. Before the first industrial revolution there were big differences in power, not in consumption.

But with the advent of manufactured goods and the ability to travel, there were things that could be purchased that actually led to substantially higher standards of living. Having a higher income came to mean something. Within-country inequality started to gain attention.

Fourth, with the advent of democracy we came to believe that all humans were created equal and that, therefore, they had an equal right to at least an equal chance at being rich—and perhaps an equal ex ante probability of becoming rich. Democracy (one person, one vote) implicitly assumes some degree of economic equality. A majority of the voters have to feel they are benefiting from the economic system if the are to see the system as fair. As a result, all democracies have a heavy redistributive social welfare emphasis in their spending patterns. Governments have to deliver something to the majority of voters.

In the United States that something is not now being delivered. Relative to the wages of the top quintile of the population, a majority of voters have falling relative wages. A very substantial number have falling wages in absolute terms. So far America illustrates that wage inequalities, if they grow slowly, can become very much larger than they were in the past without evident political kickback. Yet it is difficult to believe that economic inequality can just keep on growing without limits in democracies.

{4}

THE VOICES OF ANTIGLOBALIZATION

The violence of the protestors against globalization makes it only too evident that they are angry. But what they want to happen is not at all obvious. A retreat to "what was," perhaps? An advance to "who knows"? At the 2002 World Social Forum in Brazil—an antiglobalization meeting held to counter what participants see as the pro-globalization World Economic Forum held in Davos—the session on "positive alternatives" had no positive alternatives to offer after three hours of discussion.[1] What is it the protestors fear? They predict disaster, but what is the nature of the disaster?

The demonstrators often call for ending globalization. Ending globalization presumably means imposing government barriers to lower or eliminate trade across national borders and capital flows between countries. If that were to happen, standards of living for the average family would fall by a small amount in big wealthy countries, by a larger amount in small wealthy countries, and by a huge amount in the third world.

To see the consequences imagine what would happen if trade

and capital flows were completely shut down. Big developed countries such as the United States would quickly retool to make the low wage labor-intensive goods (toys, clothing) they now import from the third world. In this process real standards of living would decline for the average family. This would happen in one of three ways. Average wages might go down as workers were moved from capital-intensive, high productivity, high wage industries to labor-intensive, low productivity, low wage industries. Or equal wages might be paid in the two sectors and the price of labor-intensive products would rise, reducing the real purchasing power and standards of living for those who buy the labor-intensive goods. Or research and development might yield ways to make today's low wage labor-intensive goods in high wage capital-intensive ways. In the last case consumption would fall to pay for the necessary research and development. But under all three scenarios the declines in income would be small and exist for only a short period during the transition. Then normal growth would resume.

Small wealthy countries would face all of the problems facing larger wealthy countries, but they would also lose economies of scale if they had to make everything for themselves. Substantial reductions in standards of living would occur as they tooled up to make computers in mini–computer factories, TV sets in suboptimal television factories, and autos in small auto plants. Variety would certainly go down. Consumers would not have a choice among many different models of cars.

In the immediate aftermath of prohibiting international trade, oil would be the biggest problem in the wealthy industrial world. The United States produces a little less than half of the oil it uses, but many developed countries produce no oil. In the short run without being able to import oil, today's automobile-dominated transportation system would not be viable. Large shifts to electric rail and bus transportation would be needed. People could still travel, but they would have to do it in a very different style. To produce the needed electricity coal production would have to expand.

In the medium term the system would adjust. Since people like their own personal transportation system, the auto industry would convert as fast as possible from the internal combustion engine to the fuel cell engine—from the hydrocarbon to the hydrogen economy. Using solar power and sea water, developed countries have the hydrogen they need, but there would have to be massive investments in the infrastructure necessary to support a hydrogen transportation system. These investments would lower consumption standards of living as they occurred, but eventually the transition would be completed and standards of living would start rising again.

Put simply, in the developed world there would be a step or two down the economic ladder and then a return to climbing up the economic ladder.

In the developing world the abolition of global trade and investment flows would be an economic disaster. Oil exporting countries would go back to being very poor. Markets for what developing countries export, labor-intensive products, would disappear. The external funds they now get for investment would stop. The foreign technologies and foreign management and engineering skills the third world needs to complement their own local skills would not be available. Importing nothing, the underdeveloped world would not get the products (medicines, food, machine tools) they now buy from the developed world. Standards of living would fall sharply. Rather than having a chance to leapfrog into the developed world using imported equipment and technology, they would have to reinvent the wheel in industry after industry. Not being able to educate their young people abroad, technological catch-up would become virtually impossible. Abolishing trade and cross-border investment would condemn the third world to permanent backwardness and poverty as the developed world rushed ahead technologically.

The objectors to globalization often talk as if they are protecting the interests of third world countries, but third world countries understand what would happen to them if they did withdraw from globalization. They want to participate in globalization. They worry about the costs and being dominated, but they worry even more about being abandoned. They don't want to be left out and left behind.

Simply ending globalization would be bad news for all of the world and a disaster for much of the world. Protestors with signs calling for the end of globalization effectively have to be heard as screams of pain where those screaming may have real pain but don't know the sources of their pain. Not knowing where their pain really comes from is not strange.

What humans worry about is only loosely related to the objective dangers. Movies have made shark attacks seem real, but there is only a 1 in 350 million probability of being killed by a shark.[2] Stairways get little attention even though the probability of death is 1 in 195,000, or almost 2,000 times as likely. What gets our attention is often not what should get our attention. The trick is to see beyond the sharks to the stairways. There may be real dangers in globalization even if the dangers causing the anxieties are not real.

ANTI-AMERICAN OBJECTORS

As they look up at the American position at the top of the global tower, whatever their own position is in or outside of the tower, much of the rest of the world agrees that they don't like what they see as the American dominance of globalization. To them globalization is an American construction project built without their input and over their objections.

Public opinion polls show that large majorities of the world's population, even in traditionally friendly countries, think the spread of American ideas and customs is a bad idea. Fifty percent think this is so in Britain, 58 percent in Italy, 67 percent in Germany, and 71 percent in France. Only Japan, with 35 percent, comes in at less than a majority viewing American ideas and customs negatively.[3] Politicians in Germany and South Korea won elections in 2002 on basically anti-American platforms. In the words of the executive vice president of Venezuela, the United States represents a "WASP dominance that has become unbearable."[4]

Hearing such views Americans often ask, "Why do they hate us?" As they listen to these views Americans should remember that to disagree with U.S. policies is not to be anti-American. Many of us probably disagree with some U.S. policies. To be anti-American is to object to who Americans are, not to object to what America does.

Some of the anti-American feelings were produced by the end of the Cold War. The old USSR was very good at creating friends for the United States. Those who feared the USSR loved the United States. Today no one fears Russia. No German chancellor candidate would have campaigned on an anti-American platform while the Russian army was in East Germany. Today there is no one to scare other countries into being America's allies and friends.

Americans should just get used to the idea that if you are the only big guy on the block, you won't be loved, probably won't even be liked, will get very little sympathy, and certainly will be feared. Americans should remember that in any contest between David and Goliath, all of the sympathy is with David. Americans should understand that others, if they are to stop the United States from doing something they don't like (invading Iraq, for instance), have to band together against the United States—and even then they will probably fail. It is important to remember that the rest of the world is not self-confident that they can hold their own in the face of the seductive American temptations and overwhelming economic and military power. If Americans are emulated, as they are, those of us who are Americans are getting all we can ask for.

Some anti-American feelings arise because Americans are seen as getting too many of the gains from globalization. Since the global model is based on the American model, Americans have the advantage of having had the experience of playing a very similar game. Americans don't have to change very much, whereas the rest of the world has to change quite a bit to accommodate globalization. To some extent this is true. English is the language of business. Individualism with all of its risks and rewards is built into the American culture. The real issue, however, is not the need to make small changes versus the need to make big changes but the willingness to accept changes big or small.

Consider being fired. Far more Americans than Europeans have been fired in the last decade. In the booming 1990s each and every year profitable big U.S. companies laid off between 600,000 and 800,000 workers. Some of these layoffs were due to the direct productivity enhancing effects of the new technologies; some were due to the globalization produced by these same new technologies. Moving jobs to offshore production bases was new to Americans. American don't like to be fired when their jobs move abroad any more than anyone else does. Because there are less legal restrictions in America than in the rest of the world, developed or underdeveloped, when people are fired in global economic downturns both American and foreign firms lay off proportionally more of their employees in America than elsewhere. Americans could legitimately complain about not being fairly treated. It is not that Americans are fired less or care less or receive preferential treatment, it is that they are used to being fired and accept the economic uncertainty that goes with it. They have learned to accept change.

When it comes to an index measuring fears about globalization, the American index is not at zero. Real inflation-adjusted median family incomes are only slightly above where they were in 1973.[5] Economic uncertainty is very high, and a majority of Americans expect their children to have real incomes below what they have. Like everyone else in the world, Americans are worried. But it also true that the fear indexes are probably higher in the rest of the world—not because of objective realities but because of subjective realities. The rest of the world is just less used to living with such fundamental uncertainties. In 2002 despite thinking that their children will be economically worse off than they are, only 7 percent of Americans are pessimistic about the future.[6]

Consider legal and illegal immigration. America has far more of both than anyone else (about 1 million people per year), but they are less worried about it than anyone else. Americans could argue that immigrants are getting the best educational opportunities and taking their best jobs. At elite American universities, 30 to 40 percent of the undergraduate students are now Asian Americans. These are university places that Americans who came earlier don't get. Nowhere is the loss of jobs for Americans more visible than in Hollywood, where many of the stars are not originally American, among them Penelope Cruz, Russell Crow, Nicole Kidman, Jean Claude Van Damm, Catherine Zeta-Jones, Arnold Schwarzenegger, and Chow Yun Fat. Yet objections and complaints have been few. Most Americans think of these foreigners as really being Americans, even if these individuals don't think of themselves as Americans. America absorbs "foreign influences" by quickly forgetting where they come from and instead thinking of them as American influences. What makes Americans care less is not fewer legal or illegal immigration but a culture that absorbs.

Some of the fears about globalization arise because many people in other nations want to achieve the American results—high standards of living and technological leadership—but they don't want to do what Americans have to do to get those results. The fact that they cannot, logically, have both doesn't stop them from wanting both or resenting Americans because they cannot have both. It is simply frustrating to want something (the American standard of living), but not want to do what has to be done to get those results. Frustrated people often throw rocks or bombs.

To have the American standard of living, women must be full participants in the economy. In the United States, 47 percent of the workforce is female. If one looks at American family incomes, males provide about two-thirds of the average household's income and females one-third. To earn that one-third, women have to work and have to be educated. There are areas of the world, and not just most of the Muslim world, where women working outside of the home are seen as a threat to the established culture. Via the television set that to-be-resisted alternative lifestyle—the working woman—visits almost everyone's home every day.

In the aftermath of the American invasion, hundreds of female self-study groups sprang up in Afghanistan. Under Taliban rule, 85 percent of the women were illiterate. Women were, as they said, blind if they did not know how to read and write.[7] They were not permitted to ask strangers for help, and they could not tell the differences between look-alike money that had very different values. The smiles on the faces of the women who no longer had to wear the head and face coverings in Afghanistan after the defeat of the Taliban could not be faked.[8] In a real sense the women had been liberated. But there were those in other countries who saw their smiles as threatening. The pictures of smiling female Afghan faces that dominated the U.S. press were hardly seen at all in most of the Muslim world.

Long hours of work are necessary to achieve the American standard of living. Belgians, per hour worked, actually produce 7 percent more GDP than Americans, but American incomes are 24 percent higher than those in Belgium because they work one-third more hours per year. No American gets six weeks of annual paid vacation, the European norm. Many would like American incomes and European vacations, but that combination is not to be had.

Insecurity is part of the American system. Wages are high, but so is the probability of being fired. Insecurity is part of technological leadership. No one knows what will work, so many things have to be tried—most will fail. Those 600,000 to 800,000 workers who work for profitable companies yet lose their jobs every year are essential to technological leadership. One can invest in the new technologies only if one knows that the higher productivity these technologies generate will show up as quick cost reductions from lower employment.

Geographic mobility is required to achieve the American model of prosperity. When workers are fired, their next available job may be far from family and friends. Having to move far away, perhaps to

California, to get a new job is seen as an opportunity by Americans but as a threat by many in societies where one expects to spend one's life near family and friends. Still living in the same town where she grew up, my Israeli wife has many close friends who date back to high school days. Living 2,500 miles away from where I went to high school, I have no such friends.

American culture is seen to be invading and conquering local cultures under the cover of globalization. Traditionally, culture is older people telling younger people what they should believe and how they should act. What is frightening about the new American electronic culture is that it is a "for sale" culture that jumps right across the generations directly to the young. It is disruptive. In contrast to older forms of culture, this culture does not have any specific values it wants to inculcate. Those who produce this culture provide whatever sells—whatever the young will buy. It is a culture of economics (profits) rather than a culture of national values.[9] And in that sense it is profoundly different—and disturbing to many.

The American way of life, especially for the young, is seen by their foreign elders as too tempting. It corrupts. Its seductions have to be actively resisted. It leads the young to reject their historic traditions. That is why the United States is called the "Great Satan" in Iran.

This American culture can be, and is, blamed for almost anything. In the spring of 2002 a spate of mass killings hit Europe. A German high school student killed sixteen people and himself, a French psychiatric patient shot eight city councilors dead, a Swiss armed with an assault rifle killed fourteen in the regional legislature, Hungarian bank robbers killed seven. All of the killings were blamed on American influences. In Holland these events were described as "American conditions have reached us."[10] But then there are Americans who also believe that American movies cause violence. Why should Europeans be different?

It is difficult to know how to determine whether one culture is better than another. What is the cultural rank order of rock, jazz, and classical music? When it comes to public opinion polls about whether cultural changes are for the better or the worse, looking forward would yield one answer and looking backward would yield a very different answer. Our children would be horrified if they were told they had to go back to the culture of their grandparents. Our parents would be horrified if they were told they had to participate in the culture of their grandchildren. Humans tend to like what they have grown up in and gotten use to. After a certain age anxieties arise when sudden cultural changes appear imminent. Our culture is part of who we are and where we stand, and we don't like to think that who we are and where we stand are ephemeral.

Although one can argue about whether the new global culture will be better or worse than the old national cultures, there is no doubt that it will be different and will force changes in those old national cultures. The TV channel MTV is a good example of the new global culture. From country to country the songs and the languages in which the songs are sung differ, but how the songs are presented is the same: fast movements back and forth between sound and sight. The style is the same everywhere because the style seems to sell everywhere. That MTV style first appeared in the United States—but only a decade ago.

The electronic culture that frightens many in the rest of the world also frightens many Americans and has brought forth a religious fundamentalist backlash that rivals fundamentalism found anywhere else. In what other countries are there religious militia (Christian, in this case) that engage in shootouts with the police and their neighbors? One has to go to Algeria to find something more extreme.

Economically, the interesting question is why Americans seem to create more than their fair share of this new "for sale" electronic culture. American movies account for 70 percent of movies seen in Western Europe and have a more than 90 percent market share in many countries around the world.[11] Games, movies, music, and TV programs have become a major part of America's exports.

Part of the answer may be found in an immigrant society that does not have a tight conception of what constitutes American culture. Others are welcome to add to that culture. As new immigrant groups have come to America, each has changed the dominant culture. Foreign words become English words without anyone worrying about their origin. Such changes have come to be expected. Asking what potential clients (the young, in this case) want rather than trying to make them into a preconceived conception of what a young American ought to be is something a diverse country learns to do.

Because of this history American companies excel at bringing talented foreign performers into their operations and making them feel like first-class participants. Anyone good at creating cultural products that will sell is quickly invited to visit America, made to feel at home, and invited to stay. Many accept. These individuals quickly come to be seen by everyone inside and outside of the United States as an element of American culture, despite their places of birth or the national heritages they bring with them.

When a French company, Vivendi, bought a U.S. motion picture company, Universal Studios, there was no American outcry that the French were taking over American culture. Americans, if they thought about it at all, believed that Frenchmen running an American company would quickly be seduced by American influences or that they would make American culture more interesting. And exactly that belief is, of course, why there was a big public outcry in France. Instead of rejoicing that the French were taking over Hollywood, that French men and women would be the new bosses of a global motion picture studio, there was a fear that the French bosses would be seduced by what they had acquired and that Vivendi's cable channel back in France would be Americanized.

Since France has one of the world's greatest and most enduring cultures and since the French were the buyers and not being bought, French worries were illogical but not surprising. French efforts to resist Americanization have to be seen in the context of French history. France was not an army defeated by the German Wehrmacht in World War II but a society that collapsed in upon itself. Most French men and women collaborated with the Germans; few joined the Resistance until it was clear Germany was losing the war.[12] Paris had to be liberated by an Allied army. Re-establishing self-respect after collaboration with the enemy demands that one stand up to the rescuers. How else does one explain the commotion and consternation that accompanied the publication of a British cookbook in French?[13]

The movement of culture around the globe is also not as one-way as people think. The traditional American culture is not being exported to the rest of the world. A new global culture is being built, much of it in America, but what is emerging is not a global copy of traditional American practices. World football, soccer, not American football, is the global game. Pokemon is the dominant new toy. Lego blocks have replaced erector sets. Major Hollywood studios are owned by the French and the Japanese. Movie stars, as we have seen, come from around the world. Four of the world's five largest music recording companies are not American owned.[14] America's largest book publisher is German. There are more sushi outlets outside of Japan than there are McDonald outlets outside of the United States. Ask people what they would most like to buy, and European luxury goods, not American products, dominate their desires.

A UNESCO study of cultural exports (printed matter, music, visual arts, cinema and photography, games, and sporting goods) shows Japan with a net cultural trade surplus of $14.5 billion and the United States with a net cultural trade deficit of $38 billion.[15] Developing countries also export more than they import—a lot due to the production of sporting equipment, but some due to items like Cuban music and the Buena Vista Social Club, a musical group that sold a million albums in the United States in one year alone.[16]

Culture is not static but it changes over time. Globalization may reduce variety, but it also widens choices in every country. Everyone can choose to embrace cultures that are not their traditional national cultures. This freedom of choice, part of American culture, is something Americans should not be defensive about. The soft power that flows from the export of American-made cultural products to the world's young is completely legitimate no matter how frightening it appears to the elderly in the rest of the world.

OBJECTIONS TO GLOBAL GOVERNMENT

Antiglobalization feelings flow from both the need for global management and the fear of global government. Realistically, economic globalization requires a degree of political globalization. Today the world is moving from national economies to a global economy, yet there is no global government to start, lead, or regulate the process.

A partial answer to the need for global management is found in international organizations such as the United Nations (UN), the International Monetary Fund (IMF), the World Bank (WB), and the World Trade Organization (WTO). On the left, the opponents of globalization see these institutions as usurping their democratic rights to design their own national rules and rights. Environmentalists remember that despite an American law requiring the use of dolphin-friendly nets when catching tuna, the WTO approved the import of Mexican tuna caught in nets that would entangle and kill dolphins. On the right, these institutions represent a danger that might grow into some form of world government that would constrain national governments. Many Republican senators and much of the Bush Administration have this view. The United Nations should not be in the business of trying to tell the U.S. government what it may do in Iraq or elsewhere.

In fact, international organizations have been restricted by national governments to ensure they do not become some form of quasi-world government. They were set up by national governments to enforce the global rules and regulations those same national government negotiated and wrote. These organizations can interpret rules, but they have no power to write new rules independently. It is true that international institutions are not democratic institutions with directly elected global leaders. No nation would agree to direct democracy. They are deliberately non-democratic international organizations created by democratic national governments.

For similar reasons they are not international institutions where each country has one vote. No one is going to agree to let such institutions independently collect taxes. Without the power to collect money, international institutions are empty shells. A World Bank with no money isn't a World Bank. As a result, national votes are distributed based on the funds contributed. Because of weighted voting, these institutions are often accused of being too American and too much under the thumb of the U.S. Treasury. But if someone else were able and willing to provide alternative sources of money, the weights would be different. It is always the lenders and not the borrowers who call the shots at any lending institution.

In early 2003 Japan informally suggested that it should give less money to the United Nations and the United States should give more money to the United Nations, since the proportion of the UN budget Japan pays is greater than its share of world GDP while the proportion paid by the United States is less than the American share of world GDP. The reassessment is not going to happen, but if it were to happen, America would simply have more influence at the United Nations.

Since national employment quotas are in effect at all of these international institutions, none of them can employ too many Americans. Yet the institutions are often accused of being too American. If America is overrepresented within these institutions, it is a reflection of America's soft power. Many foreign nationals working at these institutions have gone to American universities. The highest-ranking example is the United Nations' Kofi Annen, a graduate of MIT and Carlton College.

Since some institution has to worry about the big picture and make sure that the global economic system works, the only alternative to the disliked global institutions is to let an even more disliked globally dominant power, the hegemon, call the shots. By default the hegemon is assigned the task of managing the global system in areas not under the jurisdiction of formal international institutions. The result is what might be called a loose imperial state. The hegemon does not rule a large empire or pick its neighbors' leaders. But in the end it is the hegemon that is the global policeman. The loose imperial state differs from the imperial states of the past, since it does not want to control land—the old source of wealth. The new imperial state wants to control ideas and knowledge—the new sources of wealth. One can argue that such a loose imperial state is both necessary to global success and unfair, since some groups of people end up with more influence on globalization than others. Both arguments are true.

America plays the role of hegemon because it is by far the world's biggest economy and it is the globe's predominant military power. The role will be played by the United States, or else it won't be played. The reason is simple: the only country that can pressure the United States to play by the rules of the game is the United States. No one else has the necessary power. But many consider this reality unfair—and in some ways it is unfair.

Since a world government does not exist, the global economy is governed by a shifting combination of these two possible systems. There are international institutions whose rulings the hegemon agrees to follow. The United States accepts rulings against it at the World Trade Organization, an international institution where every country does have only one vote. When a ruling is made against it, the United States changes its behavior or pays the required fines. But the hegemon also watches over those areas where national governments have not agreed on the rules and the institutions. Since global economic institutions have advanced much further than the globe's political institutions, most of the hegemon's activities are in the political sphere and not in the economic sphere.

The role of the hegemon is not to solve all of the world's problems but to deal with those problems that threaten the world's economic or political stability. This means political hot spots such as Israel-Palestine in the Middle East, Kashmir on the Indian subcontinent, and North and South Korea in East Asia get priority. These hot spots cannot be allowed to blow up the global system. Places such as central Africa, where equal numbers of people die, are ignored since they do not threaten the world's economic or political stability.

The Middle East gets more attention than Sub-Saharan Africa not because there are more Jews than blacks in America or because they are more influential. Neither is true. The reasons lie elsewhere. American blacks are not highly concerned about wars in central Africa, whereas American Jews are highly concerned about wars in the Middle East. Wars in the Middle East also threaten world energy supplies. The United State would not have moved 350,000 troops around the world and defeated Iraq in 1991 if the Persian Gulf had no oil. The United States was not protecting Israel. Neither those being invaded (Kuwait) nor those doing the invading (Iraq) were democracies. Without oil, the region would have been treated as the Sudan is treated; there, horrible events go on, more than 2 million die, and the world looks the other way.[17] A war in Kashmir started to receive similar attention only when both sides proved they had nuclear weapons and would probably use them.

Economic interventions occur for the same hard-nosed reasons. Aid from the International Monetary Fund is designed to protect the global financial system and not help individual countries solve their internal financial problems. Interventions are not triggered by "do good" feelings. They are not intended to help someone else. Argentina, for example, was ignored economically after it was determined that its 2002 economic meltdown would not trigger a global meltdown. In its 1994–1995 crisis, Mexico got a direct emergency loan from the United States without having to wait for IMF study teams or having to submit to IMF conditions, since Mexico's stability threatened the United States' stability. It was feared that an economic collapse in Mexico would lead millions of

Mexicans to start moving across the border. (Mexico, by the way, has completely repaid the loan.)

"Do good" interventions are one of the unexpected side effects of global communications. The Somalia intervention (the subject of *Black Hawk Down*) was triggered by global television. First world citizens do not like to watch third world people being killed in real time on their TV sets. Somalia had no strategic significance, but UN and U.S. military troops were sent nonetheless. Those same TV watchers, however, did not want their own sons killed for "no reason." A very small number of deaths caused the world's military hegemon to pull out with its tail between its legs.

Television probably increased the pressure to do something in Kosovo, but the real reasons for the intervention there were strategic. The Balkans sit on the flank of the European Union and NATO. The hegemon—the United States—was reluctantly forced to intervene, since what happens in Europe is important to the United States, even though the Balkans lie far away and what happens there does not directly affect the United States.

Not surprisingly, the world community spends some of its time urging the United States to intervene more vigorously in places like Somalia, Kosovo, and Central Africa and some of its time arguing that the United States is doing too much intervention, as in Iraq and Cuba. In the Israeli-Palestinian dispute both arguments are simultaneously made by both sides. And one can certainly argue that a great power with responsibilities for global leadership cannot let the two sides gets as close to an agreement as they did at the Camp David and Tabba talks in the last half of 2000 without using its economic and military muscle to impose a solution to settle the remaining details.

A settlement is important to the hegemon, since the conflict permanently poisons relations between the Muslim world and the United States. The Iraqi war vastly magnified this reality. The poisoning of U.S.-Arab relations is just too high a price to pay when there are only small substantive differences yet to be reconciled. Both the Palestinian suicide bombings and the Israeli invasion that followed can partly be blamed on a hegemonic power that was unwilling to do what it was suppose to do. Now new hardline leaders have been elected in Israel, neither side trusts the other, and any settlement would, to some extent, have to be imposed by outside powers with U.S. troops in the middle to guarantee adherence to any solution. In the end the region is too psychologically strategic to leave the two sides to kill each other as scorpions in a bottle—not pleasant to watch, but ultimately not important either.

From the end of the Vietnam War until the World Trade Center attacks, most of the pleas from the rest of the world were for more U.S. intervention. Since then the rest of the world has feared that the success in Afghanistan has made the United States too prone to intervene. President Bush's desire to get rid of Saddam Hussein gathered little worldwide support. Saddam was hated everywhere, but many countries were not interested in seeing the United States get a taste for changing governments it does not like. The ease with which Saddam Hussein's armies were defeated has already raised fears in Syria and Iran that they might be next on the list.

North Korea illustrates the other side of the equation. The rest of the world wants the United States to deal with North Korea, but it does not want the United States to start a war with North Korea. Essentially, the rest of the world wants to set the parameters for discussions with North Korea but does not want to take any responsibility for achieving a successful outcome. What happens if North Korea uses nuclear weapons or provides them to others? It is not an issue that can be ignored.

More fundamentally, just how does one deal with a regime that kidnaps an 8-year-old Japanese girl off a beach in Japan and holds her prisoner in North Korea for decades. The initial act wasn't a rational act. While dean at MIT, I had to deal with a similar case where North Korea kidnapped a South Korean MIT Ph.D. student in management while he was on vacation in Europe at Christmas. This is also not a rational act. What possible benefit did North Korea get or expect to get from an MIT Ph.D. candidate? Only recently did the North Koreans tell MIT that the student had died while being held in North Korea. What are the probabilities that a healthy male kidnapped at age 27 dies before age 43 of natural causes? If one has had to deal with the North Korean regime at a personal level, it is not at all clear what negotiations mean when the other side is not rational and does not believe that treaties are to be honored. Yet someone or some institution has to deal with the irrational players that exist in the game.

When it comes to world government, there is another institution, the World Health Organization (WHO), that will have to deal with an irrational player—severe acute respiratory syndrome, better known as SARS. SARS illustrates the necessity of a global approach to health, where individual countries are not allowed to run their own health institutions unsupervised by the rest of the world. A disease that might have been stopped if reported and identified when the first cases were known in China may now spread to become a worldwide killer of potentially enormous proportions. It did not have to happen. SARS may do for the world much what 9/11 did for the United States—simply change the way the world looks at itself, the power it is willing to give to global institutions, and the actions it is willing to take to interfere with national sovereignty. Not much imagination is needed to see the WHO as the strongest international organization dictating policies to all of the world's governments in the next few years. China illustrates what can happen when countries run their health systems unsupervised, and no one wants a repeat of this experience.

RELIGIOUS OBJECTORS TO GLOBALIZATION

One antiglobalization group is easy to understand. The Buddhists who put nerve gas in the subways of Tokyo, the Hindus who tear down ancient Muslim mosques in India, the Christians who blow up government buildings in Oklahoma, the Muslims who attack the World Trade Center in New York, and Jewish fanatics who machine gun down praying Muslims in Israel know exactly what they want and why they are against globalization. They want the creation of a religious utopia, their religious utopia, not some other religious utopia, in their area.

As we have seen in Iran and are now seeing in Iraq, Shiite clerics want to set up inward-looking theocracies that shun the rest of the world. They want to withdraw from globalization into a spiritual ghetto. They don't like globalization because they see it as carrying ideas that threaten their view of the world. They are not alone. On a Polish Catholic radio station, Radio Maryja, globalization is declared to be "the communism of the 21st century," since via the Internet and the electronic media it seduces Polish youth and leads them to secularization.[18] Those with these religious views want to control what is seen on the TV set and how much their people know about the rest of the world. Otherwise, as we have seen in Iran, the young grow restless and start to see their religion as their oppressor.

There is no doubt that parts of the world are going to stand aside from globalization to practice their religious beliefs. How much of the world falls into this category remains to be seen.

There are always religious leaders who want to withdraw themselves and their followers from this earthly world. That is what monasteries are all about. The real question is why these religious leaders are sometimes listened to and influential and at other times not listened to and not influential. Why does the option to withdraw into a theocracy look attractive to the potential followers? That is the real question. Understanding why people follow these religious leaders is much more important than understanding the motivation of the leaders themselves.

In many ways the rise of religious fundamentalism is simply the return of the world that existed two or three century ago. Religious wars were common between the fall of the Roman Empire and the first industrial revolution. Muslim military conquests spread Islam to North Africa, central and southern Asia, and southern Europe, starting in the 7th century with the collapse of the Sassanian rule in Egypt. Christians fought back at the time of the Crusades and later against the Moors and the Turks. Hindus fought back against Muslim rule in India and are still winning elections today by being anti-Muslim. Who can count how many wars were fought between Protestants and Catholics after the Reformation?

These religious wars were not brought to an end by settling religious issues about central truths (who has the right way to heaven) or by a rise in religious tolerance. The religious fires of earlier centuries were extinguished in the ideological battles between capitalism and socialism that arose in the 19th and 20th centuries. How to organize a geographic area economically became the fighting issue that replaced the battles over how to organize that area religiously. Hitler justified his invasion of the USSR as a war against communism. The Cold War between communism and capitalism dominated the last half of the 20th century. Hot wars between capitalism and communism were fought in Korea and Vietnam. The virtues or vices of socialism versus capitalism fueled almost all of the third world wars in the last century. The United States organized several invasions (Cuba, Grenada) and revolutions in Latin America (Chile, Guatemala) under the rubric of fighting communism.

It is not surprising that the death of communism brought with it the return of religious conflicts. If things aren't going as we would like, we all seek an ideological banner under which to fight. To be willing to die, we must have a cause that is bigger than we are. This requires an overarching ideology. Without an overarching ideology, potential revolutionaries are simply criminals—even to themselves. The need for an ideology is more important than the precise content of the ideology.

There are many historical examples. The cause of socialism led Nasser and his supporters to overthrow the feudal king of Egypt in the early 1950s. Three decades later Islamic fundamentalism was the ideology used to justify assassinating Nasser's successor, Anwar Sadat, and attempting to overthrow the Egyptian socialist state. Both sets of revolutionaries were unhappy; both needed an ideology to justify their actions. The same pattern is seen in Iraq. Saddam Hussein was part of a revolution backed by communists who overthrew the Iraqi monarchy. For most of his rule, Hussein feared a Shiite Islamic revolution more than an American invasion.

Twentieth-century revolutionaries fought under the banner of socialism. Socialism is dead. No one can fight under its banner. Twenty-first century revolutionaries needing a banner under which they can fight have picked religion. Their choice is not surprising. At the moment no other alternatives exist.

The fact that today's fanatical religious leaders have followers is also not surprising. What a religious guru offers is "certainty." Do what I say and you will go to heaven. Certainty is what the average person wants in a period of uncertainty. And in the middle of globalization, the third industrial revolution, and the worldwide shift to capitalism, uncertainty is everywhere. Certainty is precisely what the secular world cannot offer. The earthly world is not certain. The only certainty to be found is in a heavenly world. That certainty is very appealing to many in both the first and third worlds.

The 9/11 terrorists used religion as their ideology. A few decades earlier they would have used socialism as their ideology. But they also illustrate another reality. Although actual terrorists may swim among the poor and use them to justify their activities, they are very seldom poor themselves. Sociological studies show they are frustrated middle-class individuals who have not been able to achieve what they think they are entitled to achieve.[19] The 9/11 terrorists are perfect examples. Of the nineteen terrorists involved in the 9/11 attacks, fifteen came from Saudi Arabia. All Saudis are well off even by U.S. standards. All of the onerous jobs in Saudi Arabia are done by millions of guest workers. The other four terrorists were Egyptian middle-class young men. The father and sister of Mr. Atta, the 9/11 leader, are both medical doctors. Atta's main frustration with the world seems to have been that he was not admitted into his first choice German university. But he was studying in Germany. Egypt is a prime recruiting ground for terrorists since its education system turns out more college graduates than its economy can absorb, and these frustrated graduates who do not get jobs that correspond to what they believe their stature entitles them lash out at the world.

OBJECTIONS FROM THE LEFT

Antiglobalization is not a traditional left-right political split. Both sides juxtapose their understanding of the good society to the American variant—"cowboy capitalism" on the left and "mongrelization" on the right. Except for their dislike of globalization and the invasion of what they see as a dangerous American culture, the two groups agree on little else.[20]

In the immediate aftermath of the 9/11 attacks, an antiglobalization article appeared in the *New York Times Magazine* asserting that the spread of terrorism was a violent reaction to globalization.[21] According to the article the attack on the World Trade Center was just a quantum jump in a rising crescendo of smaller such events—the first attack on the World Trade Center, the bombings of the U.S. embassies in Africa, the attack on the guided missile destroyer *Cole* in Yemen. To contain these terrorist attacks, what had been a system of informal American imperialism would have to become a system of formal American imperialism. The world would resist. The march toward economic integration would lead to political disintegration. A new energy crisis would arise and further widen already widening economic inequalities within and between countries. Globalization would be overthrown.

The article was not a one-of-a-kind, off-the-wall response. It echoed what are, in fact, the standard charges against globalization. Job choices narrow in rich countries as operations are moved to poor countries. Company threats to move even more of their operations to poor countries force first world workers to accept wage reductions.

In poor countries global firms run sweatshops (unlivable wages, child labor, unsafe and unhealthy working conditions). Capitalists in poor countries grow richer by operating those sweatshops, and capitalists in rich countries grow even richer by sucking most of the gains from higher output in poor countries out of those poor countries.

Large national firms are replaced by even larger global firms. Monopolistic power grows. Much as the landed aristocracy in England used the enclosure movement to throw the peasants off land they had occupied for hundreds of years under feudalism, so global corporations are using intellectual property rights to stop average citizens in both the first world and the third world from claiming their rightful inheritances in the new knowledge economy.

Like a farmer who grows only one crop, poor countries become ever more dependent upon a narrow range of exported products. Economic risks grow and financial crashes become more frequent and severe. Economic inequality rises within as well as between countries. Worst of all, the new global system prizes profits over people.

From the left the future predicted by today's antiglobalization groups and Marx's predictions about the future of capitalism 150 years ago are almost identical.[22] If Marx had read the post-9/11 article in the *New York Times,* he could be forgiven for thinking he had written the article.

In the mid-19th century Marx predicted a crisis in what was then a new form of economic organization called capitalism, which was replacing feudalism. In the shift to capitalism, Marx believed, the poor would get poorer and become ever more numerous as machines replaced skilled craftspeople. Wages would be forced down to subsistence levels. Businesses would become concentrated into ever larger and more rapacious monopolies. The new capitalist system would be marked by frequent financial and economic crises, In response to poverty and these repeated economic crises, small-scale terrorism would break out. Eventually a major economic crisis would arrive, and this economic event would spark a general political revolt of the poor against the rich. By force of numbers the poor would seize power. Global imperialism and capitalist monopolies would be overthrown.

Marx understood that there was no going back to feudalism. Technology had changed how the world operated. The steam engine had been invented. The future belonged to industrial and not agricultural economies. And he would not have wanted to go back even if this had been possible. Things might be bad under capitalism, but they had been worse under feudalism.

In addition to outlining the process whereby the system of capitalism would end, Marx went on to recommend a new system, communism, which would, he believed, eliminate the evils of capitalism. He never said much about the transformation of capitalism into communism, but in his vision of communism (outlined in an article entitled "Utopia") it would create a new society where economic fairness and personal freedom reigned.

Like Marx, left-wing antiglobalizers say little, other than the need for a revolution, about the transition from what is to what they want. Unlike Marx, they say almost nothing about what they want. They don't even have a name for it.

Marx was both reflecting and amplifying public opinion when he made economic inequality into the central economic issue in his communist manifesto. "To everyone in accordance with their needs. From everyone in accordance with their abilities." His manifesto is no longer read, but his anger and beliefs about inequality are alive and well.

It is important to remember that what Marx predicted "would happen" did not just "not happen." The bad effects he predicted proved to be true, but they were offset by government actions he did not foresee. Capitalism survived and made Marx's predictions wrong precisely because his predictions were taken seriously. Those who controlled capitalism built a different capitalism than what was evolving in the mid-19th century. Governments intervened with a wide variety of policies to prevent the distributions of income and wealth from moving to greater and greater inequality as capitalism progressed. As a result, the ever rising inequality that Marx and others predicted did not happen.

The survival-of-the-fittest capitalism of Marx's day and age was replaced by what we know as the social welfare state but what might better be known as the social educational state—for education was the most important of these new activities. Publicly financed (free to the student), mass, universal, and eventually compulsory education was invented by an owner of textile mills in Massachusetts in the 1835. He noticed that productivity went up when he had educated workers. Compulsory state-financed education broke the link between parental income (or attitudes) and education. Children with poor parents could acquire skills and not be forced to sell just raw labor. Poor people could become educated people—and eventually rich people. (I suspect public education is humankind's second most important social invention after reading and writing.)

Many of the government programs to alleviate the inherent inequality of capitalism were adopted by conservatives as programs necessary to save the capitalistic system. Aristocrats interested in saving the capitalistic system invented new roles for governments. Roosevelt was the first to use monetary and fiscal policies in controlling macroeconomic fluctuations. Unemployment insurance (adopted by Churchill when he was chancellor of the exchequer in the early 20th century) was invented to support family incomes during the inevitable recessions and financial crises of capitalism when many workers weren't going to be needed. Government health care and old age pension systems (first adopted by Bismark in the late 19th century) looked after people when capitalism did not want them—when they were ill or when they were old. In this rebuilt capitalistic economy, those not needed by capitalism were not going to be thrown into starvation.

Progressive income taxes were adopted to directly redistribute income by forcing the wealthy to pay more than their proportional share of the social welfare benefits that went mainly to middle income families. Inheritance taxes were introduced to reduce the economic head start that those born in wealthy families would otherwise enjoy in the relay race of life. Those who got ahead in the economic relay race in one round would have their lead reduced in the next.

Regulations such as antitrust laws and other limits on monopolistic behavior were adopted to reduce capitalism's ability to raise prices and extract income from middle income consumers.

Public investments in infrastructure (transportation, power supplies) prevented countries from dividing into poor and rich geographic regions. The Tennessee Valley Authority economically opened up America's south. East of the Mississippi River railways were built with private money; west of the Mississippi River they had to be built with public money. City electrification was a private affair; rural electrification was a government program (the Rural Electrification Administration, or REA). Water reclamation projects to raise farm incomes were everywhere in government affairs.

But it is also true that technology did not move in the skill-destroying way expected by almost everyone—not just Marx—in the mid-19th century. Machines did, as expected, replace some skilled artisans and forced them to become unskilled workers, but to a much greater extent they created a host of new jobs that required educated workers. In the aggregate, technology moved in a skill-using and not skill-destroying direction.

By taking the problems flowing from capitalism and what its critics were saying about those problems seriously, the system of capitalism was effectively saved. People built a different form of capitalism–the social welfare state combined with active fiscal and monetary policies and free education—that controlled the widening income inequalities and economic instabilities inherent in capitalistic systems. The same can be done for globalization.

As the close parallels with Marx indicate, much of the protest is about the substructure of capitalism rather than the superstructure of globalization. On the left the effects of moving from socialism to capitalism are often confused with the effects of moving from national economies to a global economy.

The charges made by the antiglobalizers are sometimes true. Financial crises do occur. Inequality within and between countries is rising.

But as we have seen, the possible causes are not limited to those of globalization. Economic instability can be traced back to capitalism. As capitalism widens its global spread, periodic financial crises engulf more and more of the globe. As we have also seen, rising inequality can be traced to multiple causes—to the shift to capitalism, to the shift to a knowledge-based economy where education matters more, and to the shift toward globalization.

Even those smart enough to know they are to a great extent really protesting against capitalism, and not globalization, cannot overtly focus their protest against their real enemy, capitalism. With the collapse of communism, all forms of socialism or quasi-socialism have been discredited. To oppose capitalism one has to have a viable alternative to recommend. One cannot just be against something. At the moment no noncapitalistic alternative has any credibility. But protestors can object to globalization because they do have something to recommend—a vague return to relatively isolated national economies of the past. Objectively, this may not be possible without a big cut in standards of living, but it is not a completely discredited option. It also resonates with many people who would like to return to those national economies even if they do not understand the extent to which doing so might reduce their own standards of living.

Consider the central charge often seen in left-wing street banners: *Globalization puts profits over people.* If the global economy is based on capitalism, as it is, the global economy is guilty as charged because capitalism does put profits over people. That is, in fact, why the system is called capitalism. Labor is a rented, hired, commodity. Capitalists get to make the economy's important decisions whether the capitalism is national or global.

Consider the charge: *Much of the world is not benefiting from globalization.* True! Sub-Saharan Africa's per capita GDPs are down rather than up. In 1980 the richest 10 percent of all countries had incomes seventy-seven times those of the poorest 10 percent of all countries. By 1999 that number was up to 122.[23] But as we will see in the case of China, some of the world's big winners are the third world. The problem is not being crushed but being left out.

Consider the charge: *Globalization leads to financial instability.* Protestors often talk as if they are motivated to protest globalization because of the financial crises that have shaken the third world in the last two decades. But financial crashes both in the first world and in the third world were occurring long before globalization was even a word, much less a reality. And they will continue whether the world has many national economies or a single global economy. One only has to look at the Japanese crash in the early 1990s or the U.S. crash in 2000 to see this reality.

OBJECTIONS FROM THE RIGHT

On the far right, the fear is immigration and the threats it poses to national culture and ethnic homogeneity. Antiglobalizers see the nation to which they are attached, and with which they identify, slowly disappearing. As it does, they lose their sense of importance as someone different and better than someone else. These fears are strongest in Europe, since the disappearance of traditional nation-states is happening rapidly with European political and economic integration.

The loss of nationality (Who am I?) comes up most clearly in the issues surrounding immigration. Third world immigration (France, where there has been a lot) or the threat of immigration (Denmark, where there has been very little) is seen as something that threatens changes in the ethnic composition of the country. Politicians arise—Hader in Austria, Le Pen in France, Kjaersgaard in Denmark, Fortuyn (murdered) in the Netherlands, the Vlaams Blok in Belgium, and Blocher in Switzerland—who promise to stop immigration. All implicitly and some, like Le Pen, explicitly promise to withdraw totally or partially from European or global integration if elected. Why? "Little people ruined by Euro-globalization," Le Pen charges.[24] In their view faceless European institutions are defining national monetary policy and even telling people what to eat and how to dispose of their garbage. Clearly, if their views on foreigners were not tied to hard-right political plat-forms on other social and economic issues, these politicians would be even more popular than they are.

The same views exist outside of Europe. The prime minister of Australia, John Howard, promises control of immigration to stop the ethnic composition of Australia from changing. Australians should stand up to the "yellow peril" from the north.[25] He hires remote Pacific islands (Nauru and Papua, New Guinea) to serve as holding pens (before World War II they would have been called concentration camps) to prevent illegal immigrants from setting foot on his soil.

Although not close in intensity to those found across Europe, the same fears of immigrants are seen in the political fights across America as to whether English should be taught through total immersion or bilingual education. These aren't really fights about the best way to learn a new language. They are the product of fears that in the end the new Americans won't become "real Americans." Yet all studies show that current immigrants are becoming "real Americans" at the same pace as those in the past.

If the charge against globalization is that it promotes ethnic mingling, globalization is simply guilty as charged. Globalization does promote and encourage immigration. It does make stopping illegal immigration harder.

There are, however, positive offsets. The individuals who migrate obviously benefit from higher wages, but countries hosting immi-grants also win. Immigrants bring a lot of talent and energy to America. Whereas 21 percent of American legal immigrants have some graduate education, only 8 percent of native-born Americans have some graduate education.[26] Those who come are the stars—those right at the top of their local university graduating classes.

In the high-tech boom of the late 1990s, Germany suffered a shortage of talented people for its high-tech industries that the United States did not suffer. In America H–1B visas let companies import the highly skilled workers they needed to be successful. In 2000, American companies requested the admission of 300,000 workers and 260,000 were admitted.[27] Native-born Americans win in this process because they end up being employed in larger numbers when skilled labor bottlenecks do not slow company expansion plans. The employment of skilled immigrants and the employment of less-skilled native-born citizens is usually complementary, not competitive.

The positive effects are much bigger than simple measures of the number of talented foreigners who move to the United States would indicate. If foreigners are accepted as Americans in America, it is much easier for talented foreigners to be hired by American companies for assignments in their American subsidiary abroad. American recruiters can honestly tell these talented individuals that if they go to work for a local American subsidiary, they have a chance, if they wish, to go to the top of the American company. The recruiters can point to real CEOs at big American companies (Coca Cola, Intel, Ford) who grew up living outside of the United States. And in a global economy, being able to recruit the most-talented foreigners into a business team is vital to global success.

America has also learned something about unskilled third world immigrants. They may not be highly educated, but all have the "get up and go" to be successful in America since they "got up and went" from their poor villages. This wave of immigration from Asia and Latin America is not harder to digest than previous waves from Europe. Studies show that Latin American immigrants are joining the American culture and learning English at the same pace as earlier European immigrants. First generation immigrants, then and now, often don't learn English. Their children can typically speak both languages but cannot read or write the language of their parents. In the third generation, most cannot speak their grandparents' native language. So it is with Hispanic immigrants to the United States. Two-thirds of the third generation speaks only English.[28] Spanish-language movie theaters are closing in Los Angeles.

This does not mean that America should open the doors and not control illegal immigration. Even in America, there are limits to realistic absorption rates. If rules cannot be enforced physically or won't be enforce politically, there should not be rules. Unenforced rules breed disrespect for all laws. It is also too easy to take advantage of illegal immigrants, forcing them to work in unhealthy situations under the threat of reporting them to the border police.

In the long-run exporting countries also benefit.[29] Taiwan is full of very successful companies with Chinese founders who have returned to Taiwan after a period of time working in the United States. Morris Chang, founder of TSMC (Taiwan Semiconductor Manufacturing Corporation), is the most visible example, since his company is the largest one in Taiwan, but there are many others. What they have learned in the United States is vital to their success in Taiwan.

Although difficult to classify as either right-wing or left-wing, there is another antiglobalization argument that revolves around ethnic fear and hatred.[30] From this perspective, much of it associated with the writings of Amy Chua, globalization and democracy intensify ethnic conflagration. Much of the third world has "market-dominant minorities"—the Chinese in Southeast Asia, Indians in eastern Africa, whites in southern Africa, Ibos in western Africa, lighter-skinned and taller people in Latin America, Jews in Russia. These market-dominant minorities wield "outrageously disproportionate economic power relative to their numbers." While globalization raises the incomes of the poor majorities by small amounts, it raises the incomes of already well-off market-dominant minorities by huge amounts. Previously existing economic gaps widen and become more noticeable. Important groups of the poor majorities—American Indian corn and bean farmers in Mexico, for instance—also find themselves in industries and occupations that lose when the more advanced technologies of globalization and free trade arrive. Economic resentments soar.

The animosities have always been there, but they were previously held in check by local majority group dictators who essentially received kickbacks from the market-dominant minorities. These latent animosities are unleashed when real democracy arrives. Democracy empowers the poor majorities, giving them control over the police, and they then violently lash out at the rich minorities. Demagogues like Mugabe in Zimbabwe scapegoat the resented minority—rich white farmers, in his case—and use democracy to take over the country. Murder, rape, and ethnic cleansing are the result.

Those who share this perspective want to slow down both globalization and democracy, since the social welfare, affirmative action, and education programs that rich countries have used to narrow income differentials either don't work or take too long to work when the country is poor and the poor are the majority. Basically, this argument holds that irrational prejudices in certain parts of the world should be allowed to dictate behavior to the rest of the world. The rest of the world should not globalize because the Chinese are hated in Indonesia. Unfortunately, there is no evidence whatsoever that a slower advance of globalization will moderate such long-seated ethnic animosities. Periodic attacks on ethnic Chinese go back centuries in countries such as Indonesia.

CONCLUSION

Of all the voices objecting to globalization, none may end up being as convincing as SARS. Globalization requires travel. SARS prevents travel. NIKE announced in the spring of 2003 it would have to move the production of its next generation of running shoes out of China if its managers and engineers could not travel to China. NIKE is not alone. Japanese companies rapidly closed several plants temporarily. Offshore supply chain costs soar if executives are ordered to spend ten days away from work, as was happening in the spring of 2003, after they visited a location that has SARS. If the situation continues, some of the offshore activities will move back onshore. As a result of such decisions, China lowered its estimated growth rate for 2003 by one percentage point.

Tourism is one of the world's biggest industries. Taking vacations is not going to end, but global tourism and global conventions could very well end. Because of cancellations by tourists and conventions, Canada lowered its estimated 2003 growth rate by half a percentage point.

Fewer foreign students are going to obtain visas to study at American universities. The effects are not immediate, but in the long run soft power makes a difference.

Looking forward there are optimistic, pessimistic, and pessimistic-pessimistic scenarios for SARS.

In the optimistic scenario China and everyone else succeeds in stamping out the disease. With a delay global tourism recovers. Firms for a while are cautious about putting too many of their supply chain activities in countries such as China and seeks to diversify their supplies, but this caution also eventually disappears. Fortunately in the summer of 2003 this looks like the most probable outcome.

In the pessimistic scenario SARS gets into China's rural areas and it cannot be stamped out. To protect itself the rest of the world has to quarantine all of China. No one is allowed to travel in or out of China. If anyone goes into China, they are not allowed to come back out. Products can only be shipped from China to the rest of the world when they can be thoroughly disinfected. The transportation vessels (planes and ships) used to transport Chinese imports or exports would have to go into quarantine for a substantial period of time at some remote uninhabited Pacific Island. Under these conditions little would, in fact, be exported to or imported from China.

In the pessimistic-pessimistic scenario SARS cannot be stamped out in China and spreads to other countries where it also cannot be stamped out. In this scenario everyone retreats to isolated autocracy where countries try to have as little contact as possible with the rest of the world. SARS basically ends globalization but that would be the least of the world's problems given the death rates that seem to be associated with SARS.

SARS reminds us that the completely unexpected often has the biggest effects. There will be other unexpected events in the development of globalization.

In more normal circumstances, what ultimately counts in successful globalization are mental attitudes and social values that accept what globalization brings; a mindset that quickly comes to think of those necessary changes as good things and not bad things imposed by an outside "foreign" world. It remains to be seen what parts of the world other than the United States have these attitudes. It is in large part a matter of internal self-confidence and has very little to do with whether a country's per capita GDP will rise or fall as the result of globalization.

If the charge is that globalization forces you to accept change and embrace foreign influences, then globalization is guilty as charged.[31]

For those on the left, stopping globalization is not going to stop the forward march of capitalism. Socialism defeated itself and cannot be revived under the cover of returning to more nationalistic economies. For those on the political right, the electronic media make it impossible to persuade the poor in the third world that they should not attempt to move to the first world. They see a standard of living they want. Border patrols can stop these attempts to move only if a country's citizens are willing to do their own unattractive jobs and refuse to employ illegal guest workers. As long as citizens participate as employers of illegal immigration, border controls are impossible.

In the end the antiglobalization protestors don't tell us much about what the world can do or what it should do. What the left wants—the end of capitalism—it cannot have; what the right wants—no immigration—it should not get. Keeping out the global culture is possible only if a country is willing to cut itself off electronically so its citizens cannot surf the Internet or get satellite TV.

No one is going to do this. Isolated national cultures are headed toward extinction if they are not already extinct.

As seen in Iran, religious gurus rapidly get into trouble when they win. They then become responsible for delivering an earthly paradise and not just a heavenly paradise—and that is impossible.

Anti-American sentiments don't matter unless Americans start to let these beliefs influence America's judgments about what America should do and what its role should be. One can argue as to whether the United States should have 37,000 troops in South Korea fifty years after the Korean War is over, but whether the troops stay or go should not be based on some anti-American street demonstrations or a presidential campaign with anti-American overtones.

If the South Korean president asks us to leave, we should of course leave. And perhaps U.S. troops should leave, whatever the South Koreans think, just to make clear that nuclear weapons in North Korea may threaten South Korea, Japan, Russia, or China, but they do not threaten the United States. The threatened nations should be left to solve their own problems, but they won't do so as long they can make the need for finding a solution an American responsibility.

Arguments that globalization should be slowed down have to answer the question how. Countries can opt out of globalization, but globalization is not a process where governments can dictate the pace of events. Private contractors, not governments, determine the pace of the construction of the global economic Tower of Babel.

Forces for change automatically create counterforces of resistance. Humans are creatures of habit and willingly change their standard operating procedures only slowly in response to economic or technological forces. They resist being forced to change rapidly. Major changes seldom come willingly if they are rapid—and globalization is a rapid event. The result, as we can see in the voices of antiglobalization, is a peculiarly human mixture of the rational and the irrational.

Fears that an invasion of some American-dominated global culture will change a local culture makes sense only if the locals believe they have a culture that is ultimately unattractive to their own young people. Similarly, fears that immigrants will destroy a local culture make sense only if locals believe their culture is ultimately unattractive to outsiders. The rational response for anyone with these beliefs is to work to make their local culture more attractive. Attacking globalization as a vehicle for keeping out global culture and immigrants is an irrational response, but a very human response.

{5}

REAL DANGERS TO
THE GLOBAL TOWER

Before they can be bought or sold, products should have gone through a process of destructive testing so both the buyer and the seller know the ultimate limits of the product. Ideally, social and economic systems should also undergo destructive testing. What are their limits? If they fail, what happens? Destructive testing isn't done, since social and economic systems have no samples to test. There is only one system, and deliberately stressing it is just too dangerous. But it is possible to mentally engage in the same process, conducting what the Germans call "gedanken" experiments. What could blow up globalization? What happens if it blows up?

Studying the weak points of a system is not pessimism. It is wisdom. If we are willing to study potential disasters and organize the institutions that can lead us to use what we have learned to change our behavior, we can enhance performance on many dimensions. Predictions about the future can be improved. Disaster prevention is sometimes possible. Crises can be better managed. Survival rates can be higher and damage lower. Improvements can be made in cleaning up the resultant physical or economic messes. There are lessons to be learned for rebuilding more robust systems that won't so easily crash next time.

In the last twenty years, financial and economic crises have come, gone, lingered, and returned. These crises were not organized by design, but effectively globalization has undergone a lot of unplanned destructive testing. None of these crises have come even close to slowing down the pace of globalization, much less blowing it up. The overall integrity of the global economic structure has withstood each of these tests. The system seems to be incredibly robust.

Third world global economic crises are as old as the Mexican crisis of 1982 and as new as the Argentine crisis of 2002. Southeast Asia and South Korea had big meltdowns in 1997. Mexico had yet another crisis in 1995–1996. Large countries such as Argentina and Indonesia have been knocked down and have been unable to get back up economically. Their economic problems were ignored precisely because they did not threaten the global system. In late 2002 economic storm clouds were bouncing back and forth between Argentina, Brazil, Uruguay, and Paraguay. The global system did not miss a heartbeat.

With the exception of China, the second world has had a rocky transition from communism to capitalism. A decade after abandoning communism, many of the countries in central and Eastern Europe have production levels below or near their communistic peaks. Russia itself had a big financial crisis in 1998. Because of its nuclear weapons, many expected the world would come rushing to its rescue. The world didn't. The global system did not break! It did not even bend!

In the first world, foreign exchange crises hit Italy, the United Kingdom, and France in the summer of 1992. George Soros became famous because of the billion pounds he made in a few minutes speculating against the British pound. Japan, the third biggest economy in the world, had a stock market crash bigger in real terms than that of 1929 and a huge property crash followed by a decade of no growth. In each case the global economy moved forward.

America had its Savings and Loan crisis in the mid-1980s, a sharp stock market crash in 1987, a more lengthy stock market crash between 2000 and 2002, and recessions in 1991 and 2001. The global system was tested to see if it could withstand internal American financial crashes and economic downturns. It could.

There were no shocks or aftershocks to globalization from any of these third, second, or first world crises.

But none of this means a crisis could not occur that would shake the foundations of the system. The 9/11 attacks happened because Americans could not imagine them. "Fly me to another country" was what hijackings were all about. Very few people had ever died in airline hijackings prior to 9/11. Pilots were told to cooperate.

In many ways the current economic situation is similar to the many small terrorist attacks that occurred prior to 9/11. These smaller terrorist attacks were annoying, but they were like mosquito bites. Mosquitoes should be swatted, but they do not cause major upheavals because they don't threaten anything important. But the 9/11 attacks changed that view. This type of mosquito was suddenly seen as the kind that carried malaria. Whole swamps of terrorists had to be drained to prevent real damage in the future.

What, if anything, is the equivalent in global economics? What are we not imagining that we should be imagining so that we can prevent it from biting us before it actually bites? We have already examined one possibility—deflation. As we have already seen in our examination of Japan, deflation, if not stopped, stops economic growth.

Otherwise, the big disaster, if there is one, has to be some serious international crisis at the heart of the global system in America. It is clear what this disaster is. It is a run on the dollar where the value of the dollar rapidly plunges.

In the spring of 2003 the dollar has persistently and continuously fallen almost 30 percent vis-a-vis the Euro in a little more than a year. Worries started to surface that a falling dollar might become a plunging dollar. The possibility of a run on the dollar was a crisis, much like an early report that a comet was headed towards the earth but no one could yet calculate whether its trajectory would lead the comet to actually crash into the earth.

The optimists pointed out that the Euro was just back to where it began when the Euro was adopted in January 1999 and that overall the declines in the value of the dollar were much smaller (6 percent) vis-à-vis a basket of currencies that represented all of America's trading partners. The pessimists pointed out that overall declines were small because most Asian currencies are linked to the dollar (they cannot decline) and the Japanese government was busy buying dollars to stop any significant rise in the value of the yen. If the Asian currencies were allowed to float, the declines in the value of the dollar would have been much bigger.

Optimists and pessimists agreed that slow persistent currency declines almost always become rapid declines. The last person to sell dollars loses the most and no one wants to be last. They agreed that there were real reasons to worry. But they also agreed that no one could yet determine whether a crash was inevitable nor, if a crash were to occur, the magnitude and precise nature of the damage.

The second potential crisis facing globalization, the gradual erosion of intellectual property rights, is an epidemiological crisis much like the AIDS virus or SARS. Without assurance of being able to earn a decent return, no one wants to invest in new technologies. The economic system, global or national, gradually sinks into stagnation as it loses much of its energy to generate new technologies. Most significantly, without intellectual property rights we won't even know what it is that we are missing in our lives. Unknown things that could have been invented won't have been invented.

Imagine our world without television. It was invented because the inventors wanted to get rich. Fighting about who actually invented television and who would actually get rich occasioned a patent case that went all the way to the Supreme Court. Filo

Farnsworth won out over RCA (the Radio Corporation of America), but because World War II intervened and his patents had expired before the war ended, he never got rich.[1]

At the same time no one should be deprived of the technologies (AIDS drugs) that might keep individuals alive or the technologies that might allow countries to catch up with the income levels of the developed world. The inherent tensions between having the incentives necessary for the invention of new ideas and the free, widespread use of new ideas has to be solved.

A CRASHING DOLLAR

Until the early 1980s the United States ran roughly balanced trading accounts. It had large surpluses in the years immediately after World War II, but these disappeared in the late 1950s. In the 1960s small trade deficits allowed the rest of the world to build up needed international reserves. In the 1970s America shifted from the gold standard to a floating dollar when the rest of the world's desires for gold reserves threatened to outstrip America's supply of gold.

In the 1980s America started to run large trade deficits. In the last twenty years the only exceptions to this pattern of large deficits is found in the early 1990s during the first Persian Gulf war when Japan and Germany were paying the United States very large sums of money to compensate for the fact that no German or Japanese troops were helping to protect Middle Eastern oil supplies. In economic terms America was balancing its balance of payments by selling an export service—soldiers to defend Germany and Japan's oil supplies.

Because of these persistent large trade deficits, the United States shifted from being a large net creditor nation in 1981, when it owned $700 billion more assets abroad than foreigners owned assets in the United States, to being a very large net debtor nation in 2001, with $2,300 billion fewer American assets owned abroad than foreign assets owned in the United States.[2] As America's net investment position becomes more and more negative with continuing trade deficits, net dividend and interest payments to foreigners will be growing rapidly in the years ahead. As a result, the American current account deficit is expected to rise from its current 4.5 percent of GDP into the 7 to 8 percent range by the end of the decade, even if the trade deficit does not increase. These are levels far above the levels where other countries have always gotten into trouble.[3]

As in all markets, the value of the dollar is determined by the price at which the dollars for sale exactly match the dollars to be bought. How many dollars do people want to sell? How many dollars do people want to buy? There are two flows of currency into the market for dollars.

The first set of flows comes from the "current account." How many goods and services do Americans want to buy from the rest of the world? To buy these goods they must sell dollars to get the necessary foreign funds. How many goods and services do foreigners want to buy from the United States? To buy these goods they must buy dollars to get the necessary funds.

The second set of flows comes from the "capital account." How much money would Americans like to invest in the rest of the world? To invest in the rest of the world, Americans must sell dollars to get the foreign currencies they need to make foreign investments. This activity generates a supply of dollars. How much money would foreigners like to invest in the United States? To invest in America, foreigners must buy dollars to get the funds they need to make American investments. This generates a demand for dollars.

The value of the dollar is the price at which these different demands and supplies match. Since the overall supply and demand for dollars has to balance, the balance of payments as a whole is always in balance. If there is a deficit on the current account (the supply of dollars flowing from American purchases of foreign goods is bigger than the demand for dollars flowing from foreign purchases of American goods), there must be an equally large surplus on the capital account (foreigners' demand for dollars to make American investments exceeds American supplies of dollars to finance American investments in foreign countries). Although the flows always balance mathematically, there is an issue as to which of these two accounts is the driver and which is the adjustor in determining the value of the dollar.

When I first took graduate courses in international economics in the 1960s, my Harvard professors taught us that the current account was the driver of the value of the dollar. American desire to buy foreign goods determines the supply of dollars, and foreign desire to buy American goods determines the demand for dollars. Private capital flows were small since they were then severely restricted by law in most countries. Since the world was on a system of fixed exchange rates where governments supported the value of their currencies vis-à-vis the dollar by buying or selling dollars out of their foreign exchange reserves, the only capital flows that mattered were government decisions to intervene in the foreign exchange markets.

In this world an American trade deficit would have quickly led to a fall in the value of the dollar (supply exceeds demand) if governments did not intervene. With a lower-valued dollar, foreign goods would become more expensive for Americans to buy and American goods cheaper for foreigners to buy. Americans would quickly cut back on their purchases of these foreign goods; foreigners would quickly increase their purchases of American goods. The current account would swing back into balance with the value of the dollar stabilized at a new lower level consistent with a current account balance.

Forty years later a very different world exists. When I am teaching international economics, I teach that the capital account is the main driver of the value of the dollar. A market-determined system of flexible exchange rates has replaced a government-determined system of fixed exchange rates. Financial markets are now global. Capital controls have been removed. The private capital flows that used to be very small are now very big. Every year $5,000 billion worth of goods and services cross national boundaries, but every day $1,200 billion goes through the world's foreign exchange markets. In just four days the world's capital markets move as much money as all of the world's exports in 365 days. And on a big day the financial markets can move a lot more than $1,200 billion. If foreigners should get worried about the dollar's future value and wish to take their money home or if Americans should get worried about the dollar's future value and seek the safety of foreign currencies that could be expected to rise in value relative to the dollar in a crisis, truly enormous amounts of money would start leaving the United States.

If capital flows drive the system, the dollar rises in value when foreigners want to make more investments in America than Americans want to make investments in the rest of the world. With a higher-valued dollar foreign goods are cheaper for Americans to buy and they buy more. American goods are more expensive for foreigners to buy and they buy less. Exports fall, imports rise, and a trade deficit appears. Conversely, if a net capital outflow occurs, the capital account surplus becomes a deficit, and the value of the dollar falls. Imports fall as a much lower valued dollar leads to much higher prices for imports and much lower prices for exports. The current account deficit shrinks and becomes a surplus.

Americans find it hard to imagine an international financial crisis involving the dollar. One has never occurred. America's foreign economic activities used to be a very small tail on a very big economic dog. A friend, Lester Taylor, and I in late 1965 were the writers of the chapter in the 1966 *Economic Report of the President*, which set out to forecast the path of the American economy for 1966. He and I did not mention the rest of the world once in that chapter. What happened in the rest of the world did not make any difference to America's performance. America was then an oil exporter and did not import anything really important.

Today there is a new reality. Since 1965 imports plus exports have gone up from 5 percent to 30 percent of America's GDP and America now imports more than 60 percent of its oil. Events in the rest of the world are central to forecasting what will happen to the American economy in 2003 or 2004.

Both America and the rest of the world have become highly dependent upon America's trade deficit and the inward capital flows necessary to sustain it. For Americans these inflows have to be very large, since they have to cover both the trade deficit (about $450 billion) and American desire to invest abroad. Over the last five years Americans have been investing between $350 billion and $600 billion per year in the rest of the world. To keep their economies moving forward, the rest of the world has become dependent upon the $450 billion worth of net demand that flows from the American trade deficit and the capital inflows that build local factories. If those inflows were to quickly disappear, the damage would be extensive.

Any sharp fall in the value of the dollar would blow up the existing supply chains for both American and foreign firms. With a falling dollar, what were cheap places to manufacture components would become expensive places to manufacture components. What were very profitable places to sell manufactured products would become unprofitable places.

A sharply falling dollar is a comet crash where the point of impact is located in the United States but where the greatest economic damage is done elsewhere in the world. When the dollar falls, the rest of the world will rapidly lose $450 billion worth of demand as the American trade deficit disappears. At American levels of productivity, the loss of $450 billion in net sales represents the loss of 9 million jobs, but the countries that export to the United States have much lower levels of productivity. Something on the order of 20–25 million jobs would be at stake in the rest of the world.

Autos are a good example. With a sharp fall in the value of the dollar Americans would not be able to afford the 2.9 million cars they imported in 2000. If the dollar fell 40 percent, these cars would be approximately 40 percent more expensive. How long would it take American car manufacturers, including the American factories of foreign firms, to make an extra 2.9 million cars? They now make almost 15 million cars and they would need to raise production only 20 percent. It could probably be done in three months, since the manufacturers would start running three rather than two shifts a day. How long would it take the foreign manufacturers of the cars now exported to America to find alternative markets in which they could sell those 2.9 million cars? The answer is that it cannot be done. They would have to shut down the foreign facilities that are now producing those cars.

The inflow of foreign funds is also important to Americans. They allow Americans to consume and invest more than they produce at home. Without those funds, American consumption and domestic investment would both have to fall.

A lower valued dollar is not a possible event, it is an event that will happen. The laws of financial arithmetic tell us that no country can forever run a large trade deficit. Every year money has to be borrowed to pay for this year's trade deficit and to pay interest and dividends upon the borrowings of the past. As the trade deficit continues, the borrowings necessary to make interest and dividend payments upon past borrowings grow larger and larger. Mathematically, there has to come a point when the rest of the world either cannot or will not lend the necessary sums. On this point there is no disagreement.

In 1999 the U.S. Congress grew worried about the American trade deficit and appointed a U.S. Trade Deficit Review Commission that consisted of six Republican appointees, including Donald Rumsfeld, now secretary of defense; Robert Zoellick, now America's trade negotiator; and Anne Krueger, now the number 2 person at the IMF; also appointed were six Democrats (I was one). The commission reported back to Congress on November 15, 2000.

The report has a series of points agreed to unanimously. They include the conclusion that although no one can predict when the end might come, it will come. In the words of the six Republican commissioners: "The trade deficit, relative to GDP, cannot continue to increase without end. At some point the situation will reverse itself."[4] The bottom line is simple: what must happen will happen. The dollar has to go down. This is true even if it has not

yet happened and even if everyone up to now has been wrong
about how long the system can go on before it happens.

Disagreements among the twelve commissioners arose over
whether the end would come as a "soft landing" (a slow and gradual change in the value of the dollar and hence the trade deficit
over a period of years) or a "hard landing" (a precipitous fall in the
value of the dollar and the rapid elimination of the trade deficit in
a few months). Again in the words of the six Republican commissioners, "A disruptive end, with adverse effects throughout the
economy, cannot be totally dismissed but it is highly unlikely."

The six Democrats saw a hard landing not as a certainty but as
much more likely. "If the current account deficit continues to
grow, at some point in the near future we are likely to reach the
limit of our ability to borrow abroad in order to finance trade
deficits. This could force the United States to reduce the deficit
quickly and risk a 'hard landing' or an abrupt correction with the
clear possibility of triggering a recession. This would have enormous repercussions not only for the United States, but also for the
world economy."

To minimize the danger of a hard landing, the Republican
commissioners recommended that "these risks could be best
addressed by increasing national savings." With higher American
savings, America would have less need to import so much capital
and the chances of a run on the dollar would diminish.

American personal savings rates are certainly low and should be
higher. With higher rates, growth would be enhanced and the dangers of a currency crisis would be reduced. Personal savings rates
declined from 9 percent in 1992 to 1 percent of disposable personal income at the end of 2000. Business savings went up, but not
enough to entirely offset the fall in personal savings. As a result, the
private savings rate fell from 15.5 percent to 13.4 percent of GDP.
But government savings (state, local, and federal) was rising at the
same time from −1.1 percent to +7.8 percent of GDP. The net
result was a higher national savings rate, up from 14.4 percent to
18.6 percent of GDP.[5] Add in the net capital inflows, and Ameri-

can investment rose from 16 percent to 22 percent of GDP between 1992 and 2000 despite a fall in personal savings. The economic boom and the dramatic increase in productivity growth in the last half of the 1990s partly flowed from this rise in investment spending.

Even though some of the commissioners are now major figures in the Bush administration, nothing has been done to raise America's national savings rate. The Bush administration's large 2001 tax cut moved in precisely the opposite direction. When governments are running surpluses, effectively any tax cut is a deliberate policy decision to lower the American savings rate. Some of those tax-cut dollars will go into consumption. If national savings are to be cut by running federal deficits and if domestic investments are not to fall as a consequence, those advocating a policy of budget deficits must believe the extra savings necessary to finance existing levels of investment can be found abroad. More capital has to flow into the United States.

The necessary foreign funds are not apt to be available. In the late 1990s two-thirds of the investment funds flowing across national borders were coming into the United States. To make the economic arithmetic work, the rest of the world must either be willing to direct a larger portion of their total savings into international markets or those markets must be willing to allocate a much larger portion of the existing funds to the United States. Neither is likely to happen.

Adopting fiscal policies that require large capital inflows is equivalent to putting more pressure into a pressure cooker already at, or above, its rated capacity. This is especially true when slow growth and a falling stock market are also discouraging inward financial flows.

Because of its role in the global economy, American deficits are fundamentally different in nature from those of other countries. Conditions that would have long ago produced a crisis in any other country in the world have not yet produced a crisis in America.

Although economists talk about "borrowing" money to pay for

trade deficits, America really does not so much borrow money from the rest of the world to finance its trade deficit as it sells assets. When Mercedes buys Chrysler, the funds paid to Chrysler shareholders pays for our current account deficits. When the Japanese buy property in the United States, they pay for the U.S. trade deficit—as does a Saudi who buys dot.com shares. America has a lot of assets to sell—approximately $30,000 billion of private assets. Even if the United States has already had net sales of $2,300 billion, there are still a lot of assets left to sell.

And even when the United States does technically borrow money from the rest of the world, there is a difference between America's borrowings and the rest of the world's borrowings. Everyone borrows in dollars, but only America can print dollars. As a result, there is no risk of an American default on its loans.

A variety of factors have produced the American trade deficit, and the exact combination of these factors has changed over time. In the 1980s high American interest rates were the chief attraction for foreign investors. To get those high interest rates, the rest of the world poured money into America, raising the value of the dollar. In the 1990s the interest rate differential disappeared, but the world's investors turned their attention to America's booming stock market, higher growth rates, and leadership in the new industries of the third industrial revolution. There was the feeling that the rest of the world was falling farther and farther behind America and that it was important for wise investors to have some of their capital in America. Funds flowed in at record rates and the value of the dollar rose, leading to soaring trade deficits.

In addition to the rising value of the dollar, a variety of other factors have contributed to the American trade deficit (or the rest of the world's trade surplus). The large deficits in the 1990s can be traced partly to an American economy that was growing faster than the economies of the rest of the world. With incomes rising faster in America than anywhere else, imports into America grew faster than their imports (our exports). The effects of higher growth were compounded by an American propensity to buy imports from the rest of the world as our incomes go up, that is 35 percent higher than the foreign propensity to buy American exports as their incomes go up.[6] With a faster growth and Americans' higher propensities to import, the American trade deficit gets large very fast.

Yet if one puts all of these factors into an economic model designed to predict trade deficits, the result is still a substantial underprediction of the actual deficits. There is powerful upward thrust to the American trade deficit that flows from four structural realities.

(1) America used to be a net oil exporter, but domestic oil production is on a steep downward slope while usage is up. Sixty percent of America's oil is now imported and accounts for more than 10 percent of America's total imports. When oil prices rise, as they did in 2002, the result is a steep deterioration in America's current account deficit.

(2) American firms are leading the drive to globalization. They are simply moving much faster to offshore production bases than are firms in the rest of the world. Almost 50 percent of America's imports come from the offshore production facilities of American companies, and in some industries, such as telecommunications, this percentage is over 70 percent.[7] As these firms bring into the United States the products they used to make at home, imports rise faster than a simple analysis of income changes in America and the rest of the world would predict.

(3) One can argue whether there are more American government restrictions on imports or foreign government restrictions on American exports. Some countries have more restrictions, but there are also many countries with fewer restrictions. Comparisons with the rest of the world depend upon exactly how restrictions are measured, and, in any case, the differences aren't large. America is a lot more restrictive than most Americans believe. Think of President Bush's recent new restrictions on steel imports.

Where the big differences occur is not in official "openness" but in the degree to which America's private economy is more open and easier to penetrate. Foreign auto manufacturers do not have to build a chain of car dealerships (the normal circumstances in the rest of the world) when they want to sell cars in America. They can sell cars through existing dealers. Retailers, such as Wal-Mart, are much faster to junk American suppliers and to replace them with cheaper foreign suppliers than is the case for retailers in the rest of the world.

(4) If some countries have decided to run trade surpluses as a matter of economic policy, as they have, it is mathematically true that someone else has to run trade deficits. Globally, trade deficits and surpluses must equal zero. If in 2001 Japan is to have its $64 billion surplus, China its $31 billion surplus, Europe its $185 billion surplus, and Korea and Taiwan their $51 billion surpluses, then someone else has to have a $331 billion deficit. The only someone big enough to absorb their combined surpluses and those of the rest of the world is the United States.

At some point the systematic and persistent deterioration in America's trading position is going to have to be confronted. There are only two open questions. When will the inevitable correction occur? When it does occur, will the United States have a hard landing or a soft landing?

The timing is unknown. It is, of course, possible that the necessary adjustments will not have to be made in the next few years. A big trade deficit might go on for another twenty years. That outcome is unlikely—but it is not impossible.

Everyone knows what a hard landing would mean—a rapid flight from dollar-denominated assets by both foreigners and Americans and a plunge in the value of the dollar that would make imports so expensive that Americans could no longer afford to buy them. Suddenly losing $450 billion of aggregate demand, the rest of the world would plunge into a recession. The higher interest rates necessary to stem capital flight from America would quickly produce a sharp economic contraction in the United States. Together they would lead to a sharp global downturn.

Given trade deficits of the magnitude now occurring in the United States, there are no historical examples of soft landings. If these deficits were occurring in any other country, a hard landing would be considered a likely event. Because a hard landing would be both an American and a world economic disaster, a hard landing tends to be dismissed not because it is impossible but because it is unthinkable.

Whereas the implications of a hard landing are both clear and well known, the economic implications of a soft landing have not been equally clearly spelled out. In a soft landing trade imbalances are solved by a gradual fall in the value of the dollar and by a reduction in the American growth rate relative to that in the rest of the world. When closely examined, a soft landing is almost certain to quickly accelerate into a hard landing.

Those who believe in the soft landing argue that the United States is different. Since the United States borrows in its own currency, dollars, it can never run out of the foreign exchange reserves necessary to permit the repatriation of capital. True, there are no default risks on American debts. But it is not the prospect of total default so much as the prospect of large losses that drives investors to run for the exits. Few foreign investors would just sit still and accept, persistent falls in the value of their dollar-denominated assets, even though they know that default is impossible. Investors usually flee when they feel the market value of their investments is about to fall. They don't wait to panic until they think their investments are about to be wiped out. The first individuals to move their wealth out of dollars win; the last to move lose. The very real incentive to be a first mover is what causes hard landings. Those incentives explain why soft landings are few and far between.

Borrowing funds in your own currency is, in fact, not much of an insurance policy against capital flight.

Believers in a soft landing often assert there is no other place to go for those who might wish to leave the United States.[8] But that is not true. Together Japan and Europe have an economy bigger than that of the United States. The yen plus the Euro are viable alternatives to the dollar. There are rational places to go. But even if there were no rational places to go, long-run rationality is not in large supply in the midst of financial panics. Those who get out first win even if everyone cannot succeed if they all try to leave at once.

Believers in a soft landing also argue that foreign governments would not let a hard landing occur, since foreign governments understand that the damage to their own economies would be far larger than the damage to the U.S. economy. Foreign governments undoubtedly do understand this reality. But it is not foreign governments who will start the rush out of dollars. It is private investors—and not necessarily even their own private investors. When the outflow begins, it is apt to be led by Americans seeking to protect their wealth by moving out of a currency (the dollar) they expect to depreciate. In foreign exchange crises it is almost always the locals who run first. They are watching local conditions more closely, have the most to lose, and lead the charge to the exits.

In the view of those believing in soft landings, realizing what they had to lose, foreign governments would rush to buy dollars to prop up the value of the dollar. Perhaps, but the interventions would have to be both rapid and massive. Governments would also have to be able to explain to their citizens why their taxpayers, who on average are poorer than Americans, should have their money used to prop up the American standard of living. It is the right thing to do from the perspective of other countries, but explaining why it is the right thing to do would not be easy.

Taking the pressure out of the system is difficult, since getting the current account deficit back into balance faces a very large existing difference between America's export of goods and services and its import of goods and services ($974 billion versus $1,392 billion in 2002).[9] If foreign capital inflows stop, balance requires a fall in the dollar large enough to eliminate the trade deficit and large enough to create a trade surplus that could cover the net interest and dividends payments owed on foreign assets in the United States ($14 billion in 2002), unilateral transfers such as foreign aid and remittances ($59 billion in 2002), and net American investments abroad ($179 billion in 2002). The one study that has focused on this issue estimates it would take a 40 percent fall in the value of the dollar in the short run and a 25 percent fall in the value of the dollar in the long run to bring about the necessary balance.[10]

These estimates assume the financial markets would not overshoot, but that is precisely what financial markets usually do. The dollar would likely plunge right through the 40 percent estimate as it moved from being overvalued to being undervalued. Even if an overshoot did not occur, there is every reason to believe that this 40 percent estimate is an underestimate of what would be required. What would have to occur cannot be deduced from econometric studies of past marginal responses. It is simply not a marginal adjustment.

Since manufactured goods account for 80 percent of world trade, balance would require more manufactured exports and fewer manufactured imports. American manufacturing would need an enormous one-third expansion in output. America does not currently have the necessary manufacturing capacity. The problems go beyond the large required expansion in capacity to the creation of new manufacturing competencies that do not now exist. What the rest of the world might want to import (machine tools, for example) and what America now imports (electronic components, for example) are not what American manufacturers now make.

It would take a substantial amount of time to build the new competencies and capacities. New plants would have to be constructed. A large diversion of labor and management to new exporting or import competing sectors of manufacturing would have to occur. Investors in these activities would require the certainty that the dollar would stay down for a long enough period of time for adequate private returns to be made on their new investments. It all takes time.

Oil compounds the problems. Oil is today priced in dollars, so technically a fall in the value of the dollar would not affect the price of oil for Americans. It would make oil much cheaper for the rest of the world, however. But if the value of the dollar were plunging, the oil exporting countries would have an enormous incentive to shift to pricing oil in other currencies. If they did not reprice, they would suffer a big reduction in their own standards of living.

Should the oil exporters shift to other currencies, oil imports would become much more costly for Americans. And American demand for oil is very inelastic—a 30 percent increase in the price of oil leads to a 3 percent fall in the quantity purchased.[11] There are no domestic supplies now or in the future large enough to replace what must be imported. As the dollar cost of oil imports rises, the fall in the value of the dollar necessary to eliminate the trade deficit grows bigger. The 40 percent fall necessary to restore balance assumes oil continues to be priced in dollars.

It is often suggested that the needed exports could be found in the service sector, where America has a trade surplus. This suggestion runs into the reality that international trade in services is small and restricted by foreign government regulations.

All of these factors mean that even a 40 percent fall in the value of the dollar is unlikely to cure America's current account deficit. And even if this is the right number, it is certainly big enough to cause a rush out of dollar-denominated assets by both Americans and foreigners. What started as a soft correction would be converted into a hard landing as investors came to realize how much the dollar had to fall.

Slower growth, the second route to a soft landing, is an even less attractive option. To correct the current account deficit with lower growth would require a huge American recession. Using standard estimates of America's demand for imports, rebalancing America's trading accounts would require a more than 20 percent reduction in America's GDP.

Even if Americans were willing to take a one-time 20 percent cut in their incomes, problems would remain. Because equal increases in income cause America's demand for imports to rise faster than the rest of the world's demand for American exports, America would forever have to grow more slowly than the rest of the world if growth is to be the equilibrator in the current account. Of the seven recent studies that have tried to estimate American income elasticities of demand for imports and foreign income elasticities of demand for American exports, only one found them to be approximately equal.[12] Six found large differences. Averaging all seven leads to the conclusion that if the rest of the world were to grow at 4 percent per year in the long run, the United States would have to grow at 3 percent per year forever to balance its current account. Let me emphasize the word "forever." America would have to be willing to accept living standards that are permanently falling relative to the living standards in the rest of the world. What would have to be accepted in a soft landing is unacceptable.

In addition, investors, American and foreign, would know that America was going to be permanently growing much slower than the rest of the world. This knowledge would by itself convert a soft landing into a hard landing. Why would one want to invest in a country that is growing much slower than the rest of the world? Capital inflows would stop and outflows would begin.

The problem is not what to do, as we shall see in chapter 8. The problem is getting ourselves to do it. Predictions of a U.S. balance-of-payments crisis have been heard so often, without anything in fact happening, that these cries of alarm are now completely ignored. The U.S. Trade Deficit Review Commission's report was ignored. No one is going to believe an American balance-of-payments crisis is possible until it happens. In that sense they are exactly like the reports of possible terrorist attacks President Bush was briefed upon prior to 9/11.

Whatever the objective dangers, "do nothing" is the policy of choice.[13] Recommendations suggesting Americans should "restructure their economic system to produce higher savings rates" are going to be ignored. The Bush administration ignored calls for higher savings rates even though its own cabinet officers made such a recommendation just as they were being selected for office.

In crises the unexpected is to be expected. Undoubtedly, there are aspects of a flight from the dollar that today cannot even be imagined. At the same time it makes sense to have contingency plans. This was one of the recommendations made by the Democratic members of the U.S. Trade Deficit Review Commission, but as far as anyone knows it is being ignored by the Bush administration since the Republican members of the commission did not agree with that Democratic recommendation.

Put simply, a plunge in the value of the dollar has the potential to do to the world what a collapse of the banking system did to the United States at the onset of the Great Depression—it could start the global economy plunging downward. The Hoover administration didn't know what to do after the stock market crash in 1929 and as a result it did nothing. Doing nothing, the money GDP fell 46 percent and the real GDP fell 31 percent. In this case the "do nothing" option is even more likely. In the 1930s America had a national government that had both the responsibility and the power to intervene. When a 21st century American currency crisis hits, there will be no world government with either the responsibility or the power to step in to attempt to control the downward spiral.

The only country big enough and with the necessary global mind-set will be the country in crisis. Like all peoples and their governments in a foreign exchange crisis, Americans and the American government will quickly blame foreign speculators for the problems. There will be enormous political resistance to letting foreigners tell Americans how they should run their affairs. Tell the foreigners to "go to hell."

What happens to globalization in the midst and the aftermath of a big fall in the value of the dollar? The truth is no one knows. But if there is an economic crisis that could destroy the global system, this is it. Putting up trade and investment barriers and retreating back to more isolated national economies might start to look very good.

INTELLECTUAL PROPERTY RIGHTS

The private ownership of productive assets and the ability to own the output that flows from those assets lies at the heart of capitalism. Property rights are what allow businesses to buy and sell their goods and services. Without them a market economy cannot exist. In capitalism everyone has to know who owns what and who has the right to sell what.

Property rights are what give businesses an incentive to invest in productive facilities to make more goods and services. No one plants apple trees unless they have some guarantee that they will own the apples that grow on the trees. Property rights are why people invest in improving the value of existing facilities. Investments can be recouped when the renovated properties are sold. Property rights provide the incentives to use assets wisely. A case in point: Ocean fishing is destroying itself because of an absence of property rights. Everyone has an incentive to catch the most fish possible and let someone else worry about overfishing. If they don't catch all of the fish in the ocean, someone else will. Pollution also flows from a lack of property rights. Everyone has an incentive to dump their wastes into the air or water, since no one owns them and no one has to be paid if they are used to dispose of wastes.

To get the first industrial revolution started, physical property rights had to be more clearly specified. The enclosure movement, converting common land to private land, was an important step. Feudalism could live with vague collective ownership, but capitalism could not. Someone had to own and have an incentive to invest in the coal mines necessary to power the steam engine.

Similarly, systems of intellectual property rights lie at the heart of today's knowledge-based economy. Knowledge does not come free. Investments have to be made to extract it. Just as gold miners do not mine gold unless they will be allowed to keep the gold they extract, so intellectual miners do not mine knowledge unless they are allowed to keep the knowledge they extract. Progress in mathematics, software, biogenetics, and business methods depends to some extent upon patent, copyright, and trademark protection.

In the third industrial revolution intellectual property rights are becoming more important as other sources of competitive advantage become less important. Firms used to win because they had better or cheaper access to raw materials. Today raw materials are available to everyone at competitive world prices. Steel firms located in countries without iron or coal (Korea) can be the world leaders. Geographic location used to be key to success, but today markets can be served from anywhere in the world. Similarly, no one is going to win simply because they have more capital than anyone else in their industry. Capital can be borrowed.

The only remaining source of true competitive advantage are technologies that others do not have, copyrights they cannot infringe, or brand names that set one apart. None of these is possible without systems for protecting patents, copyrights, and trademarks.

The history of private property rights is a history of legal systems gradually inventing new property rights to catch up with advancing economic systems. Systems of land ownership weren't necessary until agriculture was invented. Hunter-gatherer nomads don't need them. Systems of mineral rights weren't necessary until mines could be dug. For the same reason, no one today worries about who owns the moon. There is no point in owning something no one can use. Conversely, with deep-water oil well drilling, ownership of the seabed has become a fighting issue.

Whereas physical property rights have slowly expanded over a long period of time, intellectual property rights are a relatively new human creation. The ancient Greeks did not think that knowledge was something that could be owned or sold.[14] Premodern Chinese,

Islamic, Jewish, and Christian societies all rejected the idea of human ownership of ideas. Knowledge was a divine gift. The invention of the printing press first created issues about intellectual property rights. Who owned the ideas and language published in books? Previous copying techniques had been too expensive to make the ownership of ideas worth disputing. Markets were too small for anyone to make money selling ideas. Only gradually did authors come to claim they were creators of their own works rather than transmitters of God's eternal truths.[15]

At each step in the expansion of property rights, the opponents of greater property rights have argued that God gave land, food, music, stories, technology, whatever the resource, for everyone to use equally. It was against God's design to allow individual humans to own that particular resource. Today the same arguments are heard about biotechnology: It isn't right to allow individuals to patent a plant, an animal, or a piece of the human genome. God created living things.

There are options to systems of private property rights. Communism did not have them. Where private property rights do not exist, some collective entity, most often the state, makes the necessary investments in production facilities, improves and maintains existing properties, controls overusage, and, most important, pays for inventing the new things that make life better. To a great extent private property rights and socialism are alternative means of arriving at the same end.

No real economy has ever been an economy of just private property rights. There are always some things managed collectively—roads and education, for example. No real economy has ever been an economy with no private property rights. There are always some things managed privately—personal effects in a kibbutz, for instance. There is always an issue of the exact balance between collective ownership and private ownership. Where should the line be drawn? It can be drawn in different places, but capitalism simply doesn't work unless it is clear where the line actually is drawn.

In the end, state investments under communism did not prove to be a good substitute for private property rights under capitalism. Communism wasn't so bad at investing in new production facilities, but it was horrible when it came to maintenance. New apartment buildings quickly became shabby. Pollution went uncontrolled. If socialism is retreating, it logically follows that there has to be an extension of private property rights to fill the gap.

In most developed countries, government spending on research and development is falling as a fraction of total R&D spending. As governments withdraw from the job of providing new knowledge, it logically follows that private industry has to step up its activity levels if total activity is not to fall. But this won't happen unless private companies see a system of intellectual property rights where they believe they can recoup their investments and make good returns.

As a result of all these factors, intellectual property rights are more central than they were in the past. This can be seen in the explosion in the use and importance of patents. In the developed world the demand for international patents at the WTO was up 25 percent in the two years from 1999 to 2001.[16] In the United States, patent applications have doubled in a decade.[17] American firms earn more than $36 billion from patent licenses.[18]

There are today three major problems with the existing system of intellectual property rights.

First, the current system was not built to deal with today's technologies. What fit the 19th-century world of mechanical engineering does not fit the 21st-century world of biotechnology. New technologies have created new potential forms of intellectual property rights. What ownership rights exist when someone discovers what a gene does? Can genetic pieces of plants, animals, and human beings be patented? Who owns the new plants and animals that will be created? What ownership rights exist when humans build new genes that replace defective natural human genes?

Second, new electronic technologies have also made old rights unenforceable. When books, music, and movies can be freely downloaded from an electronic library, what does a copyright mean? If software's look and feel cannot be patented, software can be legally copied as long as one does not use exactly the same programming codes. What does a software patent mean in this case? Laws that cannot or will not be enforced are worse than no laws at all, since they breed contempt for legal systems.

Third, there is no global system for enforcing intellectual property rights. Negotiating a global system was one of the central goals of the GATT Uruguay trading round. A TRIPS (trade-related aspects of intellectual property rights) agreement was negotiated, but most provisions have yet to be implemented; some items don't take effect until 2016. Since the Uruguay Round it has become clear that intellectual property rights are more important economically than was thought at the time. As a result, in today's context no one likes what was negotiated or lives up to those provisions that have come into effect. Poor countries think they don't get any benefits and rich countries think they don't get any protection.

In the upcoming Doha WTO round of trade negotiations, refining TRIPS is on the agenda. The current discussions focus on weakening TRIPS, even though most of its provisions have yet to be implemented. Preliminary agreements state that TRIPS is not to stand in the way of public health and restrictions are to be placed on the patenting of new plants and animals.[19] It is not obvious TRIPS will ever be implemented or enforced.

As a result, there are no agreed-upon rules, no enforcement agencies and no judicial systems for settling global disputes. And unless the system of intellectual property rights is global, it simply isn't an enforceable system. Illegal activities simply move to geographic places where they are legal or where the laws are not enforced. The losses are large. Piracy is estimated to cost the world's companies more than $200 billion per year.[20] The world leader in software piracy seems to be Vietnam, where 97 percent of the software is pirated.[21]

India does not recognize patents on pharmaceuticals. Even as large as the country is, copies in India don't just displace the inventor's products in India. "Made in India" and "Sold in Africa" might be signs hung in most pharmacies in Africa. But that failure to respect patents means that an inventive domestic drug industry cannot develop in India, since everyone knows the money they might spend on developing drugs for the Indian market cannot be recouped because other Indian companies would copy them.[22] One can understand the reasons for not respecting patents on life-saving pharmaceuticals, but the Indians give no more respect to copyrights on music CDs, where life and death is not the issue.

Today's solution to the absence of a global system of intellectual property rights is basically for the United States to go around the world hitting countries over the head and telling them they should protect intellectual property the American way. China and Israel are at the top of the U.S. State Department's list of the biggest violators of intellectual property rights. Until it joined the WTO, China had never formally signed on to any system protecting intellectual property rights, although it had often informally agreed to crack down on pirates. But it never did. In China 95 percent of the software is pirated. Microsoft and others lose $16 billion in potential sales in China alone.[23] Israel formally adheres to the U.S. system of intellectual property rights but enforces nothing. Go to the central bus station in South Tel Aviv and there you will find dozens of shops full of nothing but pirated goods. The bus station is full of security guards guarding everything but the security of intellectual property rights. Israel is not alone. Many countries formally adhere to one of the existing systems but don't enforce their own laws. Put simply, national systems that have been developed for advanced countries such as the United States are not going to evolve into de facto world standards.

Even in the United States, Europe, and Japan there are differing systems of intellectual property rights. The biggest difference is that in the United States the patent goes to whoever can prove they were first to invent, whereas in Japan and Europe the patent goes to whoever was first to file for a patent. The U.S. system favors the independent inventor, and the European-Japanese system favors large corporations who can afford to file a lot of patents before they know for sure which ideas will really work and which will really be valuable. They just patent all of the technical possibilities knowing that one of them is likely to be valuable.

The losses will be enormous if the world does not have a viable system of intellectual property rights. No one wants their mother or father to fall victim to Alzheimer's disease. If a cure is to be found, it will take enormous investments in biotechnology. Those investments are not going to be made unless investors have a way to recoup their investments and make a profit. We don't want to wait years for the organ transplants that can save our lives, but many of us are going to wait and many of us are going to die unless money is invested in transgenic animals for growing transplantable organs. That money isn't going to be invested if those who invent the transgenic pig cannot own the transgenic pig they create.

All of us want the fun and excitement of books, music, and movies. As they are now known, they are going to die out unless ways are developed for protecting the rights of the authors, artists, and producers. What has happened in music is about to happen to movies.[24] Movies not yet released to the theaters are now available for downloading, and the technology for rapid downloading is developing very fast.[25] Within a short time downloading a movie will be as easy as downloading a CD. Half a million movies a day are already being downloaded from the Internet. It takes just several hours of downloading that can be done by your computer while you sleep. Yet the cost of making an average movie is $80 million. It will not take too many more downloadings before many fewer movies will be made.

Authors, artists, and producers have to eat. If they cannot earn money from being imaginative, they will have to spend most of their time doing other things. There will always be part-time amateurs who produce books, CDs, and movies, but theirs will be amateur productions—low quality, lacking the professional touches we enjoy. How much are amateurs who cannot charge to watch their movies going to be able to invest?

Without a legal system to protect intellectual property rights, secrecy becomes the system of intellectual property rights by default. But secrecy is a bad system, since people waste a lot of time reinventing what has already been invented rather than building on what is already known. And to keep the secret, whatever has been invented, these new goods or services have to be produced in very limited quantities and sold at very high prices.

In any system of intellectual property rights, the issue is to balance two conflicting objectives. First, systems have to have strong incentives to create new intellectual property. Second, systems should rapidly spread knowledge once new knowledge has been invented or discovered. Historically, the balance has been found by giving inventors a monopoly on the use of their inventions for some limited time, and at the end of that time everyone gets to freely use what they have invented.

LIFE SAVING DRUGS

What the current system lacks most is the ability to put into the public domain things so important that everyone should have access to them immediately, even though they were discovered or created in the private domain. Some pieces of intellectual property are too important to deprive anyone of their use even for limited periods of time, yet these pieces of intellectual property won't be created without some system of private incentives.

The prime example is drugs for treating AIDS. Of the world's 40 million cases of AIDS, 30 million are in Africa, with a doubling expected in the next five years.[26] Infection rates may be as high as 25 percent in South Africa.[27] In Africa 75 percent will die, and most of those individuals will be in the prime of life.[28] The loss of experience, talent, and education is an enormous jolt to economic development. Life expectancy in Botswana has fallen from over age 60 to under age 40.[29] Output in Botswana is expected to be down 32 percent by 2010 because of AIDS. India seems to be following the African path. Indonesia's HIV prevalence in blood donations has risen eightfold in two years.[30]

A year's supply of a cocktail of chemicals for keeping AIDS under control is sold in America for $10,000 but can be manufactured for $700. Why shouldn't poor Africans who might be able to afford $700, but certainly could not afford $10,000, be allowed to save their own lives? Clearly, they should.

Getting life-saving drugs to poor people who need them is a good illustration of the complex interactions produced by a global knowledge-based economy. Since World War II, pharmaceuticals have consistently been the most profitable industry in America. Their average rate of return on invested capital has been higher than that of any other industry. Sales have been growing at about 8 percent per year and are now over $400 billion per year. But their very old, very successful business model is in the process of being blown away by three hurricanes.

One of the hurricanes comes from Doha. Something has to be done about the cost of drugs for diseases like AIDS in poor countries. The alternative currently being discussed at the Doha trading round calls for letting poor countries simply override patents on drugs for major debilitative diseases. Poor countries would be allowed to make and buy drugs at marginal manufacturing costs.

Here there is a minor issue as well as a major issue. The minor issue is smuggling. With low prices in Africa and high prices in America there are enormous incentives to buy drugs cheaply in Africa and sell them for much more money back in the United States. The major issue is political. American families with AIDS don't want to spend $10,000 for the drugs they need when they know others are getting the same drugs for $700. Ten thousand dollars is a lot of money for most American families. Why shouldn't they also have cheap drugs? Many of the people needing the drugs in the first world are poor even though they live in wealthy countries. And middle-class voters in wealthy countries simply aren't going to put up with a two tier pricing system where foreigners get cheap drugs and they have to pay a lot. Perhaps they could afford to pay more, but none of them wants to pay more. Politically, they are going to demand that they be allowed to buy their drugs at the same prices available in the third world.

A second hurricane comes from the first world's elderly. Governments want to do something about soaring health care costs, and drugs are now the single biggest element in health care costs. As a result, there are now enormous pressures to regulate and hold down drug prices in the first world as well as in the third world.

The third hurricane is biotechnology. It is revolutionizing the search for and manufacture of drugs, but the payoffs have been agonizingly slow in coming and also expensive. Those drugs easily found seem to have already been found. The pipeline of new drugs does not have much in it, and of the top 100 drugs in the world, 53 are scheduled to come off patents in 2005. In 2000 only thirteen came off patents.[31] Revenues are going to plunge when these drugs come off patent. Budgets for research and development have skyrocketed in an attempt to find good replacements, but the launch of new chemical entities has fallen for reasons that remain unclear. And among that smaller number of new chemical entities found, fewer now pass their clinical trials than has been true in the past. Bottom line: among the big pharmaceutical companies few are discovering enough new drugs to cover their current costs of bringing new drugs to the market. Their old, very profitable, business model is disappearing.

If everyone gets the cheap drugs they want, the current system of paying for the development of new pharmaceuticals collapses. Innovative pharmaceutical companies have not yet cut back on investments in new drugs, but they soon will. Like music, their business model will have been blown up and they will have found no replacement. In the end, under capitalism someone has to pay enough to make investing in new drugs profitable or the new drugs for treating old diseases won't be invented. At the moment no one wants to be that someone who pays for new drugs, yet everyone wants to be the someone who gets those new wonder drugs cheap.

Huge differences between manufacturing costs and selling prices are not evidence of rapacious drug companies. They reflect the reality that most of the costs of producing pharmaceuticals are not incurred in manufacturing drugs. They are incurred in inventing the drug, in the costs of trying to invent drugs that never work, in passing the clinical trials necessary to prove that drugs are safe and effective without too many adverse side effects, and in the many drugs that fail to repay the costs of bringing them to market. On average, it takes $800 million and twelve years to bring a successful, profitable drug to market. Most drugs, some 99 percent, won't repay that $800 million.[32] A few blockbuster drugs that are very profitable are needed to cover all of these costs. If pharmaceutical companies are not allowed to cover their real costs through their blockbuster drugs, they simply won't invest in inventing new drugs.

The best example of this reality is malaria. No one invests in developing drugs to cure malaria, the world's third biggest killer after AIDS and diarrheal diseases, since everyone would lose money on any such investment. Because malaria is a disease of poor people in poor countries, there is no potential market. Drug companies also believe, rightly if one looks at AIDS, that if a cure for malaria were found, no one would be allowed to charge enough to cover their total costs. Consequently, no research is done on one of the world's most important diseases.

The same harsh economic reality applies to vaccines. Private drug companies don't invent new vaccines for preventing disease since there is "no money in them." No one can charge enough for that one vaccination to cover the costs of developing that vaccine and incurring the liabilities from possible side effects. Most vaccines, as seen in the current discussions of smallpox vaccinations, adversely affect a small percentage of the population to which they are administered. Those individuals adversely affected will sue. When a sick person suffers from adverse side effects, the lawyers can argue that the benefits exceeded the costs. But in this case a healthy person has been made sick by the vaccine. No lawyer can argue that the benefits to that person outweigh the costs to that person even if there are enormous social benefits. As a result, the small amount of work that does occur on vaccines is all in government-financed laboratories.

Malaria may also be a good analogy when it comes to the effects of trying to run a world without an agreed-upon and enforced system of intellectual property rights. Malaria has a huge negative impact on economic development. All of the world's countries with serious malaria problems are poor. The disease kills people very slowly and is so debilitating that long before individuals die, they don't have the physical energy to effectively take care of themselves. Since the victims linger on, family members must devote large amounts of time to taking care of them. They then have less time to do their own normal work. After malaria takes its toll on the victims and caregivers, there simply isn't enough energy, time, and money left to successfully pursue economic development. Although there is no medical cure for malaria, with the right social organization—draining swamps and controlling mosquitoes, for instance—malaria can be stamped out. That is what rich countries in warm climates have done. Malaria used to exist in the American south.

In constructing the Panama Canal, the French were defeated by malaria whereas the Americans succeeded because they first focused on controlling malaria and only then on constructing the canal. Success requires the right social organization focused on the right sequence of goals. It might also be pointed out that although AIDS has no medical cure, changes in social organization and behavior can bring AIDS epidemics to an end.

But success is not achieved by denying poor countries access to the drugs they need. The anthrax scare and the U.S. government's threat to seize patents to give Americans access to cheap drugs if they needed them should have persuaded Americans that both sides of the argument are right. What is needed is a system where the poor get the drugs they need but where their access to cheap drugs does not stop the invention of new drugs.

ACCESS TO IDEAS NECESSARY FOR ECONOMIC DEVELOPMENT

Although a global system of enforceable intellectual property rights is necessary to make a knowledge-based economy work, what different countries want, need, and should have in a system of intellectual property rights is very different depending on their level of economic development. Everyone copies to catch up. As today's developing countries argue, they are doing nothing that today's wealthy countries weren't doing when they were developing. The Americans blatantly copied the British textile mills in the 19th century. The Japanese blatantly copied the U.S. auto and consumer electronics industries in the 20th century. To prevent copying would be to prevent those now behind from ever catching up.[33]

At the moment everyone feels aggrieved. From the perspective of the developed world, intellectual pirates are stealing property that belongs to them; from the perspective of the developing world, those seeking to enforce intellectual property rights are trying to deprive them of the knowledge they need to develop or to be healthy. Building a robust global economy means building an enforceable system of intellectual property rights that meets the needs of everyone on the globe—those economically behind and those economically ahead, those selling drugs and those needing drugs. Developing countries need some rights to copy to catch up, yet developed countries need some protection to prevent copying to ensure adequate rates of return on investments in research and development for pushing knowledge forward. A global system will have to allow for a diversity of economic positions.

The world is not going to succeed in getting rich unless it deals with intellectual property rights. No one will be able to run a successful global knowledge-based economy over the long run unless intellectual property rights exist and are enforced. Unlike a run on the dollar, the absence of a system of global intellectual property rights will not blow up the system. It will instead just slowly debilitate the economic health of a global knowledge-based economy, making it much less than it could be. Advances of knowledge slow down as the incentives to invest in creating knowledge are undercut. And as a result, our future economic condition ends up being just a fraction of what it could have been. The creativity and energy that should be there, and could be there, won't be there.

It is true that humans are inherently creative animals, but it is also true that there are, and have been, lots of uncreative societies where nothing new is invented or created. Creativity does not blossom evenly around the world today. Historically, there have been long periods of time in human history when little new was invented. Creativity is not something that comes automatically. The conditions that create it have to be socially organized. Creative and inventive environments have to be socially organized, and the right set of intellectual property rights are a necessary part of that social organization.

{6}

LOOKING UP AT THE
TOP OF THE GLOBAL TOWER

Third world economic development is often portrayed as if the task is hopeless. No one knows how to do it. This ignores countries such as South Korea that have succeeded and countries like China that are succeeding. Everyone knows precisely what must be done economically. The mechanics of development are straightforward. The problem is execution. Execution requires social organization, and that is precisely what most third world countries lack.

Execution begins with an important mental mind-set. Economic development requires the mentality of a marathon runner and not that of a sprinter. The catching-up process is long. No one does it quickly. It took the United States a hundred years to catch up with the per capita income of Great Britain. Japan has been chasing the United States for more than a hundred years and still hasn't caught up on purchasing power parity measures of per capita GDP. Taiwan has had half a century of 7 to 8 percent growth rates, yet its per capita GDP is still less than two-thirds that of the United States.[1]

It takes a long time to catch up because the world's economic leader is not standing still. Almost by definition, the world's most successful country is rapidly moving forward. Leaders can easily be moving forward faster than those attempting to catch up. This happened in the 1990s when America was sprinting ahead and widened its lead over almost everyone.

Education is another reason why the catch-up process is slow. Countries cannot quickly move from illiterate workforces to well-educated workforces. Brazil will proudly tell you that 90 percent of its children are now in school, but the average level of education in the Brazilian workforce is 4.5 years and only slowly rising. Unless something dramatic is done about adult education, illiterate workers stay in the economy for forty to fifty years.

Many nations are looking for the quick fix. They want a twenty year, or at a most thirty year, catch-up plan. There are none. Brazil is a good example. Frustrated that they haven't caught up after less than a decade of moving toward freer markets with less government intervention, the Brazilians elected a new president in 2002 who promised a different, faster, as yet unspecified model of economic development that will involve more active government participation and less hardship. Brazil shifts so fast from strategy to strategy that nothing has time to work—and then its people wonder why the country is falling behind.

Among the economic leaders in the developed world, per capita incomes are rising at about 2 percent per year. A country with a 4 percent growth rate and a 1 percent rate of population growth has a 3 percent annual rise in per capita income and is only slowly catching up with the industrial world at the rate of 1 percent per year. The same country with a 3 percent rate of population growth is falling behind at the rate of 1 percent per year. To catch up, low rates of population growth are essential. It is simply impossible to catch up with high population growth rates.

If one looks at wealthy countries, one sees they have all had a century or more where population growth rates did not average much more than 1 percent per year. The reasons are simple. Before per capita incomes can go up, the new individuals added to any society have to be provided with those items necessary to generate the society's already existing per capita GDP. Newborn citizens must be fed, housed, and given medical attention until they enter the labor market and can support themselves. Entering the labor force on average at age 20, they need $8,000 per year in living expenses for twenty years if they are to have the average American childhood. To get an average job they must be given the average amount of education. American elementary and secondary education costs $7,200 per year, and higher education $14,700 per year. A little multiplication will tell you what must be invested in education if everyone is to have twelve years of education and 34 percent of the population is to have some college education. To create an American average job requires $122,700 in capital equipment. About two-thirds of the adult population works. Social infrastructure, such as roads and airports, requires another $21,000 per person. Adding it all up, total investments of a little less than $400,000 per person are needed to make each new American into an average adult American.[2]

Human populations can at their maximum grow at about 4 percent per year. No country has ever had a 4 percent population growth but some, like Mexico, have come close for a while. Suppose America's population were growing at 4 percent per year. This would mean 11.3 million new Americans every year and a required investment of $4.4 trillion per year. But the American GDP is only $11 trillion. Forty percent of the American GDP would have to be devoted to making these new Americans into average Americans. This would require a big reduction in the standards of living of existing Americans. They simply would not accept it. The necessary investments would not be made, and the average per capita American GDP would start to fall.

In poor countries the investment numbers in each category are different, but when one divides by the local GDP the percentages come out about the same—somewhere near 40 percent. As a result, with population growth rates much above 1 percent it is essentially impossible to catch up. This is one of the main reasons to be optimistic about China's economic prospects and pessimistic about India's economic prospects. One country has its population under control and the other does not.

Countries need both social capital and social capabilities to engage in economic development.

Working together, individuals have higher productivity than when they work alone. Social capital refers to the social networks individuals join to raise their standard of living. It is estimated, for example, that bilateral trade between ethnic Chinese countries is nearly 60 percent larger than it would be if both sides were not ethnic Chinese.[3] Trust, culture, social solidarity and language make a difference. At a more local level, rural irrigation systems raise output, but they require farmers willing to work together to build and maintain the irrigation canals and to share the available water supplies.

Social capabilities refer to the ability to get organized—to set up village schools, to separate drinking water from sewage water, to take preventive actions to stop AIDS from spreading, to establish the institutional frameworks (political, social, and legal ground rules) necessary for economic development.[4] This cannot be done by outsiders, no matter how well intentioned. No country can organize a school system for another country. This is a task each country must do for itself. Some countries are much better than others when it comes to this task. Egypt and Ecuador have the same per capita income, yet illiteracy is only 9 percent in Ecuador and 40 percent in Egypt.[5]

If the third world can organize its schools, the first world can help pay for those schools. Without the third world's internal ability to organize, however, first world money simply ends up in corrupt hands and Swiss bank accounts. First world outsiders can help with financial resources, but third world insiders have to do the hard lifting—the basic organizational work.

Not long ago my wife and I visited a number of Mung villages along the Mekong River with a local agricultural economist as a guide. All of the villages had about the same amount and quality of land to use in their coffee farming. The density of TV antennas seemed similar. But it is only a slight exaggeration to say that some villages looked like little Switzerlands, with drinking water and sewage separated, children cared for, and houses neat and tidy, whereas others were chaotic, with drinking water and sewage mixed, children uncared for, and houses a mess. The difference was local leadership and the villagers' willingness to work together. Some villages had social capital and social capabilities, whereas others did not.

Local countries have to provide for personal safety and be able to control crime. Capitalists engaged in the business of creating wealth need protection from criminals. If the protection is not there, capitalists won't be there. Crime destroys capitalism essentially by being an unpredictable erratic tax on economic success. Studies indicate that the effects of corruption are similar to tariffs, with a 10 percent increase in corruption leading to a 5 percent reduction in output.[6]

But the story is complex. Capitalism seems to tolerate some kinds of corruption easily yet be completely intolerant of other kinds of corruption. In a recent ranking of corruption China, currently the most successful country in the developing world, ranked fifty-ninth out of 102 countries. Above China with less corruption were many economic failures: Belarus at 36, Jordan at 41, Ghana at 50. The most honest poor country is Botswana, in the twenty-fourth position. In terms of honesty it is rated ahead of the far wealthier France or Italy.[7] Greece at number 44 ranks as the most corrupt among relatively wealthy countries. All of the least corrupt and most honest countries at the top of the list are wealthy, but what is the direction of causation? Does honesty cause wealth to grow, or can the wealthy simply afford to be honest?

Issues of personal safety, such as the kidnapping or murder of foreign executives, are even bigger deterrents to economic activity than are bribes. Both threaten lives and take a lot of executive time. Not too long ago, I ran into a Japanese friend who manages a large auto parts manufacturing firm's activities in North and South America. He told me that he had just spent the previous two months, the worst two months of his life, negotiating with Columbian kidnappers who held two of his executives. What do you think my Japanese friend is going to do when he gets his executives back? The answer is simple: pull out of Columbia. Business people have better things to do with their lives and their time.

All of the indicators of personal safety show big differences among Africa, Latin America, and Asia, with Asia being much safer than the other two. Assaults and robberies are five times as likely in Sub-Saharan Africa as in Asia. In Latin America most kidnapping involves citizens, but in Africa the majority of those kidnapped are foreigners (80 percent in Nigeria).[8]

Corruption is something outsiders find much harder to deal with than do locals. Corrupt systems are by definition not transparent. No one publishes the rules. Locals know the local rules of corruption (whom to bribe, how much to pay, when to say no, who can really deliver what they promise), outsiders do not. When periodic political crackdowns on corruption do occur, it is also true that outsiders are much more apt to be arrested than insiders.

If one looks at countries with a lot of corruption, government officials, including the police, are usually paid very low wages by the standards of their own countries. Being paid very low wages, they have to find ways to supplement their family incomes. Demanding bribes is the easiest way to get more income; being paid very little, they have little to lose if caught and fired. The Cambodian police officer takes you to the temple you want to see, though it is not open to the public, if he gets the right sum for "protection." If government officials are paid high wages, as they are in Singapore, they have much to lose and don't need bribes to feed their families.

But it is also true that corruption is an area where history plays a big role. Once endemic, corruption is very hard to stamp out. Few throw their trash on the streets when the streets are clean, whereas almost everyone will throw their trash on the streets that are already dirty. So too with corruption. Few want to be the first to test whether the system will tolerate corruption, but many are willing to participate in corruption when it is clear that the system is corrupt.

Some global industries have learned to live with murder and terror. The oil industry operated right through the Nigerian civil war. Today it operates in the chaos of central Asia. Other extractive industries are operating and investing in the midst of Africa's current civil wars and chaos. If the investors in extractive industries don't get the official protection they need, they know how to hire private armies. They are tough enough to kill a few people to prove they should be left alone.

Normally these arrangements are kept very quiet but occasionally they pop into public view. According to a recent press report a very profitable mining company supplemented the salaries paid to the regular army in its neighborhood in Indonesia to get protection. Soldiers were said to have high expectations when assigned to the mining company's area and to have been very disappointed when the mining company reduced their pay and perks.[9] In retaliation for this reduction in pay, two American schoolteachers were killed and eight wounded in army attacks designed to convince the company to restore their previous pay scales. But most global investors have neither the profits nor the stomach to take on such activities.

All of these factors are magnified in the case of systematic terrorism. Investors are going to avoid or withdraw from places where their employees feel physically threatened. Murdered missionaries in Yemen mean that no global firm is going to invest in Yemen. A disco blown up in Bali means that no global firm other than those involved in natural resource extraction is going to invest in Indonesia. Killing a journalist and blowing up Christian churches in Pakistan forecloses investment in Pakistan. If the Muslim world is seen as dangerous, all of the Muslim world, except that part that produces oil, will be left out of globalization. There are a lot of other places to go where terrorism does not exist.

There is a clear economic bottom line on corruption and personal safety even if the exact location of that line is murky. Beyond some point corruption and issues of physical safety become so large that capitalism cannot and will not tolerate them. Capitalism needs governments to stamp out corruption. Firms cannot do it by themselves since their incentives lie on the side of paying bribes. In the short run paying bribes is less costly and less time consuming than banding together to force governments to stamp out corruption. But most firms also cannot live with corruption. As a result, their only option is to move to other, less corrupt locations. And that is exactly what they do—leaving corrupt countries outside of the global economy.

Corruption has to be controlled locally. First world laws prohibiting first world companies from paying bribes or ransom in the third world don't work. Those laws cannot be enforced, and where there is an effort to enforce them, firms simply decide that avoiding or leaving corrupt countries is easier than reforming corrupt countries. Business firms are not in the business of making countries honest. It is expensive and time consuming.

Social capital and social organization are not synonyms for great political leaders. America is the best example. Most Americans can remember none of the names of the presidents from Lincoln to Theodore Roosevelt in the second half of the 19th century. The presidents cannot be remembered because they did not do anything worth remembering. Yet the United States caught up with Great Britain economically during this period. The names that Americans do remember from the late 19th century are those of the great industrialists—Edison, Rockefeller, Eastman, Carnegie, Vanderbilt, and Morgan—who actually led the American economic advance. They were more important than the presidents—not just for their successful businesses but for their pioneering activities when it came to using their fortunes after they had made them. The idea of charitable foundations came from these men. Carnegie put libraries in every town. Rockefeller and Eastman built universities. They were leaders both when it came to making money and when it came to giving it away and making their societies better places in which to live and work.

Presidents Truman and Roosevelt will be remembered in the history books for their activities in the Great Depression and World War II, but a hundred years from now the 20th century is apt to be like the 19th century. Few presidents will be remembered. The names that will dot the history books about the 20th century will be those of Ford, Sloan (GM), Watson (IBM), Hewlett and Packard, and Bill Gates, and not the presidents. Leaders are essential, but it is not necessary that they be political leaders.

Once the social foundations are in place, all economic growth depends upon improvements in technology. Successful countries go through three stages in acquiring technology. In stage 1 they mobilize human and capital resources to fully exploit existing technologies. In stage 2 they copy existing technologies from more advanced countries to catch up. And in stage 3 they build new industries based upon the advances in knowledge that flow from their own research and development.

Since Japan is the only non-oil country that has gone from poor to rich in the last century, it is worth examining its economic development.[10] After the Meiji restoration, Japan began by mobilizing its capital resources to produce a high savings society. It was fortunate to start its economic development with a population as well educated as that of the world's economic leader, Great Britain. It did not need to build a school system.[11] It had one. Its population growth rate was low.

All of the successful economies of East Asia in the last half century have followed the Japanese pattern. Starting with large labor forces, they organized themselves to produce very high savings rates so they could afford massive investments in new capital equipment. China, with its internal savings rate of 30 percent, is only the most recent example of a country on this path.[12]

With a reverse twist, the same pattern is visible if one goes back to the United States in the last half of the 19th century. Having a shortage of labor, America mobilized labor rather than capital. Foreign workers were actively recruited as immigrants from Europe and China. Millions of farmers moved from farms where they worked relatively few hours per year to factories where they were working almost 3,000 hours per year.[13]

Education is the second part of resource mobilization. Those who study how the United States caught up with Great Britain's per capita GDP in the early 20th century trace much of the catch-up to a better-educated workforce.[14] People talk about a digital divide between rich and poor, but the real divide is an educational divide. Any country that can afford an army, and all do, can afford to provide the hardware part of the digital divide. It is just a matter of priorities. The educational divide is more serious. Technology cannot be absorbed without an educated workforce and, as a result, all societies that wish to develop must organize to educate their labor forces.

For a country to really upgrade educational skills, women must be educated and their talents fully utilized. Americans would not have an American standard of living if only men worked outside of the home. But it is skills and not numbers that are important. Americans would not have an American standard of living if its women weren't educated.

A branch of the Muslim religion in northern Pakistan, the Aswali Muslims, associated with the Aga Khan, believes in educating girls. They place a simple slogan on many of their schools: "Educate a man, educate a man; educate a woman, educate a family." Men with illiterate mothers are not going to be well-educated men. The same can be said for fully using the talents of minorities. India's caste system retards development. The issue is not theoretically legal rights but actual practices. Whatever its laws, as long as India has its caste system (and one in six Indians are in practice treated as untouchables), India will not be rich.

The third part of resource mobilization is building the infrastructure that lets a country's existing productive resources more fruitfully interact with each other. America's investments in transcontinental railroads were central in creating the American economy in the 19th century. Electrification played a big role in the early part of the 20th century. Interstate highways and airports were important in the second half of the 20th century. Communication systems in the 21st century are what the railroads were in the 19th century. Labor, capital, and natural resources were made more productive by tying them together more efficiently.

After mobilization the next step is motivation. Communist countries were good at mobilizing large numbers of workers (by law all women worked in the USSR, and those of us old enough can still remember picture of millions of Chinese being mobilized to build dams, one handful of dirt at a time), but not much was produced because the individuals saw no payoff for themselves in working hard. That is why the USSR imploded and Communist China decided to move toward free markets. Countries have to build individual incentive systems that work.

It is at this point that capitalism becomes a necessity. Socialism simply does not provide the necessary structure of individual incentives. One has only to look at Israeli kibbutzim: they have capital, skills, and infrastructure in abundance, but they cannot maintain motivation from one generation to the next. As a result, they have failed economically and are gradually fading out of the Israeli economy. In the short run, individuals will sacrifice their own self-interests to help their neighbors, but no one has been able to organize a society where individuals will do so in the long run. In the long run, humans work, invest, and sacrifice to help themselves.

After mobilizing capital, educating the workforce and tying it together with the necessary infrastructure in a system with strong individual incentives, countries can move on to stage 2, where they start to acquire new technologies. Everyone begins by copying technologies from those who already have them. Great Britain, as the initial industrial leader, is the only exception. Americans were famous for being copiers in the 19th century, just as the Japanese were famous for being copiers both before and after World War II.

Whom one copies depends upon your model of technological

development. Until the Japanese provided an alternative model, what was called the "product cycle" was seen as the standard way technology moved around the world.[15] Over time high-tech industries become low-tech industries as any particular technology slowly moved from the most-advanced countries to the least-advanced countries.

Textiles were the prototypical example. Starting as a high-tech industry in Great Britain in the early 19th century, they moved on to become the economic starting point for Britain's closest followers, Germany and the United States, later in the century. Eventually, almost two centuries later, textiles have become the place where every poor country starts its industrial and technological development.

In the product cycle model of economic development, countries copy the countries immediately ahead of them—one stage farther along in their economic development. The newly acquired technologies are then used in an import substitution model of economic development. Products previously imported because they required technologies a country did not have are replaced with products produced locally.

The Japanese demonstrated that it was possible to develop a leapfrogging model. Instead of following historical patterns and looking at the countries just slightly wealthier than they were, the Japanese looked at where the economic leaders were and where these leaders were going. Japan then charted a technology path for intersecting with the leader's technological path without following it. In this model economic followers quickly become technological competitors with the economic leaders.[16]

To succeed in this strategy, countries need technological policies to speed up the copying process. In the 19th century, official Japanese delegations were sent around the world to study what were believed to be the leading models of social organization and technological development. These models were then brought back to Japan to be adopted and then adapted to Japanese conditions.[17]

After World War II a wide variety of specific policies were put in place to accelerate the copying process.[18] A productivity center was established in Washington to translate scientific and engineering articles into Japanese and to send them to the Japanese companies that might benefit from their content. Students already working for private companies were sent to leading American universities to master American technologies that were relevant to their employers. In the aftermath of a 1957 antitrust decree that ordered the Bell Labs of AT&T to freely share their technologies, a Japanese office was set up in New Jersey to monitor and transfer the Bell Labs technologies back to Japan. Camera-equipped Japanese on factory tours of American plants were so common that they became a subject for jokes by late-night TV comedians. When technologies had to be purchased, the Japanese government acted as a monopsonistic buyer using its bargaining power to buy cheaply and then broadly share the purchased technologies across the entire Japanese economy.

Japan understood that historically there is no tight connection between scientific leadership and economic leadership. The per capita GDP of the United States exceeded that of Germany in the first half of the 20th century, although Germany was the scientific leader of the time. The technological gap between Germany and the United States wasn't small. It was huge. At the last global physics conference held before World War II (the Solvay conference in 1936), only one individual from America was invited.[19] Scientifically, America was far behind. If one looks at Europe today, the rank order of spending for research and development is not closely correlated with the rank order of per capita incomes.[20] In purchasing power parity terms, Luxembourg has Europe's highest per capita GDP but is in no sense a scientific leader.

The central issue is acquiring engineering knowledge. Basic science can be learned from textbooks. Engineering knowledge is difficult to acquire because much of it is acquired from informal on-the-job experience rather than from what one formally learns in a school of engineering. One cannot competitively design and manufacture semiconductor chips based upon what one learns with a degree in electrical engineering.

Japan's development strategy did not stop with just copying engineering know-how. It invested heavily in improving engineering knowledge. It spent about the same fraction of its GDP on research and development as did the United States, even though it was much poorer. But the spending patterns were very different. Two-thirds of Japan's R&D money was spent on improving products and processes, whereas the United States spent two-thirds of its money on developing new products. The Japanese strategy was to copy a technology from the rest of the world, learn to make those copied technologies work 10 percent better or 10 percent cheaper, and then use that margin of superiority to outcompete those who had first developed the technologies. Robots and copiers are good examples. The Japanese invented neither, but in just a few years they had become leaders in both.[21]

The recently acquired and improved technologies were then used to support an export-led model of economic development. Japanese companies that successfully exported products made with their new technologies were rewarded with protected local markets where high profits could be made to offset the losses necessary to penetrate foreign markets.

Because of the economic reversals of World War II, Japan's per capita income had fallen to less than 10 percent of that of the United States in 1950. By 1989 Japan had a per capita income above that of the United States in currency terms ($36,966 versus $25,980) and below that of the United States in purchasing power parity terms ($18,880 versus $23,223).[22] Inside and outside of Japan, the Japanese were widely seen as a technological equal to the United States at the beginning of the 1990s.

South Korea is the best example of a developing country that has explicitly followed the Japanese model to catch up. The model requires a high degree of social organization if it is to be successfully implemented. An educated workforce and high levels of spending on process technologies are both necessities if copied products are to be successfully exported. The products being copied have to be more cheaply made or have better performance characteristics than the originals. Not surprisingly, South Korea is the only country in the developing world whose R&D spending equals that of the world's biggest spenders as a fraction of GDP and exceeds that of many of the much richer industrial countries.[23] Global brand names have to be established. Establishing brand names is both difficult and expensive. South Korea makes the necessary investments.

Japan was lucky in that for a few decades after World War II copying was particularly easy. The U.S. government actively encouraged copying to create prosperous Cold War military allies. America even helped pay for foreign students to study at its leading technological universities. From the U.S. Cold War perspective, Japan needed American help so it could be a prosperous unsinkable aircraft carrier off the east coast of the Soviet Union. In the aftermath of the Korean War, South Korea was similarly seen as a country to be helped.

American business firms did not closely guard technology, since technology was not seen as central to economic success. Economic success flowed from the control of natural resources or from economies of scale. Those with well-situated iron and coal deposits dominated steel production. Those with economies of scale dominated auto production. Controlling the dissemination of technology was not central to maintaining a country's or a company's competitive advantage.

American arrogance also contributed to the ease of copying. America's technological lead after World War II was so big that American companies saw themselves moving on to the next generation of technologies before those in the rest of the world had mastered America's last generation of technologies. As a result, they did not worry about those who were trying to copy their current technologies.

Perhaps it is an exaggeration to say that the Japanese route of direct copying-to-catch-up is no longer open, but it is certainly a much harder route to follow than it used to be. Japanese and European success in the 1970s and 1980s erased American arrogance. Technology is much more guarded, since controlling the dissemination of technology is now seen as central to future success.

If one looks at more recent economic success stories—Singapore, Taiwan, Ireland, Malaysia, China, and Thailand—the copying-to-catch-up comes via a very different indirect route. Countries seek to attract global companies wishing to establish foreign production facilities to reduce their costs. In these offshore production facilities, global companies will employ their latest, or close to their latest, technologies. Local workers are taught the necessary production skills and, over slightly longer periods of time, local managers are trained to replace expatriate managers. Copying is the end result, but one is "taught" the latest technologies more than one "copies" the latest technologies.

Realistically, economic development today depends upon a country's ability to attract foreign direct investment (FDI). Such investment is not important because it brings money. Any country can easily borrow money. Global companies possess markets, technology, and scarce management or engineering skills that developing countries must have if they are to participate in the global economy. Without FDI, markets are difficult to penetrate, new technologies are hard to acquire, and missing engineering or management skills are impossible to find. By themselves, developing countries cannot produce at the quality levels demanded in high value-added industries and cannot market what they produce even in low value-added industries such as textiles or shoes.

There is a close link between being able to attract FDI and being economically successful.[24] It is no accident that China is the world's largest recipient of FDI in the third world and the world's most successful developing economy. It is likewise no accident that the United States is by far the largest recipient of FDI and the world's most successful developed country. Without FDI the

United States would have been a lot less successful than it is. In the twelve years from 1990 to 2002, the United States received $1.27 trillion in direct foreign investment—more than Japan, Germany, France, and the United Kingdom combined.[25] German and Japanese auto plants have been central in maintaining the U.S. position in the auto industry. Some auto makers, like Honda, have almost become American companies. At every level of economic development there are new things to be learned, and the easiest way to learn them is to have an experienced teacher.

If one looks at FDI as a fraction of the country's gross capital formation, the importance of FDI is clearly visible. In Ireland, the most successful country in Europe in the 1990s, FDI accounted for 88 percent of capital formation. Despite its huge size, FDI contributed 11 percent of total investment in China—as it does in Mexico. In contrast, FDI accounts for only 2 percent of gross capital formation in India.[26] Very little of the world's foreign direct investment goes to the world's poorest countries because they do not have the characteristics business firms need.[27] Africa gets almost none. When the required characteristics vanish, as they did in Indonesia, global corporations quickly move on to better locations. In Indonesia an inflow of more than $2 billion per year in foreign direct investment in the first half of the 1990s had become an outflow of almost $4 billion per year in 2000 and 2001.[28]

Attracting foreign direct investment has the advantage that it requires much less social organization than the direct copying approach. Local companies do not have to start by gaining the ability to compete against the world's top producers. Countries do not have to find ways to acquire technologies from foreign owners who do not want to share those technologies. Instead, countries have to set out to make themselves into what the world's global corporations see as desirable production bases.

When making their investment decisions, global corporations are looking for low cost production bases, but "low cost" is not a synonym for the world's lowest wages. They want relatively low-waged but well-educated workers, engineers, and managers. Singapore spends more than anyone else in the world on education. Ireland offers a good education system and a plentiful supply of relatively cheap engineers. Taxes and market access play a role. Ireland offers a very low corporate tax rate and access to the European common market. Mexico offers access to the U.S. market. Companies considering investments want infrastructure, such as dependable electrical power and reliable transportation. Singapore claims to have the world's best infrastructure. They want social order, including safety from criminal behavior and the control of corruption. Taiwan gives it to them.

It takes time and money to set up a subsidiary in a new country. Among developing countries, there typically is a 20 to 1 difference between the countries that take the most time and the least time for basic activities such as land acquisition and other entry requirements.[29] Time is money. Monetary costs rise and production opportunities are lost if it takes a long time to get organized in a new country.[30] How easily outsiders can deal with local bureaucracies explains many of the differences in foreign direct investment.

If the right conditions are in place, global corporations will transfer the specific production technologies and market linkages necessary to participate in the global economy to their local subsidiaries or to their local subcontractors. These subcontractors are usually local workers and managers who have previously worked for and been trained by global corporations and then encouraged by the same global corporations to set up their own companies to do contract manufacturing for the original equipment manufacturers (OEMs). The OEMs directly transfer to local companies the technologies necessary to make the components they wish to purchase from the local companies. Over time the components produced by the local companies become larger and larger portions of the total product being sold to the foreign company. Local companies move up the supply chain to become what are called tier one suppliers. As can be seen in the case of Taiwan, eventually these local companies are producing the entire product (laptops, scanners, etc.), and only the brand names of the OEMs remains.

Ultimately, local third world firms need to acquire direct foreign market access and their own brand names. In many ways market access seems to be harder to obtain than technology. In principle one of the new technologies, electronic retailing, should make it easier to acquire foreign markets. Potential exporters do not need to build up a brick-and-mortar infrastructure of retail stores. Before the Japanese downturn stalled the process, it looked like L.L.Bean would make catalogue and electronic retailing models work in Japan, but as yet no one has succeeded in using electronic retailing as a method for penetrating foreign markets. The real problem is not local distribution but brand name. Stores like Wal-Mart make it easy to distribute foreign products, but they do so under their own brand name in arrangements where Wal-Mart essentially gets all of the profits.

Within the developing world it is skilled workers who have the most to gain from globalization. As foreign investments flow into a country, average wages rise but skilled wages rise more than those of the unskilled. In both China and India the incomes of relatively skilled urbanites are rising rapidly vis-à-vis the stagnant incomes of their unskilled rural hinterlands.[31] The net effect is higher but more unequal wages.

As they search for the cheapest places to make their products, firms move technology around the world. But technology can flow only to developing countries that have the human resources to absorb them. This is why China gets a lot of FDI and Africa gets almost none. The result is a harsh reality. Those who need technology the most get it the least.

This problem is only going to get worse. Of the 6 billion people on the planet, 1 billion are illiterate using the most basic definition (you can read and write your own name), 2 billion are illiterate on a slightly tougher definition (you can read and write a sentence about your own daily life), and probably more than half of the world is functionally illiterate (you can operate at a fourth grade level of performance).[32] Half of Sub-Saharan Africans and 60 percent of the Indian subcontinent are illiterate on the second definition. Yet fifty years from now there will be little demand for illiterate workers in either the first or the third world. Robots to mow our lawns already exist, and robots to clean our houses will soon exist. As long as most of the workers in the world are unskilled, global inequality is going to rise.

In principle the shift from industrial economies to knowledge-based economies should make the catch-up process easier. There are places where the new technologies should be able to speed up the development process enormously. Normally, creating an educated workforce is a slow process since teachers are not available in the large numbers required for K–12 education and most of the existing workforce is too old for conventional education. If a workable system of electronic education could be developed to reduce the number of classroom teachers required in K–12 education and to reach the adult workforce, the upgrading of educational skills could occur at a much faster rate than has ever been possible in the past.

Industrial economies to a great degree depended upon having a lot of natural resources relative to population densities. It is not surprising that Asia lagged behind when this was the only reality. Economies poor in natural resources cannot become rich in natural resources, but economies poor in human resources (education and skills) can become rich in human resources. There are many examples of countries—Taiwan, Korea, and Singapore—doing just this. It is possible to leapfrog technologies and make it into the developed world. China, with one-quarter of all the people in the developing world, seems to be in the middle of such a leap.

If one looks at the statistics on national per capita incomes, an interesting pattern jumps out from the data. Some countries succeed, others fail, and a very few remain in between. The world's richest countries have per capita GDPs approaching $40,000, and there are twenty-eight countries with 847 million people where per capita GDPs are between $15,000 and $40,000.* At the same time there are 169 countries with 5 billion people where per capita incomes are below $7,500. In between there are only eleven countries with 130 million people whose per capita incomes is between $7,500 and $15,000.[33]

Any normal distribution has many more countries in the middle than in either the upper or the lower tails. The sparsely populated middle-income group of countries is not hard to explain. If the basics of development are present, it is not difficult to stay in the first world. If the basics are present, countries catch up. Japan, Taiwan, South Korea, Singapore, Hong Kong, Ireland, and Finland have done it. China, Malaysia, and Thailand are doing it. If a country does not have the basics, it stays in the bottom group. Many don't have the basics, and that is why the bottom group is so large. The few countries in the middle-income category all have the basics and are in the process of moving into the developed world. Being successful, they will soon leave this middle income classification. No country stays a middle income country very long. That is why the group is small.

In the end the world knows what to do when it comes to economic development. The doing is hard, but the "what to do" is both straightforward and well known.

BOOMING CHINA

Since China is the current great success story among developing countries, it is worth looking at the sources of its success. What should other developing countries and those interested in promoting economic development learn from its success? Unfortunately, China is more feared than emulated because it has the size to be everyone's major competitor in the third world. Talk to business

*Just to reference these numbers, the World Bank thinks that a GDP of $5,000 per capita is necessary for a country to provide its citizens with the basics—food, shelter, education, health care. Above this level countries are buying luxuries, not necessities.

leaders or government officials in any developing country and the conversation quickly turns to worries about Chinese competition and stories about local industries that are moving to China. China is the "great sucking" sound. Scare headlines abound: "Asian Tigers Fear Last Supper Thanks to Ravenous China"[34] and "Seoul Feels the March of Chinese Capitalism."[35]

China does look formidable as a competitor. It is attracting most of the foreign direct investment that is going to the developing world. In 2003 it may attract more FDI than the United States. Because of its huge size China's supply of low wage labor won't quickly disappear, even if China grows very rapidly. Its supply of educated labor is large enough that with the injection of the technology, management, and markets that come with foreign direct investment, it can quickly make products now made in the developed world. As China's growth speeds up, those who fear China see the rest of the developing world's growth slowing down.

The fears and competitive threats are grossly exaggerated. The Chinese story must begin with both an injection of reality and the understanding that China's economic success does not threaten the rest of the world. But when a country the size of China (20 percent of humanity) that had cut itself off from most of the rest of the world for thirty years suddenly decides to rejoin the global system, it does change the game—as we shall see later.

Some analysts see a military threat flowing from China's economic success. China is already an important military power, perhaps number two in the world behind the United States and certainly number three behind the United States and Russia.[36] China will be a great power politically and militarily in the 21st century. No one should doubt it. It is the dominant regional military power now if one leaves out the United States. Absolute size determines military power, and China is very large. But the growth of this threat is only very loosely connected to economic development. The problem is not China's capabilities but its military intentions vis-à-vis its neighbors.

Economic power is a very different matter. It depends upon per capita GDP—not absolute GDP. Leading edge products are sold to leading edge consumers, and leading edge consumers have to be high income consumers. In 2000 China's per capita GDP was $847 using exchange rates to convert yuan to dollars. America's was $36,868. Economic change starts in America precisely because America has those high income consumers. China may become an important economic power in the future, but that future is distant.

To demonstrate this latter point to yourself, take out your hand calculator and key in both China's per capita GDP and America's per capita GDP. Then key in the speed at which you expect the United States to grow over the next century (in the last century per capita GDP grew at 2.1%) and the growth rate you expect from China over the next century. Remember that no country has ever averaged more than 3 percent per year per capita over a full century. Then calculate what China's per capita GDP will be in the year 2100 relative to that of the United States.

Unless you key in something quite unlikely for China's growth rate over the next century, you will find that in 2100 China will still have a per capita GDP far below that of the United States. Since China has more than four times as many people as the United States, its absolute GDP will probably be above that of the United States in 2100, but that fact is irrelevant. Per capita GDP is the name of the game. There may be a Chinese economic century, but if there is, it will be the 22nd and not the 21st century.

These calculations take nothing away from China's current or future economic success. They are simply to say that economic success goes to the marathon runners, not to the sprinters, and that China has yet to prove that it is a marathon runner and not a sprinter. And even if it is a marathon runner, it has a marathon that it must run—and win.

It is also important to understand the strengths and weaknesses of China's current position. China's past growth rates are not as good as they look, current growth rates are not as high as announced, and future growth rates will not be as good as those in the past.

THE PAST

The Chinese economic miracle is found not in the booming cities everyone visits but in its countryside. In 1978 China began its reforms by abolishing the communes and giving every peasant family a piece of land. Technically, the peasants were given fifteen-year leases for annual crops and fifty-year leases for tree crops with the right to transfer (sell) land leases under the "family responsibility" system. But in reality every peasant knows that the land is permanently theirs and that the state isn't going to get it back. Abolishing the communes improved the incentive structure and led to a big jump in agricultural output with no investments in irrigation, fertilizer, machinery, pesticides, or transportation. In just six years, from 1978 to 1984, China's agricultural output rose by two-thirds.

The service of a porter carrying someone else's bags at the airport was not a legitimate activity in the eyes of communism. Services were part of the old feudal and capitalist systems of exploitation. The linguistic roots of "services" after all are found in the Latin words for slaves and slavery. As a result, services weren't valued under communism, weren't counted as output in Communistic statistics, and were grossly underprovided. Count what was always there, let the private sector provide the services communism would not let them provide, and there will be a one-time boom in service production with almost no required investment.

Communism made massive investments that did not pay off because of poor incentive systems. A hotel building that long existed can, if given good management and good service, easily become a real productive hotel. Correct communism's industrial inefficiencies with better incentive systems, and the investments of the past can often be made to pay big returns with very little new investment. The effect is a little like repairing the bridges across the Rhine River after the World War II. A single bridge repair allows a lot of previously existing investment to go back into production. But this is a one-time, unrepeatable, leap in output. Eventually the amount of investment necessary to support any particular growth rate soars.

Count what was happening in services, add to it what was happening in agriculture, improve incentives in existing industries, and China's reported double-digit growth rates in the 1980s become eminently believable—but not repeatable.

THE PRESENT

But in China's economic statistics they were repeated. Published annual growth rates of 9.7 percent grossly exaggerate Chinese success in the decade of the 1990s. A detailed investigation of Chinese statistics and correlations with variables that are closely related to GDP growth, like electricity consumption, point to a growth rate of 4 to 5 percent.[37] This is a great result for a big country, but it also has the advantage of being a believable result.

If China can sustain something close to a 5 percent growth rate combined with a 1 percent growth in population for a century, it will come to hold the record for the highest long-term growth rate in per capita income in human history—4 percent. Japan, the previous record holder, managed to grow its per capita income at only 3 percent over the course of its first century of industrial development.

The exaggerated numbers for the 1990s do not mean that anyone in Beijing is deliberately inflating the data. Local officials in China get bonuses and promotions depending upon the growth rate of their regions. Those same local officials are in charge of calculating and reporting local economic statistics. Local officials write down the numbers they think their bosses in the central government want to hear. Who wants to be the first to send in nega-

tive data? You'd have to be a saint not to exaggerate your own success, and local Chinese officials are not saints.

Periodically, Beijing punishes some local official for exaggerat-
ing his area's economic performance just to keep the whole system
quasi-honest. In 2001 there were 60,000 admitted violations of
reporting procedures, and the head of central statistics admitted that
every province but one reported growth rates of more than 8.5
percent in 2001 and that he marked the average down to 7.3 percent—but on what basis was not reported.[38]

Parts of the Chinese economy are clearly booming and other
parts are just as clearly stagnating.

No one denies that its export production economy is booming
or that China's large coastal cities are doing very well. Exports
from China to the United States have grown at 82 percent over
the course of the last five years, and one can visibly see the boom in
the coastal cities.[39] What is less visible is what is happening in the
countryside, where most Chinese still live. With 73 percent of
Chinese employment in agriculture and 80 percent living in the
countryside, it is difficult to have a rapid national rate of growth
unless agriculture is advancing rapidly. Yet in the last decade, by the
admission of Beijing, agricultural output has stagnated. With
incomes not growing for 80 percent of the population, mathematically a national growth rate of 10 percent requires the incomes of
the remaining 20 percent to grow at 50 percent per year. It is not
possible.

THE FUTURE

Even a 5 percent growth rate will be difficult to match in the years
ahead. China has some big economic problems looming ahead.

Communism invested in a lot of projects that are simply making things that people don't want at costs that would dictate losses
in a capitalistic society. Many of these factories are losing massive
amounts of money and can survive only with public subsidies.

These plants have no long-term future. State industries own 63 percent of China's industrial assets, produce 70 percent of industrial sales, employ 40 percent of the urban workforce, and most important, pay 74 percent of its taxes.[40] At least one-third of these state industries will eventually have to be shut down. When these big state-owned enterprises (SOEs) are shut down, they will become a subtraction from the statistics of economic growth.

The potential shutdowns are not limited to the firms that now officially lose money. Under communism many things (transportation, raw materials, energy) were free or heavily subsidized by the state. When China completes its movement to the market, many of the inputs industries buy will rise dramatically in price and what now look like profitable firms will quickly become unprofitable ones that must be shut down.

The nonviable state-owned firms continue to exist courtesy of subsidies that come via the banking system. Banks are forced to make huge loans to money-losing large state industries to stop urban unemployment from soaring. On the day they are made, the loans are known to be bad loans that will not be repaid. As a result, China's banking problems with the SOEs are sometimes described as a big Enron waiting to happen. The banking system will implode because of bad loans that aren't repaid. Depositors will lose their money.

It won't happen. The depositors can easily be repaid. The government simply provides the banks with the cash to repay the depositors. Since the government prints money, there is no shortage of cash. Since the local banks in China are all government banks, there are no private shareholders to be wiped out. The real problem is finding alternative work for the hundreds of millions of urban people employed in the SOEs. Twenty-seven million people were laid off from these firms between 1998 and 2002, but tens of millions more will need to be laid off.[41] The problems with SOEs are economic and social, not financial.

For those firms that can be made viable, the necessary restructuring costs will be huge. The investment funds to maintain current levels of output for these viable SOEs will have to come from somewhere else, and growth will slow down in the areas where investments are reduced.

Initially, growth could be allowed to occur along the coast, where little infrastructure was needed, especially along that part of the coast that could use the infrastructure of Hong Kong. But China is a big continental country where large investments in infrastructure will have to be made if incomes are not to stagnate in the interior of the country. Because of its history, China has less infrastructure (communications, transportation, and electrification) than have even smaller, poorer countries such as India. China is three times as large as India yet has 20 percent fewer miles of railways. In India the British army built railroads in the 19th century so that it could efficiently garrison the country. China had the disadvantage of being a quasi-colony, where none of the colonizing countries—among them Britain, France, Russia, Germany, and Japan—took responsibility for building its national infrastructure.

In addition, because of Chairman Mao's experience in fighting the Japanese during World War II, he believed in regional self-sufficiency and did not build the transportation infrastructure that was built in other Communist countries such as the Soviet Union. China's regions were to be self-sufficient, so that no country could conquer China militarily. Using resources from these self-sufficient regions, the Chinese army would simply retreat until the invader did not have enough soldiers to occupy the country.

Infrastructure problems are made worse by what can be described only as regional economic warlords. Regional officials attempt to monopolize economic growth for their areas by being unwilling to spend their money on cooperative regional infrastructure projects that would in the long run lower the costs for everyone. Although China needs more ports and airports, it already has ports and airports that are grossly underutilized because they were built in the wrong places. The four new airports in southern China near Hong Kong are the best example of this. Building just one airport with high-speed rail connections to the major towns in the area would have been cheaper and would have provided an area-wide transportation grid. But it did not happen. What is going to emerge is a lot of debt and a lot of unused capacity located at the wrong places. China cannot afford to spend money on duplicative facilities or poorly located facilities.

China is also wasting a lot of money by not using the money flowing from its foreign trade surpluses for something more important than foreign exchange reserves. In the last decade China has consistently run big trade surpluses and had accumulated $331 billion in foreign exchange reserves in early 2003 (Hong Kong has an additional $114 billion).[42] China is too poor to run such trade surpluses. It does not need anything like that sum of money squirreled away to run its international economic affairs. Fifty billion dollars in reserves would be more than enough to support China's international trade. When China runs a big trade surplus, poor Chinese are essentially making loans to rich Americans. It does not make economic sense.[43]

Instead of being accumulated in foreign exchange reserves, the money should have been invested in projects that would have employed millions of people doing useful things. Fifteen million people are unemployed in urban areas of China, and no one knows how many people are unemployed or underemployed in rural areas.[44] Some estimates place the number in excess of 100 million people.

Large investments need to be made in both infrastructure and plants and equipment to close the large income gaps now emerging right across China. Within the eastern cities, incomes are growing four times as fast at the top as at the bottom.[45] At the start of its market reforms, China had a 4 to 1 gap between the top and bottom quintiles of its population. That gap is now 13 to 1.[46] Much of it is a rural-urban gap. Rural incomes are stagnant, falling from a peak of 58 percent to 38 percent of urban incomes. There is a 14 to 1 gap between China's richest province and its poorest province.

Funds are needed to roll the boom out of the eastern cities into the countryside, where 80 percent of the people live. Massive investments in fertilizers, pesticides, machinery, transportation, communications, and electrification will have to be made to raise rural productivity and incomes if the Chinese who live in rural areas are not to move to urban areas (as many as 50 million may already have moved). Funds are needed to roll the boom off the east coast into the center and west of the country.

Looking forward, we can foresee that even if China uses the money now in its foreign exchange reserves efficiently, it will need to take some of the investment funds that are now going into light manufacturing or services with rapid payoffs and use them to make long-term investments in infrastructure and agriculture. When that happens, growth slows down. Since infrastructure requires large capital investments per dollar of output, the shift to infrastructure investment raises China's capital-output ratio. For any given investment level, it gets less growth in output.

For all of these reasons, China's growth rate will be lower in the future than it has been in the past.

Outsiders should view the Chinese economy as three different economies.

(1) There is the supply chain economy where components are manufactured to be assembled into products ultimately sold in the wealthy industrial world. This is a very profitable economy, since Chinese wages are very low given its exchange rate and its internal costs of living.

(2) There is a second economy where capital equipment is sold to the Chinese. Here the initial sales are profitable, but further sales depend upon whether the sellers can protect their intellectual property rights. Equipment sold has a way of being copied by local suppliers, who both take over the local market and become an export competitor for the initial seller. Those who sell and wish to continue selling must hold something back that the Chinese cannot duplicate.

This local competition does not arise by accident. Foreigners are forced to operate in China using joint ventures. Joint ventures are part of a Chinese strategy for getting technological spillovers so they can eventually learn how to make by themselves the products they start off making with their joint venture partners.

These joint ventures produce a major set of problems for the foreign partners. How do they make joint ventures with Chinese firms work when joint ventures generally don't work even when they are between American firms where cultural differences are small? Western joint ventures quickly end in one of three ways: One firm buys out the other firm. One firm becomes a silent financial partner with all of the management being done by only one of the original partners. Or the two firms are at war with each other and in that war destroy their joint venture. Every firm entering the Chinese market should have an exit (prenuptial) agreement with their Chinese partners. Few do.

(3) In the third Chinese economy, foreign firms sell directly to Chinese customers. This economy is mostly a mirage. Foreign firms see a huge market, but when they get to China the market isn't there or it doesn't last for very long. Products made in the first world are too expensive for Chinese incomes, and local firms have a way of edging aside foreign firms who attempt to produce in China. Few foreign firms make money selling products to the Chinese consumer.

A CHINESE MODEL OF DEVELOPMENT

China's advantages are many. Communism and a Confucian culture have reinforced each other's interest in education. Illiterate parents want their children to be educated. Relative to other big developing countries such as India, Indonesia, or Brazil, China is both better educated and more broadly educated. Teaching modern production skills to those with a good basic education is simply much easier than teaching the illiterate.

Management functions are very different under communism and capitalism. Under communism managers are essentially quasi-militaristic economic officers. There is a central economic plan, the battle plan, established in Moscow or Beijing. Managers are told what to make and are sent the necessary materials, components, people, and money for wages. They are notified as to when a flatcar will arrive to take what they have produced to some unknown location. They will be punished (court-martialed) if their required production is not ready. Communist managers never buy anything, never sell anything, never negotiate with anyone, never study market information, never worry about profits and losses, and never talk to a customer. They are colonels in an economic army doing what their general staff tells them to do. Business requires a completely different mentality.

In China this problem was solved by the overseas Chinese. They knew how to play the capitalistic game because they were raised in capitalistic societies. They replaced the old economic colonels of communism and headquarter functions could be performed in Hong Kong. These overseas Chinese, from Hong Kong, Taiwan, the United States, Southeast Asia, and Singapore, brought with them money and technology, but of more value, what they really brought was the knowledge and contacts necessary to play the capitalistic game. They were important to China's economic success. They were part of its social capital.

China's entry into the World Trade Organization has been widely discussed inside and outside of China. An important psychological event, it signaled to everyone inside and outside of China that the leaders in Beijing want to play the global capitalistic game. But by itself joining the WTO was not an important economic event. China's entrance into the WTO should be seen as an instrument the leaders in Beijing could use to persuade middle and lower levels of the bureaucracy to continue reforming China's economic institutions. Reforms could be defended as necessary to fulfill WTO requirements (blame the foreigners) when, in fact, the leaders in Beijing see them as necessary to keep economic progress going. If the Chinese leadership did not believe that these reforms were necessary for their own future success, they would not have joined the WTO. China was doing very nicely outside of the WTO.

In the future, if China's leaders don't believe that WTO requirements are in their long-run self-interest, they just won't conform to these requirements—just as Europe does not conform to the requirements on hormones in meat and the United States does not follow the rules when it comes to offshore tax advantages for its companies. The Chinese know they will not be kicked out of the WTO. Fines are small, just a few billion dollars, for not following the rules, and one can always find clever ways around the rules without violating the rules. Korea gave tax audits to those buying Ford Taurus cars when Korea thought too many imported Fords were being sold. Nothing in the WTO rules says anything about who can be given a tax audit.

China had a brilliant economic development strategy and executed it well. China initially limited its experiments with free markets to special economic zones rather than trying to implement market reforms in some economic big bang that would cover the entire country. As the special economic zones expanded, the geographic scope of the market expanded. The privatization of agriculture led to the privatization of services, which led to the privatization of small-scale retailing, which led to the privatization of small-scale manufacturing. The export sector was freed before the import sector. The Chinese strategy was to move forward gradually with success feeding upon success.

Step back and think about the previously discussed mechanics of development. How do they fit the Chinese case? China understands that the economic catch-up process is a long-term process. When it comes to social capital and social capabilities, China has both. The role of the overseas Chinese in China's economic development is what is meant by social capital. China has an effective government that can design strategies and can, once those strategies have been agreed upon, make and enforce decisions. It has a consistent long-run strategy that has been well executed over the last few decades. It has demonstrated its organizational abilities in setting up and expanding the special economic zones. The rural communes have been abolished and the state-owned enterprises are being privatized. Individual incentive systems are in place. China is investing vast sums in infrastructure—the big dam on the Yangtze River is only the most visible project.

China's population growth rate is under control, growing at about 1 percent per year. China's government has mobilized the factor in scarce supply, capital, and has created a poor society with a 30 percent savings rate. Although education and health standards are far better in urban than rural areas, relative to other large developing countries China has good education and health care systems. Ensuring better rural education is probably the country's biggest need, but it is not its biggest priority.

Women are fully utilized. They are educated and hold important positions in the economy and in the government.

Terrorism isn't a threat. Foreign business people have physical safety. They don't get kidnapped or murdered on a regular basis. There is corruption, but China's leaders know they have a problem and are working to control it.

The government knows it must sell China as a good place to do business. It goes after foreign direct investment.[47] Among emerging countries it gets three times as much as the next biggest recipient, Brazil, and thirty times as much as India.* By insisting on joint ventures, local firms have a better chance of learning from the outsiders.

When it comes to fitting the profile of what is necessary to develop, China fits. Because it fits, it succeeds. Successful economic development is not mysterious. What has to be done is clear. Successful working models exist.

---

*Some fraction of what is measured as FDI in China is clearly local Chinese money that goes abroad and then comes back as FDI because FDI gets more favorable treatment from government at all levels and is under less pressure from corruption than is local investment.

ECONOMIC DECLINE IN SUB-SAHARAN AFRICA

If China is a 10 when it comes to the beauty of its economic development, Sub-Saharan Africa is a minus 1. Output is up but population growth is even higher and, as a result, real per capita GDP is falling and below where it was in the mid-1960s. The denominator of the equation is simply growing much faster than the numerator. In Africa nine out of ten people live on less than $2 per day, and in the Congo more than nine out of ten live on less than $1 per day.[48] Of those in the world living under $1 per day, 66 percent live in Africa.

It wasn't always thus. When Africa received its postcolonial independence in the mid-1960s, it was substantially wealthier per capita than Asia. Today it is poorer. In the last thirty years Africa's percentage of the world's very poor has gone up from 11 percent to 66 percent, whereas in Asia the fraction has gone down from 76 percent to 15 percent.[49]

Africa is a continent geographically located in the wrong place where everything that could go wrong has gone wrong.

Physically Africa is a block continent with the world's shortest coastline relative to its area, yet economic development is a coastal phenomenon. Almost 70 percent of the world GDP is produced within 100 km of the seashore. Africa has few natural harbors. Since Africa is a large plateau with most rivers falling over escarpments in falls or rapids near the shore; rivers are navigable for only short distances. The Nile is the only exception.

Except for a few miles extending inland along the Mediterranean and Nile River, North Africa is a harsh desert.[50] South of the northern deserts Africa is almost all tropical. Except for the city-states of Hong Kong and Singapore, there are no examples of successful economies anywhere in the tropics. In countries such as Brazil that have both tropical and temperate zones, the temperate zones are much richer.

There are real physical reasons why tropical development is difficult. To get economic development started, food surpluses must be generated in rural areas and used to feed city populations. Technology advances occur in urban cultures. But productivity is very low in tropical agriculture. Lacking the necessary rural food surpluses, cities developed much later in tropical Africa than elsewhere.

The problems in generating rural food surpluses start with plant and animal pests. Winter is the great executioner, and when it is absent, controlling these plant and animal pests is almost impossible. No one anywhere has succeeded. Agricultural problems continue with heavy seasonal rains that leech the soil and make it unproductive. The soil ends up containing little organic matter. The rainy season is followed by a season of extreme drought. Soil becomes hard and difficult to cultivate. The extent of animal life depends on how many animals can be supported in these dry months. Historically, nomadic cultivation was the only way to keep animals alive during the dry season. No one could stay in a fixed location.

Diseases like trypanosomiasis carried by the tsetse fly meant that horses and oxen could not be used to pull plows. Human power could not be augmented by animal power in Africa. Porters and human power had to be used for commercial travel, and this is the most costly and least efficient of all transportation systems. The trading patterns that developed before industrialization elsewhere never developed in Africa where there was very little trade except for slavery. Slaves could travel on their own legs.

Human diseases are similarly hard to control. A large number of diseases either don't exist elsewhere or are much easier to control elsewhere. River blindness and malaria are just two of many examples.

Much later the green revolution that worked agricultural miracles in temperate countries such as China and India failed in the tropics. It, too, was defeated by the soils, rainfall, pests, and diseases of Africa.

Colonial borders were set where the British and French armies met in the 19th century. There was nothing sensible about them, neither language, nor ethnic groups, nor geographic conditions, but they could not be changed politically after independence. No one felt attached to "their" country. The local governments that followed the colonial governments were disasters everywhere. Political systems became ethnic jousts between different competing groups rather than social systems for advancing the interest of everyone.

At the bottom of the hierarchy civil servants, such as the police, receive salaries so low that they have to collect bribes to survive. Systems of law and order first became corrupt and then broke down entirely as they lost legitimacy. Why should anyone support a government that cannot deliver the most basic of public services—personal safety?

Countries where there are small educated elites—as was true under British and French systems of colonialism—easily fall prey to bad government and corruption. Small in-groups end up running the country. The in-group sees and wants the standards of living that exist in the developed world. In a poor country this requires exploitation. The sight of these in-group leaders promising to do better in exchange for more foreign aid at the G-7 summit in Canada in 2002 would have been laughable were it not so sad.

The mechanics of development, the criteria that China meets, Africa fails to meet. It does not have social capital, social capabilities, or leaders who have long-run consistent economic strategies. Population growth rates are high, personal safety is low, and the infrastructure inherited from colonialism is melting away. Savings are low, education is limited, and women are not fully utilized. Chaos destroys personal incentives to invest in one's self or one's business. Africa attracts little foreign direct investment except for its extractive industries. American firms put two-thirds of their African investments in mining. Instead of selling themselves to potential investors, countries do everything possible to repel them. Outsiders see Zimbabwe's treatment of its white farmers, for example, and stay away.

It is not hard to say what Africa should do. Reverse all of the above. It needs to start by educating its citizens and controlling its population growth rates. Only one-third of the children that should be in school are in school. Africa has to make itself attractive to foreign direct investment. To the extent that borders are in the wrong places, it either has to move the borders or teach different ethnic groups to live with each other. Corruption must be reduced and personal safety restored.

In a word, Africa must change its political and social culture. Easy to say, but how is it to be done? Where are the starting points and the points of leverage that allow it to be done? No one knows.

CONCLUSION

On average the third world is catching up with the first world. But this reality is the product of two conflicting trends. China is closing the gap with the first world economically while other smaller areas such as Sub-Saharan Africa are falling behind. When it comes to economic development the global issue is being left out, not crushed, by globalization. This reality can be seen in a China that participates in globalization and a Sub-Saharan Africa that does not.

As China and Sub-Saharan Africa illustrate, the mechanics of development are known. Countries just have to be able to execute. Most simply put, countries have to make themselves attractive to foreign direct investment. If they are attractive, they will be taught the technologies they need to advance. If they are attractive for foreign direct investment, they will also be good places for local entrepreneurs to do business.

{7}

RESHAPING GLOBALIZATION
FOR THE THIRD WORLD

The first world's ability to cause economic development and prevent financial crises in the third world is extremely limited. Each developing country has to develop the social capital whereby individuals in that country can work together to raise everyone's productivity. Each country has to organize and run its own education system. Each country has to learn how to clean up the financial messes of capitalism. No one can do it for anyone else. If countries in the third world can get organized to do so, the first world can speed up the process of economic development with open market access, financial aid, and a better international system for dealing with financial crises. But the first world cannot cause economic development or prevent financial crises in the third world.

Pressures to do something about the third world seem more pressing now than in the past because of the new communications technologies. For most of human history the world's poor lived in rural villages where they knew little or nothing about the rich urban parts of the world. But today even the poorest of villages in

China, India, Africa, or Latin America have their village TV set. They sit watching what is, in fact, an exaggerated TV view of how well the average person lives in the developed world. The glimpse of riches sets in motion a worldwide pattern of legal and illegal migration by the poor. Why should anyone sit in a Mexican village, with a per capita income of $1,000, when they can walk to California, with a per capita income of $40,000? Those with get up and go, get up and go. On average those who do go end up economically much better off than they would have been had they stayed at home.

Similarly, people in the developed world now sit watching third world poverty. The glimpse of poverty leads the rich to have vague beliefs that something should be done about global poverty, but they do not know exactly what should be done or how the wealthy in the first world could play a positive role in alleviating the conditions of the poor in the third world. At the same time, TV telecasts also allow first world citizens to see individual third world citizens who are often corrupt, are wealthier than they are, and engage in conspicuous consumption. "If they are that rich, tax them and not me, to pay for third world schools!"

Surveys show that American citizens think they are a lot more generous than they actually are when it comes to foreign aid. America is perhaps the worst of the developed countries on these dimensions since it spends less than 0.1 percent of its GDP on foreign aid and much of what it does give is given for military reasons to countries such as Israel and Egypt. The U.S. Agency for International Development spent only $6.5 billion in 2002. Except for the Marshall Plan years, foreign aid has never been large in America, and over the years the amount has gotten progressively smaller. In absolute dollars American foreign aid is only one-fifth what it was in 1949, and as a percent of GDP it isn't even remotely comparable.[1] The reasons for the decline are not hard to find. They go back to those views Americans see on their TV sets. Foreign aid "doesn't work" and it "goes to corrupt individuals in the developing world who are wealthier than we are." If this simple view were completely accurate, no taxpayers in the developed world should be willing to see their taxes go to the third world. But it isn't completely true. There are countries that merit help.

There is one place where foreign aid has unequivocally worked—health care. Life expectancy in the developing world has gone up rapidly and in most countries is not all that different than life expectancy in the developed world. The differences that still exist are almost all concentrated in the first year of life. It is also the place where all of the experts agree that with a little more money, health care could be much better.[2] And there is an economic payoff. Better health care leads to a more energetic population that can work harder. Skills don't disappear because of premature death or disability. Proponents of more foreign assistance for health care argue that annual economic output might go up three times as much as the cost of the extra health care.[3]

But when it comes to economic development, better health care is a two-edged sword. Death rates fall, but birth rates do so only with a long time lag. With higher population growth rates, it is harder to raise per capita GDPs and average standards of living. For the reasons examined earlier in the mechanics of development, health care without population control is a waste of money if economic development is the goal.

Debt relief for the world's poorest countries is often suggested, but it has to come with other requirements. If debt forgiveness allows a failed government to re-enter the credit markets to borrow again and to waste again whatever it has been able to borrow a second time, debt relief is of no value at all. If debt relief allows a country to put more resources into its military establishments, debt relief is of no value at all.

In the world of aid givers a number of truisms about economic assistance have been true, or have, at least, been believed to be true, for a long time. Givers need more coordination among themselves, noted President Truman in 1949 and the president of the World Bank in 2002. Greater selectivity should be exercised, said President Kennedy in 1963 and the International Development Association in 2001. There should be a focus on poverty, stated World Bank president McNamara in 1973 and the International Development Association in 2001. Africans need to improve their governments, declared the World Bank in 1983 and 2002.[4] What has not been said is that receivers have to have the ability to get organized. If they do not have that ability, no amount of better organization on the giver's side is going to lead to economic development.

How should people in the wealthy developed world help people in the poor developing world? The answer is to help those who have the necessary social organization. Foreign aid is not a matter of giving money regardless of outcomes or of giving money to the poorest countries. Not all poor countries should be helped. Aid should go to those who can efficiently use it. If the foreign aid doesn't go to the right countries, it simply ends up in corrupt hands.

For proof that aid without social organization does not work, look at Nigeria. It has received over $250 billion in oil revenues since its independence, yet its per capita GDP is only one-third of what it was then.[5] Outside aid is important, but it is not the starting point of economic development. The real starting point is found in social organization.

DOHA WTO TRADING ROUND

If the wealthy industrial world really wants to alleviate poverty among the poorest of the poor, it will open up its agricultural markets to free trade in the new WTO Doha trading round that has just begun. Nothing would help the third world faster. The poorest of the poor are third world farmers. The third world knows how to produce what the first world wants. It has the necessary skills. It needs only market access. In this case, making the third world wealthier is simply a matter of changing first world laws. There are no difficult cultural or educational changes to be made.

Those who are against globalization on the grounds that globalization hurts third world countries should be reminded that agriculture is the one industry where globalization is in retreat. National agricultural self-sufficiency seems to be a first world goal. These policies are a disaster for the third world.

If city people in the first world want to give money to farmers in the first world, they can continue to do so. They just cannot make the size of their gifts contingent on how much a farmer produces. One is paid for being a farmer and not for farming. Although this alternative is more sensible than the current system, the surface absurdity of having city taxpayers make payments to rural subsidy collectors who do nothing to get their subsidies explains why it hasn't happened.

Negotiating the Doha Round is going to be very difficult in the years immediately ahead. Doha is the first trading round occurring since currents of public opinion have turned against freer trade. The gains from further reductions in tariffs and quotas on manufactured goods will be very small, since the remaining tariffs and quotas that could be eliminated are very small. Moving free trade into other sectors, such as agriculture and services, runs up against politics in both the developed and the underdeveloped world. The developed world wants to protect its farmers and does not believe in free trade for agricultural. The underdeveloped world wants to protect its service industries and does not believe in free trade for services. To get the free trade it wants in agriculture, the third world would have to give up the protection it has in services. To get the free trade it wants in services, the first world would have to give up the protection it has in agriculture.

What the underdeveloped world wants in intellectual property rights, more open and cheaper access, is exactly the opposite of what the developed world wants, better protection for its patents, copyrights, and trademarks. In the first world there are demands on the left that future trade agreements cover labor standards and environmental issues. Third world countries do not want the first world setting either their labor or their environmental standards. Yet without something said about labor standards and environmental issues, it is doubtful that whatever is negotiated can be ratified in the parliaments of the developed world.

Ultimately, the issue is not designing sensible compromises in the Doha Round but dealing with the lack of a political willingness to compromise. As the next chapter will show, we can design a system of intellectual property rights that allows poor countries to copy technologies and give drugs to poor people at prices they can afford while preserving incentives to invent in the first world. Certainly the whole panoply of environmental and labor protections should not be exported from the first world to the third world, but there is a place for labor and environmental negotiations. There are areas where agreements are both possible and desirable.

Poor countries cannot afford the same environmental standards as rich countries, but there are environmental issues that hit the third world just as hard, or harder, than the first world. Economic activities that pollute drinking water are one. Safe drinking water is a proper area for global environmental negotiations if the developed world is to expand its medical aid to the developing world. Water-borne diarrheal diseases are the world's second biggest killer after AIDS. For the first world to give more aid to help pay for more health care without requiring local countries to clean up their water supplies is a waste of money. Clean drinking water is an issue properly debated at Doha.

Trade agreements should not attempt to set wages for third world countries or attempt to export the full range of labor practices seen in the first world, but they can deal with issues such as child labor. There is nothing wrong with an American worrying about very young Pakistani children sewing soccer balls for the U.S. market. These children should be in school and should be protected by adults, locally or globally. Child labor did not slowly die out in the United States as Americans grew richer. At some point Americans woke up and made it illegal. Ending child labor is in the self-interest of any country. Those who work full time as children don't get educated to become productive adults. Child labor is not going to lead anyone into the promised land of economic development. More important, it is simply morally wrong. In every country, no matter how poor, forcing young children to work outside of the home is abusive exploitation. Sensible WTO rules can be written to specify when children can legally go to work outside of the home. No one is talking about making teenage summer jobs illegal.

A significant Doha agreement was unlikely before the Iraqi war and much less likely after the Iraqi war. Opening up first world agricultural markets requires an agreement between their European champion, France, and their American protector, the United States. After the war in Iraq and the events that preceded it, such an agreement is difficult to imagine. Without an agricultural agreement and the service agreement that would go with it, other compromises are not going to be made. Logic would call for a lengthy recess in the Doha Round until tempers have cooled and normal diplomatic relations have been restored. But diplomats don't believe in public failures. Instead, they will negotiate an empty agreement that will leave everyone frustrated.

The most recent Uruguay Round lasted from 1986 through 1994 and gave birth to a mouse. After nine years of negotiations the World Bank, IMF, and GATT (General Agreement on Tariffs and Trade—the previous name for the WTO) estimated that the Uruguay Round results would raise world GDP by $140 to $274 billion within eight years.[6] The OECD was more optimistic and said $200–$500 billion within six years but it also foresaw a $1 billion fall in GDP in Sub-Saharan Africa.[7] No one has reviewed the data to see if these results actually occurred. Basically, the predicted gains are so small relative to the global GDP that it would be impossible to find them even if they did occur. Even a $500 billion gain spread over six years is invisible in a global GDP now approaching $45,000 billion.

The Doha Round will produce much smaller gains than the Uruguay Round.

THIRD WORLD FINANCIAL INSTABILITY

Much of the concern about the third world comes from their financial crises. But financial crises don't occur in the world's poorest countries. No one is willing to lend them money. Financial crises are a problem for the upper ranks of developing countries that have the credit ratings to borrow money and the desire to encourage economic development—the Mexicos and the Thailands of the world. Doing something to reform the system for dealing with third world crises is not an activity that is going to help the poorest of the poor.

Although the advent of globalization is often blamed for financial crises in the third world, the real cause is found in the shift to capitalism. As the world moves away from socialistic or quasi-socialistic forms of organization, it will on average get richer, but it will most certainly also become much more unstable. Economic instabilities existed long before globalization was invented, and they are not going to disappear with the advent of globalization. Globalization can only be blamed in the sense that the decision to participate in globalization involves a simultaneous decision to participate in capitalism.

The Mexican and Brazilian loan crises in 1982 were the first financial crises to be seen as part of globalization. Third world financial crashes accelerated in the 1990s. There was another Mexican loan crisis in 1996. In 1997 an Asia crisis started in Thailand and quickly spread to Malaysia, Indonesia, the Philippines, and South Korea. This crisis shook the foundations of the third world, since just a few months earlier the World Bank had held up the afflicted countries as the world's best models of economic development. Unlike Latin America, they did not have budgets out of control, their governments did not owe large amounts of money to foreign banks, and their savings and investment rates were high. A crisis in Russia started in 1998. There was no logical connection, but the panic spread to Brazil.

Details differ, but in broad terms all speculative meltdowns over the last four hundred years have similar causes and similar cures. The sequence of events in a meltdown is well known: Some economic variable (land prices, stock market values, debts, trade deficits, currency values, tulips, dot.coms) reaches levels far above economic sustainability. Every investor (no one thinks of himself or herself as a speculator) recognizes this reality but imagines being able to see the end coming and thus getting out in time. In the end few do.

As overvalued asset prices fall, what had been good loans become bad loans. Adequate collateral becomes inadequate collateral, and inadequately collateralized loans get called. Fearful of defaults or short of liquidity themselves, banks don't renew short-term loans that would normally be automatically rolled over. Credit markets freeze up. Suppliers fearful of not being paid demand cash before delivery rather than being willing to wait the normal ninety days for payment. Working capital dries up. Within hours of the onset of the 1997 East Asian crisis, boats loaded with raw materials for Korea were halted off the coast waiting for payments to clear before unloading. Even financially sound firms find they cannot pay their bills because they are unexpectedly suddenly asked to make loan repayments and prepay suppliers. Business firms that cannot finance themselves go broke.

Worried about preserving their wealth, insiders as well as outsiders flee to currencies that are not expected to depreciate. Vast amounts of money leave the country, and the value of the country's currency plunges. With currency values down, the real costs of repaying foreign currency loans rises. At four pesos to the dollar, a $100 million loan is an obligation to pay 400 million pesos. At six pesos to the dollar, it is a 600 million peso obligation. With everyone trying to get out of their local currency and into dollars, the local central banks eventually run out of international reserves and even companies with enough local funds to repay their international loans cannot get the necessary foreign funds to repay. A financial crisis becomes a business crisis and then a country crisis.

Fear leads to flight, but both fear and flight are the right things for individuals to do to preserve their wealth. Naval officers are taught that the brave go down with the ship. Business schools don't teach that capitalistic investors should go down with the ship. In capitalism the brave do not go down with the ship; they are taught to be the rats who desert the ship before it sinks whenever they fear their wealth is in jeopardy. That instinct is built into the genes of the capitalistic beast—a beast bred to protect its capital. The stability of the global financial system is someone else's worry.

Consider the Argentine meltdown. As always there were multiple causes. Forty percent of Argentines do not pay their taxes.[8] Businesses have looked to government for protection from competition to generate profits. Export industries are small in Argentina. The electorate is fickle and wants quick fixes. Paying off corrupt officials is standard operating procedure. No country can, without limits, incur foreign debts that grow faster than its GDP, yet from 1976 to 2001 Argentina's foreign debt went from $8 billion to $171 billion—an amount equal to almost 60 percent of GDP.[9]

Argentina had a currency board where the exchange rate between dollars and pesos were fixed at 1 to 1. No country can forever hold its currency at a fixed rate relative to another currency. To maintain any fixed parity forever, the two countries would have to have the same rates of growth of productivity, the same rates of inflation, the same rates of GDP growth, and the same propensities to import; they would have to attract identical capital inflows and have equally attractive exports that went to the same countries in the same portions. No two countries are so alike.

When capital inflows shrank and were insufficient to cover the trade deficit, dollars flowed out of Argentina. Under the rules of a currency board where the printing of local pesos is rigidly linked to the country's holdings of dollars, Argentina's internal money supply shrank. A recession resulted.

The trigger but not the cause of the 2002 Argentine crisis was a Brazilian crisis and the sharp devaluation of Brazil's currency in

2000. Brazilian goods suddenly became much cheaper. Argentina was going to sell less to Brazil and buy more from Brazil. The trade deficit got bigger, the restrictive monetary policies became harsher, and the recession grew. Politically, no country can forever run a recession to lower its own income so it purchases fewer imports. Argentina cried "uncle" when its unemployment rate got to 25 percent in 2002, when it was in its fifth year of recession.[10]

Outsiders such as the International Monetary Fund can at best play a subsidiary role in determining who succeeds and who fails in the aftermath of a financial crisis. The IMF's principle role is to lend foreign exchange reserves to the local country so it has more time to pick up the pieces, but the IMF cannot actually pick up the pieces. That is a job for the locals. The IMF also has a role to play in taking the blame for the policies that will have to be imposed. The IMF's management is not elected, so it can take the blame for good, though unpopular, policies. It can provide political shelter to the governments that have to impose these policies.

With some justification the IMF is accused of being a doctor with one set of medicines (fiscal austerity, high interest rates, freer capital markets, and privatization of state-owned industry) that are administered whatever the disease.[11] High interest rates reduce capital flight. Government budget surpluses are imposed to force savings rates up, push incomes down, and reduce imports to eliminate trade deficits. These policies may be appropriate in Latin America where savings rates are low, but they may be inappropriate in countries such as South Korea, where savings rates are already very high. (Korea has a 40 percent national savings rate.) Austerity is also inappropriate when it has to be administered to many countries at the same time since it ends up cutting worldwide aggregate demand and aggravating problems by slowing world growth.

Historically, the IMF has been very good at restoring international financial stability (its primary job) but horrible at restoring domestic prosperity (its secondary job). In Indonesia, the international creditors were rescued and order was restored, but six years later the median Indonesian family income remained below where it was when the crisis began. In retrospect, IMF predictions are always too optimistic regarding how much IMF austerity policies will cut local growth rates. In subsequent years GDPs are always below the IMF's forecasted results. None of the Asian countries forced to accept IMF recommendations to get out of their financial crises in 1997 and 1998 can point to faster growth in the five years after adopting the IMF remedies than in the five years before adopting the IMF remedies.

In America both the left and the right object to IMF policies. The political left thinks the IMF cares too much about international lenders, big businesses, and macrostability. It imposes its austerity policies without thinking about their impact on the middle class and the poor. As the left points out, it is the poor who get hurt when the IMF moves in, but it was not the poor who created the problems.

The political right thinks the IMF undercuts the realities of risk taking in capitalistic societies. It funds bailouts for lenders, borrowers, and countries that have made bad decisions. By doing so it creates a moral hazard where people knowingly take and make bad loans, confident that the IMF will bail them out. From their point of view bankruptcy is what maintains capitalistic discipline and order. The right also objects to the IMF because they see it as a first step to world government. An international agency effectively ends up running countries.

In the developing world the IMF is often accused of not understanding their problems. Perhaps it is more accurate to say that the IMF often underestimates the local citizens' distrust of their own local government. Despite the closure of thousands of banks during the U.S. Savings and Loan crisis, there were no runs on federally insured banks. Everyone knew they would shortly get their deposits back. Their money was safe. They had seen banks go broke before. Depositors always got their money back. In contrast, in Indonesia deposit insurance existed but no one believed it would protect their deposits. The system had never been tested. Who knew whether the guarantees were really true? Why should the average depositor believe these guarantees would be honored? The government's word was often untrustworthy in other areas. As a consequence, there were runs on the banks in Indonesia that the IMF did not anticipate. These runs made a bad problem worse.

The IMF also often overestimates the local government's abilities to implement what it promises. Restructuring requires a solid base of support, which did not exist in either Indonesia or Russia. Indonesia is a country much like the old USSR, with little to hold it together except military force. Unlike China it has no long national history. It has many languages, religions, and ethnic groups spread across thousands of widely dispersed islands with little interaction with each other. The initial Dutch conquest of these islands, their temporary replacement during World War II by the Japanese, and their permanent replacement by a military government in Jakarta after the war did not make Indonesia into a real country any more than Russian conquests made the old USSR into one country.

What international agencies should do in the midst of a financial crisis is a subject of controversy between those who have worked for the IMF and the World Bank—the two international agencies dealing with these problems. Part of this dispute flows from differences in institutional responsibilities. The World Bank exists to help poor countries develop faster. The IMF exists to protect the viability of the world's financial system. The IMF's standard remedies may hurt the country where they are applied but help restore confidence in the world's financial system and keep funds flowing across national boundaries.[12]

This is precisely the charge made by Joseph Stiglitz, former chief economist at the World Bank.[13] In his view the IMF is protecting global finance rather than promoting global economic stability (growth). The IMF always pushes for quick liberalization, privatization, and stabilization with austerity policies (shock therapy) that increase poverty and widen income gaps. Although liberalization and privatization may be good things, they have to be implemented slowly, in his view, since developing countries don't have the entrepreneurial talent to build or run the new industries needed when free trade destroys a country's old industries. In Stiglitz's view the IMF has forgotten about full employment and has become, essentially, a colonial ruler—over its client countries.[14] Not surprisingly, he reflects a World Bank view of the world and not an IMF view of the world. And in many ways he is charging the IMF with doing what it is supposed to be doing.

It is easy to agree that the IMF gets too deeply involved in micromanaging third world economies in the aftermath of financial crises. In the 1998 letter of intent negotiated between Indonesia and the IMF, Indonesia promised to phase out subsidies on fish meal and rice and to eliminate the import monopolies on grains other than rice. It promised to abolish marketing arrangements and territorial restrictions on livestock trading so that firms could distribute their products freely. It pledged to eliminate the regional monopolies on cloves, nuts, oranges, and vanilla; to increase the prices of kerosene, diesel fuel, and electricity; to reduce tariffs on chemicals and metal products; and to abolish administrated cement prices. It committed to canceling twelve infrastructure projects. Fiscal accounting was to be improved. Trade and foreign investment were to be liberalized. Export taxes and import restrictions were to be phased out. It does not take a person temperamentally disposed to hate the IMF to agree all this seems like a lot of micromanagement.

Partly in response to its critics, the IMF floated the idea of building a formal bankruptcy procedure for countries that would allow them to more easily shed their debts.[15] But sovereign debt is often nationalized private debts. Governments take over the debts of their firms to prevent foreign creditors from pushing them into bankruptcy and taking the local collateral to which the creditors are legally entitled. Easy government bankruptcy effectively becomes easier private bankruptcy. More important, who will run the system for country bankruptcy? Who will be the judge in charge of the bankruptcy court? Who will enforce its decisions? In private bankruptcies new management is almost always brought in to run the firm. Doing this for a country is quite different. Yet the old managers who have failed are clearly not the right managers to restore prosperity once debts have been written down.

The U.S. Treasury wasn't enthusiastic about the IMF's idea for sovereign bankruptcy, and the idea disappeared from sight soon after it surfaced.

President Bush's former secretary of the treasury, Paul O'Neill, took the view that both the IMF and the World Bank were wrong. No help should be given. Let the countries go broke to teach them and their lenders to be more careful in the future. Bailouts, in his view, encourage even sloppier behavior in the future since lenders know they will be rescued. The O'Neill approach was tested in Argentina but quickly abandoned when problems broke out in Brazil and Uruguay. In early 2003 the IMF was ordered by its member governments to resume lending to Argentina. These governments did not want to take a chance on what might happen next. In the end Argentina proved that doing nothing wasn't really an option.

The IMF and the World Bank were both originally designed in 1944 to provide functions that are no longer needed. Both need to be fundamentally reconstituted.

The World Bank was designed to provide loans for profitable large infrastructure projects that could not be financed by third world countries. Today there is no need for this function since world capital markets have plenty of funds and are eager to finance large profitable third world infrastructure projects. And if the projects are not profitable, they should not be financed by anyone. The World Bank was not originally designed to be an institute for general economic development in the third world—the function it now performs.

The IMF was designed to deal with temporary balance-of-payments problems between wealthy industrial countries. It has not performed this function since the early 1970s. It was not designed to be a world central bank providing liquidity to third world countries in the midst of financial crises—the function it now performs.

The World Bank should become a global Department of Education—a multilateral aid agency with a focused educational mission. The World Bank's many other activities should be abandoned. If there are global health issues, for example, they should be left to the World Health Organization. The world does not need an agency that gives general technical assistance on economic development and provides funds for infrastructure development.

The World Bank should have a mandate to co-invest in education with poor countries wherever those investments would actually lead to higher levels of education. Economic growth requires more education and a better distribution of education. Often this means redistributing attention to elementary education for everyone rather than spending too many funds on university education for the elite—the Latin American pattern.

No outside agency can force Africa or India to make the social changes necessary to make universal education a reality. Cultural changes, such as eliminating India's caste system, in particular untouchability, have to occur. Only local political regimes can make such changes. Governments have to be airport builders, both literally and figuratively, if the planes of the global economy are to land. Outsiders can help pay for the runways, but they cannot force the building of the necessary runways. The ultimate responsibility for managing local economies lies with the relevant nation-states. That will remain true as long as national governments exist. They are the actors that can make things happen locally. The rest of the world can give advice and should provide money when their advice is being taken, but they cannot force changes in places that do not want to change.

As a result, the new World Bank should not provide money for schools unless countries have demonstrated that they have the social organization to get schools up and running and the ability to get all of their children into those schools. The foreign aid funds that flow from rich to poor countries should also be similarly focused on countries where universal free-to-the-parents schooling is in place and underway. If a country can run a good school system, it undoubtedly has the social organization to engage in economic development. It will be attracting the foreign direct investment everyone needs if they are to succeed. Education is the right index of self-help to be used when trying to determine whether outside help should be given.

If one looks at third world financial crises, the real damage comes not during the crises themselves but in the lengthy periods of austerity that follow. Those periods of austerity can be eliminated. The IMF should continue its focus on third world financial crises. But the right answer to these crises is neither more generous, less onerous, bailouts with fewer conditions nor easier, more structured, bankruptcies. It is also not to be found in refusing to aid countries in crisis so that lenders and borrowers face up to the real risks of their lending and borrowing. Moral hazard is a phony problem.

Instead, the IMF should run a system of international liquidity insurance much like national bank deposit insurance. During normal times, before a crisis has occurred, the IMF should specify the policy mix that makes a country eligible for international liquidity insurance. If a country meets these conditions and then has an international financial crisis, it receives the promised funds without any further changes in its policies. The criteria for economic soundness are specified before there is a crisis, not in the midst of a crisis or in the aftermath of a crisis. Once a crisis is underway, the IMF cannot add any new criteria. It simply disperses the promised funds.

The insurance system might have two different levels of support. The first level would be determined by a formula that depends on the recipient country's size and the degree to which the country is adhering to the IMF conditions. The second level might be a degree of extra protection, extra liquidity, that countries could purchase by making annual payments to the IMF in currencies other than their own.

Instead of being required to raise taxes, cut expenditures, and raise interest rates during a crisis, thereby making the GDP much smaller, countries would know that their policies have been certified to be sound and that they will have the needed international liquidity to ride out any economic storm. For those eligible for international liquidity insurance, the extremely damaging post-crisis periods of austerity would be eliminated.

By imposing its own eligibility requirements—whatever it determined were the right requirements consistent with economic growth absent a crisis—the IMF could come to be seen as an agency that speeds up economic growth rather than as an agency that slows down economic growth. It would cease to be a quasi-colonial power micromanaging economies where it was not elected to do so.

THE END OF EXPORT-LED GROWTH

The most important development problem facing third world developing countries, however, is not learning how to deal more effectively with financial crises. There is a far bigger issue: everyone is going to have to find a replacement for their current export-led strategies of economic growth. Effectively, the export-led model of economic development is now being crushed between China's desire to follow the export-led model of economic development and the United States' inability to permanently run large trade deficits.

All of those countries that have been successful in their economic development in the past forty years have used the export-led model of economic development. Japan did so in the 1960s, 1970s, and 1980s. Taiwan, Singapore, South Korea, and Hong Kong did so in the 1980s and 1990s. Southeast Asia did so in the 1990s. And mainland China is doing so today.

In the export-led model, invented by Japan, local firms export their products to wealthy industrial countries where markets are so large that a small increase in market share translates into a very rapid growth rate back in the economically much smaller developing country. As a result, exports can grow much faster than the developing country's GDP, pulling its economy forward. In Japan exports grew more than twice as fast as the GDP during its years of rapid growth.

In export-led growth strategies the focus is always on pumping up exports. If exports can grow at 15 to 20 percent per year, the country's domestic economy can grow at 7 to 8 percent per year. Funds are available to buy the equipment, spare parts, and technology necessary to enable the country to become more efficient. In addition, the export-led model forces firms in developing countries to rapidly become efficient, since they have to sell their products in highly competitive foreign markets without government protection. It is a virtuous circle.

What sounds sensible when heard separately in each country—to export more—becomes nonsense when aggregated around the world, with everyone planning to export more. How can all countries increase exports by 15 to 20 percent per year when the world economy grows only at 3 or 4 percent per year? They can't. How can everyone have a trade surplus? It is not possible. Globally, deficits and surpluses have to add to zero.

By definition exports can grow faster than GDP only if imports also grow faster than GDP. In our national economic accounts, exports are added to the GDP and imports are subtracted from GDP. In the aggregate for all countries combined, the growth of imports has to equal the growth of exports. What more exports add to the GDP is matched by what more imports subtract from the GDP, and there is no net forward momentum to be imparted to the local GDP if exports equal imports.

The export-led model of economic growth dies when everyone wants to use it. Export-led growth works only when a few small countries play the game. The principle export-led growth players in the 1980s and 1990s—South Korea, Taiwan, Hong Kong, and

Singapore—together have 65 million people. Japan had 110 million people when it was playing the game in the 1960s and 1970s.

Those melting down in the 1997 Asia crisis were all following export-led growth strategies. Yet at the time of the crisis they all had large trade deficits—the prior two years' deficits were $13 billion in Indonesia, $10 billion in Malaysia, $18 billion in Thailand, $8 billion in the Philippines, and $31 billion in Korea.[16] Their swing from earlier surpluses to deficits is directly traceable to mainland China's decision to play the export-led growth game. Since China offered better-educated but cheaper workers than Southeast Asia, along with a much bigger internal market, it quickly pulled exports away from other Asian countries. As firms move their offshore exporting activities from Southeast Asia to China to take advantage of lower costs, the trade surpluses that used to be in Southeast Asia move to China. The two-year $80 billion trade surplus gained by China was lost by Southeast Asia. Countries that were supposed to be running trade surpluses under their export-led models of economic development were running trade deficits.

With the exception of South Korea, none of the Asian economies that participated in the 1997 crisis have been able to recapture their pre-crisis growth rates. Leaving the crisis years (1997 and 1998) aside and comparing the three years after the crisis to the five years before the crisis, we see that Indonesia's growth rate was just one-third of what it had been, Malaysia's just half of what it had been, and Thailand's just 40 percent of what it had been. The Philippines was a late joiner of the rapidly developing club of Southeast Asia. It had a negative growth rate in 1991 and very low growth rates in 1992 and 1993, so the pre-crisis five-year average and the post-crisis three-year average don't differ all that much. But the three-year post-crisis growth rate is 30 percent below the pre-crisis three-year average.[17]

South Korea could not muscle China aside, but a very large devaluation made it possible for South Korea to take some export markets away from Japan. But despite a recovery in growth rates,

South Korea's per capita GDP in 2002 was still well below where it was in 1996.[18]

China explains why all of the other Asian economies have per capita incomes evaluated in dollars below where they were at the start of the 1997 crisis. To lower their wages to compete with China, the other Asian economies all had to sharply devalue their currencies. And despite these large devaluations, what was happening is still happening. Dell, for example, is moving its computer manufacturing activities out of Malaysia and into China. Foreign direct investment in Malaysia is less than one-third as large as it was before the 1997 crisis.[19] And it is not alone.

To get out of China's way economically, these countries needed to go upscale in technology very rapidly, but most were not well educated enough to do so. South Korea had the educational skills, and it moved its low wage manufacturing exports to China. But without a large devaluation, South Korea could not replace these exports with high wage manufacturing exports because of Japanese competition and Japan's rapidly rising trade surplus. As has so often happened in its history, South Korea was once again squeezed between its two huge neighbors.

With China in the way, none of them can go back to their old export-led growth strategies. China is so large that when it decides to build an export-led economy, it is effectively as if everyone on the globe had decided to build an export-led economy—a mathematical impossibility. Because of the history of communism (many basic necessities such as housing were provided free or at very low cost) and an undervalued currency, China's internal cost structure is lower than anyone else's. Because of communism and Confucian beliefs in education, China has a better educated population than anyone else in the developing world. It has a much larger internal market and, because of its size, wages are not going to rise quickly as firms move their offshore production to China.

On the other side of the export-led growth equation, simply add up the net exports that various governments around the world have publicly announced as their growth goal. The sums are huge. Yet no one can have more net exports unless someone else has more net imports. There are only three places that can run large trade deficits—Japan, Europe, and the United States. The export-led model of economic development might be extended for a somewhat longer time if Japan and Europe were also willing to run trade deficits and share the deficit load with the United States. But they are not. If asked how they will recover from their current economic problems, countries such as Germany and Japan say they plan to export more to the United States. Essentially, the rest of the developed world has also decided to rely on an export-led model of economic growth, and this reliance will bring about the demise of the model even faster. This leaves America as the only available market for new exports, but America starts with a trade deficit that is already north of $450 billion. Add a few hundred billion to the already existing deficit, and the American deficit has to get scary to international investors who do not want to lose money on their American investments. For currency speculators watching those growing American deficits, moving money out of dollars has to start to look attractive.

Anyone following an export-led growth strategy faces a plunging dollar when the American trade deficit becomes unsustainable. Instantly they become a much higher cost place of doing business. Global supply chains would have to be ripped up and laid down in other places. Factories focused on the American market would become worthless since they could not profitably sell their output given the lower value of the dollar. And there would be nowhere else on the face of the globe to sell the output produced by those factories.

Because of China, the export-led growth model of economic development is dying in the Asian countries that formerly practiced it. That is why their growth rates have not rebounded after the 1997 crisis. The inventor of the export-led growth strategy, Japan, repeatedly tried to revive its economy in the 1990s with an export surge. But its attempt failed. What used to be possible is no longer possible. Latin America talks about shifting to an export strategy, but the country that moved the farthest, Mexico, now finds itself rapidly losing plants to China. Greater China is the only part of the world left with a viable export strategy. But it, too, will find that the game has come to an end when the United States can no longer run large trade deficits.

No one can predict the timing, but the game of export-led growth is definitely coming to an end. Just as most of the third world has become convinced of the merits of export-led growth, the model is headed toward extinction—crushed between China's decision to follow the model and the inability of the United States to run perpetually large trade deficits. What has been successful in the last half century will not be successful in the next half century. Those successful in the future will have to design new strategies for growth.

The replacement for export-led growth strategies is to be found in internally pulled growth strategies similar to those used by America in the 19th century. In the American model massive infrastructure investments (railroads, electricity, the telegraph) pulled the economy forward and at the same time made it much more efficient. Better and faster transportation and communications systems made it possible to create a national economy that could take advantage of the economies of scale and scope that were inherent in industrial economies. Electricity made possible the shift from the centralized power sources of the steam era to the distributed power, its source, of the electricity era. Machines, each with its own power source, could be arranged in much more productive patterns and used in small motors where big steam engines could not be used.

Internally pulled growth is not a return to the failed model of quasi-socialism and import substitution tried in most of the developed world in the 1950s and 1960s. A competitive environment is sustained by letting foreigners enter and compete under the same set of rules that apply to the country's citizens. Foreigners are, in fact, encouraged to enter and drive locally owned businesses out of business—if they can—to keep local business on their toes. This internal competition, rather than the external competition of exporting, creates the competitive pressure necessary to make firms more efficient. Industry is neither government owned, nor government financed, nor government protected.

Today the needed infrastructure investments would be very different from those in the 19th century. Investments in telegraphy are replaced by investments in modern telecommunications. But they fall into the same broad categories. Communications, transportation, and electrification investments are still needed in most developing countries to pull their economies forward and make them more efficient.

Those who win get ahead of the wave—they change just slightly before everyone else is forced to change. But being the first to give up export-led growth is difficult since it has been such a successful game for those who were the first to play it. Unfortunately, China makes it into a losing game for everyone else, and China's size ultimately makes it into a losing game for China itself. China ends up with a lot of those worthless factories that used to make products for the U.S. market when the dollar plunges.

{8}

RESHAPING GLOBALIZATION
FOR THE FIRST WORLD

Since 80 percent of the world's economic weight is in the developed world, only problems at the top of the global economic tower can threaten to topple the tower itself. Third world economic problems are important because of the human suffering they represent, but they do not threaten the existence of globalization. There are many things the first world can and should do for the third world, but the most important of them is to insure economic prosperity in the first world. Without first world prosperity and the market opportunities that are generated by this prosperity, the third world has no hope of economic development.

DEFLATION

Japan's deflation has already spread to most of East Asia. In Europe, Germany would be in deflation were it not for all of its bureaucratic rules and regulations that prevent prices from falling. To find the real rate of inflation in Germany one must look at what is happening to prices not controlled by government rules and regulations. Measured inflation is very close to zero (actually below zero in April 2003), and if one looks at prices that are free to move up and down, Germany is already in deflation. Technically, the U.S. inflation rate is positive—1.2 percent on the GDP deflator during 2002. But much of this inflation is localized in health care. Health care inflation is not caused by the same factors that cause inflation in the rest of the economy. It is driven by new, more expensive technologies for treating chronic diseases among a much larger elderly population. The normal remedies for inflation elsewhere—deliberately raising interest rates to create recessions and reduce demand—does nothing to stop it. Subtract health care inflation, and the inflation rate for the rest of the U.S. economy is 0.3 percent. The United States is not yet into deflation but it is very close.

As average inflation rates near zero, many industries face falling prices long before deflation technically sets in. On the 2002 inflation-deflation teeter-totter, computer prices were down 22 percent, used car prices were down 6 percent, and audio equipment prices were down 5 percent while gasoline prices were going up 26 percent, drugs were up 5 percent, and legal and funeral services were up 4 percent.[1] Industries facing persistently falling prices have to take the necessary defensive measures, such as focusing on paying off debts, even if the average rate of inflation is still positive. Relative to the prices at which they sell their products, the real values of their debts are going up. As inflation approaches zero, the number of industries facing the reality of persistently falling prices increases and the negative effects of deflation set in well before deflation technically arrives. That is why capitalistic economies work best with a positive rate of inflation between 2 and 3 percent.

Japan's deflation was generated by its own peculiar problems—rapidly falling asset prices and a decade of no growth—but deflation has now spread to the rest of East Asia because of wider global realities. The inflation of the 1970s and 1980s did not just suddenly disappear in almost every country in the world because of better management at the world central banks. It disappeared for some very concrete reasons.

It is a basic axiom of economics that in the long run prices follow costs. If costs fall, prices will fall. Initially, those who lead in finding cost reductions make higher profits, but eventually everyone copies their innovations and competition then forces prices down for everyone.

Inflation disappeared because new technologies were lowering costs in many industries such as microelectronics or computers. Think of scanners. They started as very expensive add-ons to computer systems and became an item thrown in free with a new computer purchase. Much cheaper computers and electronic controls widened opportunities for using these technologies in other industries. Much better computers and smarter electronic controls raised productivity and reduced costs in the industries that bought them. With no need for large investments in physical infrastructure, Internet shopping, for example, reduced retailing costs. To get customers to switch, Internet retailers set prices at levels far below those found in conventional stores. This competition in turn forced brick-and-mortar retailers to sharply reduce their prices. As just one example, electronic brokerage firms forced huge reductions in the standard charges for trading stocks and bonds in conventional brokerage firms.

Inflation disappeared because deregulation and privatization reduced costs, increased competition, and forced prices down. Trucking costs, airline fares, and the cost of long distance telephone calls all fell dramatically in the aftermath of deregulation.

Inflation disappeared because global supply chains dramatically reduced the costs of producing labor-intensive goods. If China produces items 30 or 40 percent cheaper than they could be produced in the developed world, prices are going to fall for these products.

Inflation disappeared because of downsizing. Workers were laid off, but those who kept their jobs were also paid less. For the last twenty-five years real wages have been falling at the rate of about a percentage point per year for the bottom 60 percent of the American male workforce. Wage reductions lead to lower costs and in the end to lower prices.

Manufacturing, mining, and construction could easily keep wages down because of the huge reserves of low cost labor they can tap in the service sector. Many of the people now working in the service sector would be delighted to quit their low wage service jobs and move into higher-paying jobs in manufacturing. As a result, even record low unemployment rates in the late 1990s did not lead to inflationary wage increases in manufacturing, mining, and construction.

Name any product, add up the amounts the world could produce if all of the world's factories were operating at capacity, subtract what the world is going to buy, and you will find that the world's production potential exceeds the world's expected consumption by at least one-third in almost every industry. Autos, semiconductor chips, and oil are just three of the many examples. Given normal operations, the world's auto factories could produce 22 million cars more than the world is going to buy in 2003. Part of this excess capacity comes from new technologies that have dramatically raised productivity. Part of it comes from competitive pressures that force firms to invest in new low cost offshore production capacity even though they were not short of capacity at home. With such an overhang of productive capacity, firms have an enormous incentive to lower prices in an attempt to keep their facilities operating closer to capacity.

Outsourcing reduces prices. It is common practice in America for companies to negotiate contracts that require annual price reductions from their suppliers. Auto parts manufacturers, for example, have signed contracts with the major auto parts suppliers calling for 3 percent annual price reductions. Outsourcing plays a big role in these tough contracts since it is simply easier to get tough on prices with an outside supplier than it is with an inside supplier. If an outside supplier doesn't make any money with the new lower prices, that is the supplier's problem. But if an inside supplier doesn't make any money, what the corporation gains in one of its buying divisions, it loses in one of its selling divisions. There is no gain in aggregate profits. That is why Ford and General Motors spun off their parts manufacturing activities into two new firms. They thought they could get a better deal from Delphi and Visteon if they weren't part of General Motors and Ford.

Meltdowns such as those in Asia in 1997 substantially increase downward price pressures. Countries such as South Korea have to export more to correct their trade deficits, and with much lower exchange rates they can profitably do so. If their global competitors do not want to lose market shares, they have no choice but to match the Korean price reductions. With a 50 percent decline in the value of its currency, Korean products could be sold for 50 percent less. Japanese export prices had to come down.

Stopping deflation is not easy. In the 1930s a wide variety of approaches were tried, among them instituting minimum selling prices, providing government price supports, and destroying sources of supply—plowing up planted fields before they could be harvested. They all failed.

Once deflation has set in, there is only one cure—a huge sudden fiscal stimulus. In the Great Depression it took the huge fiscal stimulus and change in expectations caused by World War II to do the job. In Japan it will require a large systematic reduction in the value of outstanding debts followed by a big fiscal stimulus. Reducing Japanese debts need not be called bankruptcy, but whatever the process is called, the debts must be reduced. A large part of the fiscal stimulus package might be directed toward writing down all debts by some percentage, say 80 percent. If the prices of positive assets (property and stocks) have fallen by 80 percent, then the value of negative assets has to be reduced by a corresponding amount.

The Japanese often point to their large existing budget deficit and argue that they can do little more. The size of the Japanese government's current budget deficit is simply irrelevant to the actions that will have to be taken. When the Japanese have blasted their way out of deflation, they can worry about restoring fiscal balance. An accumulation of past mistakes cannot be allowed to foreclose future opportunities to restart the Japanese economy.

Although nothing can be done to change Japan's past or the fact that East Asia has caught the deflationary disease from Japan, elsewhere prevention has to be the first line of defense. Prevention starts by not letting the inevitable financial crashes of capitalism expand into long-term economic disasters. What to do and what not to do are obvious if we compare the U.S. Savings and Loan crisis and Japan's Lost Decade.

The GDP data for the 1980s show no signs of the American Savings and Loan crisis. A major financial crash had little or no impact on the system's aggregate economic performance. Why? In America a czar could be appointed to clean up the mess, the funds necessary to protect bank depositors could be collected from taxpayers, families could walk away from their mortgages when they exceeded the current value of their homes, bankruptcies could be imposed, assets used as collateral could be auctioned off to the highest bidder, and those individuals who crossed the line into illegality could be thrown in jail. The system was sound. It picked up the pieces and smoothly moved on with little or no damage to short-run or long-run economic performance.

Japan could do none of the above. As a result, Japan went from being the industrial world's best performer in the 1980s to being its worst performer in the 1990s. The system was not sound. Systems that don't work have to be changed, and the changes don't happen automatically. Only the Japanese can determine whether the world is going to see the Japan of the 1980s or the Japan of the 1990s in the decade ahead. Solutions demand a change in Japan's culture, and only Japan can change its own culture.

More important, everyone has to recognize that an inflation prone era in the 1970s and the 1980s ended in the 1990s. Those running central banks have to understand that they have won the war against inflation and are now in a new war against deflation. If they don't recognize the victory they have had and continue to wage a war against inflation, they are only going to throw their country's economies into deflation.

Inflation was endemic to the economic system in the 1970s and the 1980s. Faster growth and lower unemployment quickly led to more inflation. But in the 1990s inflation rates fell even as growth accelerated and unemployment reached levels not seen in more than thirty years. The disappearance of inflation in the 1990s marked the fact that something fundamental had changed. If booms produce very low and falling inflation rates, recessions or even slow growth are very likely to produce deflation. And this became the case in 2002. Despite a reasonable recovery in terms of aggregate economic growth rates (2.4 percent) the real wages of American workers fell at all income levels in 2002—at the tenth percentile, at the fiftieth percentile, and at the ninetieth percentile.[2] A new deflation prone era has begun. The central dangers are now deflation, not inflation.

Europe should take warning from what is happening in Asia and America and start aggressively stimulating its economies with monetary and fiscal policies to prevent deflation. With downward price pressures flowing from new, more efficient technologies and from new, cheaper global supply chains, letting the second largest economy in the world operate for a long period of time at or near a zero growth rate is a recipe for producing deflation.

To cope with deflation, fiscal policies will have to be reorganized to become part of the solution to recessions and slow recoveries. To make fiscal policies an equal partner with monetary policies in turning recessions around, new procedures are needed. The issue is delay. Getting tax reductions or expenditure increases through Congress simply takes too long. One answer would be to have a congressionally pre-approved package of short-term tax and spending plans triggered by some economic index or by an independent board much like the Federal Reserve Board.[3]

In the spring of 2003 President Bush did succeed in getting another tax cut through Congress, but once again it focused on long-term tax cuts rather than short-term fiscal stimulus. Whatever one thinks about the double taxation of dividends, cutting long-term dividend taxes in half is not going to stimulate the economy in 2003 or 2004.

Similarly, Europe has to build some flexibility into its stability pact. Rigid fixed limits on fiscal deficits, regardless of the existing economic conditions, don't make macroeconomic sense.

Much of countercyclical spending should go to preplanned infrastructure projects because they have the great advantage that the extra spending ends when the projects are completed. Infrastructure projects, no matter how big, don't make long-run deficits larger. Adult education is the other place where spending should rise in recessions. Labor remains idle, and it is a perfect time to retrain the labor force. Firms should be subsidized to put a substantial fraction of their labor hours into retraining—both reducing unemployment and upgrading the labor force. Here again the spending ends when the downturn ends and workers return to employment.

America also needs to reinstitute countercyclical revenue sharing for state and local governments. Vigorous economic recoveries are difficult to engineer if state and local governments are cutting spending and raising taxes by tens of billions of dollars during the initial phases of a recovery.

Since all capitalistic locomotives have built-in stop-go economic engines, having three global locomotives (Japan, Europe, and the United States) rather than one (the United States) would do a lot to reduce global stagnation and deflation. When one engine was stopped, the other two would still be going. Here the problem is not deciding what to do in Europe and Japan but creating in those countries a mind-set that is willing to do what must be done.

A FALLING DOLLAR

The comet hurtling toward the global economy is a "sharply falling dollar." In the spring of 2003 with the overall (trade-weighted) value of the dollar having fallen 12 percent in the previous twelve months, that comet did not look like science fiction. What should be done about the dangers of a falling dollar is well known.

The American trade deficit should and will eventually disappear, of course. On that issue there is no debate. But a hard landing and a rapid swing from deficit to surplus would be a worldwide disaster. There is one, and only one, route to a soft landing however. Surplus countries have to use monetary and fiscal policies to stimulate their economies to grow faster. If surplus countries adjust, they raise their demands for goods and services and the world economy gets bigger. If the deficit country is forced to adjust, it must reduce its demands for goods and services and the world economy gets smaller. Our only choice is to eliminate the U.S. trade deficit in the context of a rising global GDP or in the context of a falling global GDP.

But recommendations that the surplus countries stimulate their economies have been made many times and are going to be ignored in the countries with the large surpluses just as foreign suggestions to raise savings rates are ignored in America. It is clear that no preventive measures either in America or abroad are going to be taken to prevent a fall in the value of dollar. Americans and foreigners are going to wait for an attack on the dollar to happen—and they will react after they see how much damage is done.

In foreign exchange crises there is a standard IMF remedy: dramatically raise interest rates to discourage capital flight and to encourage capital inflows. Raise taxes, cut spending, and generate budget surpluses to increase local savings, cut consumption, and reduce imports. If applied to America in the midst of a foreign exchange crisis, this formula is a remedy for global economic disaster. An American recession due to high interest rates and fiscal austerity would compound a rest-of-the-world recession caused by the quick disappearance of their trade surpluses.

But it will be politically difficult to argue that America should be treated differently from everyone else. Officially, the IMF will almost have to demand that the United States do what it tells everyone else to do—raise interest rates, raise taxes, and cut spending. Since America does not need the IMF's dollars to stem the crisis, the IMF will have no power to enforce any of its views on America, but calls for austerity will certainly muddle the situation.

A new model for handling foreign exchange crises will be needed, since this crisis will be very different than those in the post–World War II period. When the dollar does inevitably plunge, the appropriate response is for everyone to immediately adopt highly stimulatory monetary and fiscal policies. The Keynesian pedal will have to be pressed to the metal if the global economy is not to stall and crash. Without such actions, a falling dollar is going to lead to a big downturn in global aggregate demand.

Working out a plan in advance of the crisis has to be better than working out a plan in the midst of a crisis. The IMF and the U.S. government should draw up contingency plans for dealing with the case of a sharply falling dollar. In this case the contingency plans are for an emergency that may, in fact, be fast approaching in the spring of 2003 if one looks at the rate at which the value of the dollar is falling vis-à-vis the Euro.

INTELLECTUAL PROPERTY RIGHTS FOR EVERYONE

The long-run health of the global system depends upon an agreed-upon, enforceable global system of intellectual property rights. It is needed and it is to be had. The mantra for the design process is simple: Don't handicap those who want to develop. Find a way to provide cheap medicines for the sick who are poor. Maintain incentives to make huge investments in new ideas.

To facilitate economic development, the amount of legal copying should be made inversely proportional to a country's per capita income, going down as per capita incomes go up. The Doha negotiations should set up a fee schedule for using patents that begins at zero for very poor countries, rises as per capita income rises, and then becomes a market-determined system when a country's per capita income exceeds some level.

To get life-saving drugs to poor people who need them, the right answer is a system much like the eminent domain systems for taking land needed for national infrastructure projects. Rich developed countries simply buy the relevant patents and let everyone freely use them. If the inventing company won't sell, a court sets the fair selling price. This maintains the incentives for invention while giving low cost drugs to everyone who needs them in rich countries and in poor countries alike.

For those countries that don't adopt or won't enforce the agreed-upon system of intellectual property rights, there are simple methods to encourage self-enforcement. The United States simply announces it will keep a country-by-country record of annual sales lost to the infringement of American intellectual property rights. American firms will then be allowed to legally and freely use any patents or copyrights owned by firms based in the offending country. The American firms will continue doing so until the American sales gained by infringing on this foreign country's intellectual property rights are equal to the sales lost by their infringement of American intellectual property rights.

For countries such as Israel that now fail to obey the rules and already have substantial amounts of their own intellectual property, this formula will encourage quick adherence to the rules of the game. Countries without substantial amounts of intellectual property may continue to violate the rules of the game for a while, but they will know they are storing up enormous future intellectual property right debts for themselves if they do so. They will quickly come into compliance.

REDUCING ECONOMIC INEQUALITY

Globalization's impact on inequality depends on how, exactly, inequality is measured—male versus female, top versus middle, middle versus bottom, individuals versus families, or wealth versus income. Nonetheless, antiglobalizers' predictions that inequality will rise are certainly right if one looks at the income gaps between the well educated and the poorly educated. But the prime cause is not found in globalization. The prime cause of rising inequality is the skill-intensive shift built into the third industrial revolution. Unskilled labor is simply going to be worth less and less. That is dictated by technology.

The right answer to rising wage differentials is shrinking skill differentials. Arguments about the relative size of the roles played by globalization, capitalism, and the knowledge-based economy in generating more income inequality are irrelevant. The solution in all three cases is found in education and skill enhancements. This means an all-out push to ensure that everyone develops a set of marketable skills and the ability to learn new skills over the course of their lifetimes. Sets of skills acquired by age 18 or 22 that can be continuously used over a working lifetime are going to be few. Adult re-education is going to have to become a reality rather than a buzzword—much talked about but seldom seen. Education and training have to be the prime answer to rising inequality. Anything else is equivalent to applying cosmetics rather than antibiotics to a serious wound.

In the United States these better skills need to be coupled with mechanisms for reducing average wage differentials between services and manufacturing so that when workers move into service jobs, they don't take a big cut in wages and fringe benefits. Millions have moved into services and millions more are going to move to services.

The right starting place is to abolish the laws that allow those who employ part-time workers to avoid paying health care benefits and pensions. These laws make part-timers cheaper, but turnover rates are very high among part-time workers and as a result skill training is almost never given to part-time workers. If firms were forced to pay full fringe benefit packages to part-time workers, they would switch back to what would become cheaper full-time workers. More training would be given, and average wages would undoubtedly rise in the service sector.

Better-targeted and in some countries larger social welfare benefits may also be needed to prevent inequality. Globalization creates no competitive necessity to cut back on social welfare policies or to refrain from expanding them. It does, however, demand that the system be funded with value-added taxes and not payroll taxes. Because value-added taxes are added to imports and subtracted from exports, value-added taxes do not raise or lower the prices of domestically produced goods and services vis-à-vis the prices of internationally produced goods and services. As a result, only value-added taxes do not affect the global competitive equation. Those who are first to replace corporate income taxes and payroll taxes with value-added taxes are going to get an edge. The governments that are last to realize this reality are going to be governing nations that are falling behind.

CULTURAL THREATS

The feeling that too much of the newly developing global culture comes via the United States is an accurate perception, but the feeling that too much is an export of traditional American culture is wrong. Much of the new global culture is being created in the United States, but far more than half of the ingredients come from other places. This new global culture is changing traditional American culture as fast, or perhaps faster, than anywhere else in the world. The United States is essentially an importer of culture, a modifier of those imported cultures, and then a re-exporter of a new global culture. The goal for others should not be to keep out that American-made global culture but to become more active participants in building their share of this new global culture.

To some extent this is already happening. Part of the success of American-made TV programs was clearly transitory. Most of the world started the TV era with one government-owned and -run television network. The transition to private ownership and multiple networks was marked by a temporary shortage of world programming, and so American programs came to dominate what was watched on these new private channels in many countries. But as these new networks matured and had the time to gradually scale up their own programming, American dominance has all but disappeared. Few American programs are now shown in prime time elsewhere in the world. Local programming has replaced them. The same pattern is apt to happen in movies and in many other cultural areas as well.

Reverse cultural exports are already starting to appear. Americans already watch Taiwanese-U.S. movies (*Crouching Tiger, Hidden Dragon*) and Hindu-U.S. movies (*Monsoon Wedding*), and they will soon probably watch foreign movies that do not have an American link.

But the real answer to fears of a cultural invasion is found in self-confidence—the idea that my culture will survive and it is a great culture even if it changes with globalization.

REJECTING BUT NEEDING GLOBAL GOVERNMENT

Those who object to global government (either international institutions or an American hegemony) have an unsolvable problem. The global economy requires some global regulation, and no democratically elected national government would either accept the direct election of the leaders of international organizations or give those institutions the power to independently collect taxes from their citizens. As a result, institutions like the United Nations, IMF, WTO, and World Bank are simply needed.

Since international institutions have been set up to cover most international economic problems, unilateral American interventions are almost always generated by political and military events. Iraq is obviously the best current example. With or without globalization, geopolitical, military events such as the conflict with Iraq would occur, and there would be calls for the United States to intervene or not to intervene.

When it comes to using U.S. military power, the rest of the world is clearly ambivalent. Half of the time it asks the United States to intervene, as in Kosovo, Bosnia, and Uganda, and half of the time it asks the United States not to intervene, as in Iraq. Half of the time (Iraq) it wants the United States to work multilaterally through agencies such as the UN Security Council, and half of the time (North Korea) it wants the United States to work alone.

Whereas a lot of attention has focused on U.S. decisions to intervene or not to intervene, little attention has focused on Japan's and Europe's refusals to play roles that correspond to their economic wealth and national self-interest. Japan pays little attention to those parts of the world that do not directly affect it. Only China and North Korea get its attention. And even then it is a hand-wringing form of attention rather than attention that leads to actions to avoid or solve problems.

Europe is so focused on building and expanding the European Union that it pays little attention to most of the rest of the world. Put simply, Europe opts out on North Korea, and Japan opts out on Yugoslavia. When the best advice the Europeans can give themselves is to "wait for an American recovery," as they declared when considering how to get out of the mire of the 2001 recession, the world has a problem, but it isn't a problem of too much American leadership. It is a problem of too little global leadership from the other two big players, Europe and Japan.

Europe and Japan must be willing to act to solve some of the globe's geopolitical problems if the United States is not to end up becoming too dominant. This, of course, means being willing to spend money on maintaining their military capabilities. In the end, as Chairman Mao said, "all power comes out of the end of a gun," even if the guns are never used. In Iraq the inspectors might have been able to disarm Saddam Hussein, but they were let back into Iraq only when there were some guns in the neighborhood.

For those who wish to limit U.S. military, political, or economic power, the answer has to be found in harnessing it in a troika with Europe and Japan. And this can happen only if Europe and Japan pull their weight in the troika. If they aren't willing to do so, Americans will decide when and where to accept or reject requests to stay out or jump in. That's just the way it is as long as the United States spends more on defense than the next fourteen countries combined.

LIVING WITH DILEMMAS

Some of the globe's economic problems, such as intellectual property rights and deflation, can be solved. Many of the globe's economic problems, however, are dilemmas. Dilemmas are problems for which there are no acceptable solutions. All potential solutions have negative effects that may be as large as those of the original problem to be solved. Socialism, for example, eliminates financial crises, but it is not an acceptable solution because it also eliminates economic growth. But almost all of the globe's dilemmas can be reduced in scale and scope. Economic instability and inequality are two good examples. Neither can be eliminated, but both can be reduced.

{9}

HELP WANTED:
A CHIEF KNOWLEDGE OFFICER

With three revolutions simultaneously underway, actual economies are not smooth, predictable systems moving along some known path. To understand the effects of the new technologies that are hitting the existing system, we must recognize that the present system's previous path—its history, institutions, and culture—and the system's current momentum—the speed, size, and direction of its movement—matter. Understanding this process, what is called the hysteresis of the system, becomes central to understanding what is happening and what is likely to happen. Knowledge has to be extracted from the hysteresis of the system to build a better, more robust, more inclusive, and more productive global knowledge-based economy.

The importance of understanding the hysteresis of the system can be seen in the Japanese financial crashes of 1990–1991. No economist, including the one writing this book, predicted a subsequent Japanese decade without growth. From the perspective of normal economic analysis, the Japanese stock market and property crash was just a temporary downward perturbation, much like the

U.S. Savings and Loan crisis a few years earlier. But the Japanese system did implode. The forces hitting the Japanese economy—specifically the end of the bubble economy and the advent of the third industrial revolution—required Japan to build a new economy very different from what had existed before, but the historical, institutional, and attitudinal forces of the old Japanese economy made that change impossible.

What is important is not so much adopting policies to cope with these new events but building processes, institutions, beliefs, and attitudes that will allow individuals, companies, and countries to deal with the fast changing world that is going to confront them. To lead us in understanding what is happening and how we might respond to it, we need both a thought process and institutions that can best be described by thinking about the appointment of a chief knowledge officer, a CKO. This person leads us in understanding the hysteresis of the system in which we now find ourselves.

Much of the anxiety about globalization flows from the concern that everyone is going to have to change standard modes of operation. The concern is justified since changes will certainly be required. Individuals, firms, and nations are going to need new business models if they are to succeed economically. The realization that fundamental changes are required to survive economically is, in fact, the biggest asset any individual, company, or country can have. All have to believe that new inputs are not being put into the old system but are interacting to produce a new system where the basic structure of the system is in flux. If they really believe this is so, they will be willing to develop, explore, and adopt new business models. Humans simply won't do this as long as they believe they can remain successful by continuing what they have been doing. Human beings like to say they like change but, in fact, they hate change.

When it comes to illustrating the fundamental changes in business models that will be necessary in the old economy, the world's music industry is the best example. People often joke that the world's oldest industry is prostitution, but it is, in fact, professional music. As far as human history can be traced, people have been paid to play music at weddings, funerals, and other religious events. But the world's professional music industry is now headed toward economic extinction.

Copyrights still exist but have become unenforceable. Using MP3 technologies, young people can download music from the Internet and trade music with each other at quality levels just as good as the original. The Napsters who try to promote copying on a large scale can be put out of business with copyright infringement suits, but no one can stop millions of young people from trading music with each other. Fifteen thousand illegal music copying sites were closed in 2000, but these closings did not even slow down the process.[1] Steve Jobs and Apple are trying to save the industry by offering very cheap legal downloads ($0.99 per CD), but why should people pay anything for something they can get free? They won't and they don't. Experiments show buyers won't even pay token amounts to make their copying legal.

The sales of music are on a steep downward slide. Sales of CDs were down 10 percent in 2001 and 13 percent in 2002.[2] A big industry-wide sales drive during the Christmas 2002 selling season did nothing to reverse the trends. The ownership of CD burners is up from 14 percent to 40 percent of the population in just two years, and blank discs for recordings are now outselling recorded CDs. Simply extrapolating current trends does not lead to accurate sales forecasts, but if one does extrapolate today's downward trends, CD sales will reach zero in 2011.

The music industry has to find a new business model. Industry leaders have to use the new technologies to find ways to lock up their product so people cannot get music without paying for it. Perhaps listeners will be sold a device with an embedded debit card where they automatically pay per play. If they attempt to open the device to get at the digital code, it self-destructs. Whatever the answer, there has to be an answer or the world's oldest industry will soon become the world's newest business casualty.

What is happening to music is not unique. Sooner or later every old business will face the equivalent of the music problem. Every business is going to need a new business model if it is to remain in existence. When giving lectures I often play a game with my audiences. During the question period I ask them to give me the name of any old industry and I will tell them how the new technologies are going to blow up that industry's current business model. Music is different only in that the crises have come faster than in other old industries.

Put simply, the right business models for the world of the slide rule are not the right business models for the world of the computer. The right business models for the world of national industrial economies are not the right business models for a knowledge-based global economy. The right business models for a quasi-socialistic world are not the right business models for a much more capitalistic world.

And there is a simple bottom line for governments. When businesses change their mode of operations, governments have to change their models of governance.

THE COMPANY CKO

It is easiest to understand the role of the CKO if we start with what she or he might do in that job at a business firm. In the newly developing global knowledge-based economy of the 21st century, getting the edge in the sense of knowing where the edge is to be found is the job of the chief knowledge officer.

This is not a job for the CEO. It is not a part-time job: the CEO is too busy to do it. Neither is it a job for the head of research and development whose job it is to focus on building new technologies once the decision to build them has been made. Nor is it the job of the chief technical officer, who understands broad scientific choices and alternative technology road maps. The CKO is not the navigator, the strategist, or the tactician. The CKO brings to all of these other functions what they need to do their job—knowledge about the nature of the new system in which they will command, navigate, and plot their long-run or short-run strategies and tactics.

The CKO's job is much like that of the head of the CIA. Instead of providing honest, unbiased intelligence about foreign powers, the CKO provides honest intelligence about technology and its interaction with economics and society. Foreign affairs teach us that if the people responsible for operations provide their own foreign intelligence, they will tend to provide information and analysis that fit their preconceptions of what they want to do rather than providing the most accurate information and analysis possible. Technological and economic intelligence is no different. If it is collected by people with operational responsibilities, technological and economic intelligence will be biased consciously or subconsciously toward what operational people want to do which is to continue doing what they have been doing.

Bill Gates at Microsoft is the prototype business CKO. He demoted himself from being the CEO of Microsoft and promoted himself to being the CKO of Microsoft. His actual job title is "Chief Software Architect," but in a software firm this is the CKO. What he should do in his CKO role is being invented as he defines the parameters of his new job, but in the words of Microsoft's new CEO, Steve Ballmer, it is Bill Gates' job to see how "emerging software technologies can be woven together and parlayed into must-have industry standard products."[3] It is his job to ensure that Microsoft continues to control the channel of technology that has made it rich. Focusing on this problem and not on running the company, he can be the determining factor in Microsoft's future success or failure. His time, "Bill Capital," as it is called at Microsoft, is the firm's most valuable asset.

Historically, the role of the CKO will evolve during the third industrial revolution much as the role of the chief financial officer (CFO) evolved during the first and second industrial revolutions. Eventually the CKO will come to hold the role in the corporate hierarchy now held by the CFO, usually the second most important person after the CEO.

The CFO got the number 2 position by creating real competitive advantage for the company. When capitalism was in its infancy in the 19th century, no one understood how capital should be managed. If a firm could figure out how to manage capital before its competitors did, it could be a winner. Someone had to think deeply about how a firm's scarce resource, capital, should be managed. It wasn't a part-time job. The CEO was too busy running the company to do it.

But before the position of CFO was born, businesses first had to learn that a chief accountant was not enough, that a chief accountant plus a controller were not enough, and that a chief accountant, a controller, and a treasurer all together were still not enough. None had the position from which to formulate a strategic vision of how capital should be managed. In addition to these three jobs, the firm also needed a CFO. But it took a substantial period of time before this realization sank in. The title CFO did not come into general usage until the 1970s—more than a century after capitalism had begun.

In retrospect, that the CFO emerged as one of the dominant players is not surprising. Capitalism was, after all, called capitalism because capital was the scarce resource. It was the controlling variable. But today the management of capital is a commodity. No firm is going to win because it has a better CFO. Everyone has a good CFO. And if they don't, a good CFO can easily be hired from Goldman Sachs. Good business schools like MIT believe that the necessary financial engineering skills can be learned in eighteen months in their MBA programs.

Eventually every firm will have a CKO. Those who get there first will have a competitive edge. Today, no one knows exactly what this person should do, since the job is being invented on the job. What the person does will differ from industry to industry just as CFOs don't do exactly the same thing in every firm and in every industry. Eventually the CKO, like the CFO, will become a commodity, but in the meantime a good CKO will mean the difference between a mediocre economic performance and a great economic performance.

Although no one knows exactly what the company CKO should do, it is possible to spell out a menu of possibilities.

Should the firm buy, sell, or make its technologies? This is not a decision to be made by the head of research, whose job it is to make new technologies in the most efficient possible way once the decision to make new technologies has been made. A wider perspective of the direction of social and economic systems is necessary to make decisions about whether to make, buy, or sell technologies. Recommendations to buy, sell, or make new technologies are the job of the CKO.

Cisco decided the right strategy was to buy technology. Cisco did not do research, but it was very good at finding, buying, and keeping the people at innovative small firms that did good research. Eighteen such companies were acquired in 1999 and twenty-three in 2000.[4] For Cisco in its golden years, before the 2001 recession, when it had a currency (a high stock market value) that made buying technology cheap, the decision to buy was a highly successful strategy.

What is the biggest business mistake made in the last half century? At peak stock market values in March 2000 it was a $559 billion mistake: Steve Jobs' decision not to sell the Apple operating system. He had, and perhaps still has, a better operating system than Microsoft's. He could have been Bill Gates with a company worth $582 billion rather than having a company with the $23 billion valuation of Apple Computer.[5] There is a right time to sell.

But someone has to figure out that selling a company's technology is the right decision. It is unlikely to be the same person who invented the technology. Inventors are too attached to their inventions. Fortunately for Microsoft, Bill Gates did not invent the original DOS Microsoft operating system. It was bought from a neighboring firm that had gone bankrupt. What is bought is easily sold. What is invented is hard to sell.

Intel neither buys nor sells. It makes its own technologies. And for them that has been a very successful strategy.

The CKO knows why "buy" is right for Cisco, "sell" is right for Apple, and "make" is right for Intel.

Countries face the same choices, and so the national CKO should also know whether make, buy, or sell is the right national choice when it comes to acquiring the technologies that will allow the country's citizens to succeed.

Firms talk about bench marking themselves technologically, but very few firms seriously do it. Some operational person is given the bench marking task and predictably comes back with one of two reports: Our firm's technologies are just as good as those of anyone in the world. (If it weren't true, I would not be doing my job well and you would fire me.) Or our firm is far behind technologically and needs a lot of new investments to become competitive. (I have wanted these expensive toys for a long time.) Operating people cannot do honest bench markings. They are too closely attached to existing technologies. Bench marking is a job for a CKO who is knowledgeable about technology but is not responsible for the existing operating technologies of the company.

Countries also need to benchmark vis-à-vis the competition. The European Union recognized this reality at its Lisbon summit in 2000 when it recognized it was falling behind the United States and set itself the goal of becoming the most competitive economy in the world by 2010.

Most large firms will tell you that they have huge gaps between the most technologically advanced parts of the firm and the least technologically advanced parts of the firm. General Motors will tell you that somewhere in the world they have a plant (paint plant, engine plant) that is the best in the world at performing every function, but they will admit they are not equally good everywhere. It is the job of the CKO to ensure that technology moves around the company and that those productivity gaps are eliminated.

Technological gaps between the most-advanced and the least-advanced parts of any economy are much bigger than such gaps within any one firm. For countries, as for companies, reducing those internal technological gaps is central to global success.

The CKO keeps track of where technology is going and where new competitors may arise. Intel doesn't really have to worry that someone will invent the better electronic microprocessor. That is a highly unlikely event. The company's R&D spending dwarfs everyone else's in the field, and the company hires the best people. Intel's real worry is the Polaroid worry. Someone will invent something that makes their product irrelevant. It could happen. Researchers at MIT and elsewhere are working on molecular biologically based computers that could make Intel's electronic microprocessors irrelevant. Intel's CKO would keep track of what is happening with alternative technologies and make sure there are some biologists in the Intel laboratories.

The CKO knows what is hot technologically—and what is not. Nations also have to know what is hot and what is not.

In a knowledge-based economy patents, copyrights, and trademarks become the firm's biggest asset and its biggest source of legal problems. Billion-dollar patent settlements are common. Breaking patents before their legal expiration date is central to generic drug manufacturers' strategies. What one patents is not just a matter of how important a new idea is to the firm. Strategically, it may be necessary to establish a portfolio of patents to trade for the use of other firms' patents. IBM and HP have such an arrangement. If a firm does not have a patent portfolio, a firm has nothing with which to trade.

How does one fight the patent wars? It is not the job of the firm's patent lawyers. Patent lawyers file new patents, defend old patents, and break the patents of others after the orders to do so have been given. Defining a strategy for fighting the patent wars is the job of the CKO.

Consider three words: "*cluster*," "*picket*," and "*submarine* patents.*" If the CEO does not know the meaning of these three words, the firm definitely needs a CKO.

During the 2000 Christmas season Amazon suddenly announced

that it had a patent on "one click" checkout and sought to stop other electronic retailers from using "one click" checkout systems. Even if this patent is eventually thrown out by some judge, it significantly disrupted Amazon's competition for a Christmas season—and it costs only $15,000 for the patent. The Amazon patent was a *submarine* patent. You don't see it coming until it torpedoes you.

Dell computer has thirty-six patents on supply chain management. The company hasn't sued anyone for patent infringement but it might. What happens if Dell arrives at your firm's door one day with an injunction stopping your firm from using its system of supply chain management on the grounds that it violates Dell patents? The CKO should have figured out what the firm's response should be, and the right defense, long before the injunction arrives.

Polaroid received more than a billion dollars from Kodak in a patent infringement case on instant photography because it has a *cluster* of patents around its key inventions. One patent almost never protects an important idea. Any one patent can always be invented around. True protection of any fundamental idea requires a cluster of patents. Patent every little detail necessary to use the technology.

Someone has patented a key idea central to your firm's future. You want to use that idea. Instead of paying for their important idea, you patent a set of trivial details around their important patent—you establish a *picket* fence of patents—to stop them from using their own idea. Then you trade the use of your trivial picket patents for the use of their important core patent. The Japanese are often accused of establishing picket patents to obtain the use of core breakthrough ideas without paying for them.

Cycles of birth, growth, maturity, decline, and death among business firms are produced by a set of complex interactions between technology and economics. They are not understood with linear projections. During industrial revolutions, technology is full of periods of punctuated equilibrium, that is, long periods of slowly changing conditions interrupted by periods of sudden change. Disruptive new technologies replace old technologies. Firms face inflection points where growth rates suddenly surge or slow down. Cycles of birth and death become harder to understand for both companies and countries.

Wealthy industrial economies have potential long-run economic growth rates in the neighborhood of 3 to 4 percent. Workforces grow at 1 percent per year, and labor productivity grows at 2 to 3 percent per year. Growth companies by definition outperform the market. As a result, growth companies live in industries with growth rates in excess of 4 percent. Those keeping up with the market, mature companies, face growth rates of 2 to 4 percent per year, and those falling behind the market, declining companies, live in industries with growth rates of less than 2 percent.

The CKO understands that every product reaches the day when it becomes mature and growth rates slow down. Most industries will reach the day when their output starts to decline in both relative and absolute terms. Recognizing when these changes are about to occur and responding accordingly before the changes are obvious is as important as picking the right technical strategy in an emerging industry. Those in charge of operations always want to push on doing what they have been doing for as long as possible. The last thing they want to do is to admit that the world has changed and that they have to change what they have been doing.

Every market eventually reaches saturation and maturity. The personal computer, for example, gets to a technological point where more speed and smaller size are irrelevant for most users. Fewer and fewer buyers want a new computer simply because it is more powerful. All those who economically need or want a personal computer already have one. And every device is not a TV set, where saturation means that 98 percent of the population have one. Peak computer penetration seems to have been reached with only about two-thirds of all American households having a computer. The other one-third may see no need for a computer or rely on using libraries or cyber-cafes when then want to go online–just as many Americans go to the Laundromat rather than owning a washing machine. When peak penetration is reached, the PC market becomes a replacement market (inevitably a smaller market) rather than a growth market. It is the job of the CKO to understand this cycle and inform the firm where computers stand in this cycle. How the firm reacts to this information is the job of the CEO.

The failure of many firms to get ahead of the curve in understanding the life cycles of their industries can be seen in the 2001 recession. While American recessions are completely normal, the 2001 recession had some different characteristics precisely because it occurred in the midst of an industrial revolution. Think of the big-name companies that went broke in the 2001 recession: Swissair, Polaroid, Bethlehem Steel, K-Mart, Burlington, Chiquita, Global Crossing, Enron, WorldCom, Adelphi, Arthur Anderson, Arthur D. Little, United Airlines, and U.S. Airlines. Of the ten biggest bankruptcies in U.S. history, six occurred in 2001 and 2002.[6] In the two and one-half years after the stock market crash of March–April 2000, seventy-one firms with assets of over $1 billion went broke.[7] The crashes weren't limited to small start-up dot.coms.

Name the famous big-name companies that went broke in the bigger 1990–1991 recession. You can't. There weren't any. Normally, big companies that have survived a number of recessions don't go broke in recessions, especially a recession so mild there were arguments for a while as to whether a recession had really occurred. Arthur D. Little was the oldest consulting company in America with over one hundred years of history. It has seen many a recession. None of these companies went broke because of the 2001 recession. The recession was just that added bit of financial stress that pushed them over the line—the trigger, but not the cause.

These companies also did not go broke because their managers had suddenly gotten stupid. They went broke because a technical revolution had changed their world. Suddenly their old business models did not work. And they had not been able to discover the new models that might work—often because successful new business models did not exist in their old industries.

Polaroid went broke because of the invention of digital photography and one-hour developing, not because of general recession–induced cutbacks in consumer spending. One can argue that Polaroid should have been more aggressive in its attempts to get into digital photography, but the company clearly saw digital photography coming and made what can only be called an all out effort to get into digital photography. It predictably failed. Why? How is a company with all of its technological strengths in chemistry going to be the leader in a new electronic technology when it is up against the world's best electronics companies, companies such as Sony? It had no chance of winning the race in digital photography. Spending money in an attempt to win was equivalent to throwing money into the Charles River.

Since Polaroid's core business, instant photography, was declining only slowly, Polaroid could have profitably slowly ridden down its sales curve to a very comfortable ending. It would not have been an exciting growth company with a high price-earnings (P/E) multiple on the stock market (in 1968 it had a P/E of 95), but it could have returned a lot more money to its shareholders and provided a lot more jobs to its employees if it had not attempted to resist the inevitable. What Polaroid needed was a skillfully managed strategy for decline.

But almost no one can develop or execute such a strategy. Skillfully managed decline is not a management failure, but it is widely seen as a management failure. If a firm can be a last survivor, there is often a very profitable niche to be found. General Electric, often described as America's best-managed company, can be seen as a collection of last survivors: electric locomotives, power systems, and aircraft engines.

There are more horses today in America than there were in 1900, and providing services, such as making horse shoes, for what is now a luxury industry catering to the rich is a lot more profitable than providing services to what used to be basic transportation. Someone is making a lot of money making a limited number of very expensive horse carriages. At the end of the line there is often a lot of money to be made.

Consider the problems faced by Swissair as it went broke. Just a decade earlier it was one of the world's most profitable and admired airlines. Its Swiss mangers did not suddenly suffer from amnesia and forget how to run an airline. Globalization forced a change in how successful airlines must be managed. In the airline industry of the 21st century there is room for big global alliances such as the Star Alliance, flying hundreds of planes to many destinations, and there is room for low cost point-to-point airlines using secondary airports—Southwest in the United States or Swissair's own Crossair subsidiary in Europe are good examples—but there is no room for midsize national airlines with eighty planes.

Swissair hoped to join one of the big global alliances, but those global alliances wanted bigger and better European partners. Not being asked to dance by the big guys, it tried to create its own global alliance by buying up airlines (Sabena) no one else wanted. But there were reasons why no one else wanted these firms: They weren't the building blocks necessary to create an effective global airline. In attempting to build its own alliance, Swissair just lost money faster and went broke faster than it would have had it remained on its own.

There was a winning Swissair strategy. In the midst of an industrial revolution, the correct strategy for many firms is to sell their valuable assets and exit their industry. If Swissair had sold its very valuable landing slots at some of the world's busiest airports (Kennedy, Heathrow, and Narita) in the mid to late 1990s, exiting its core business, it would have had a lot of money to distribute to its shareholders. It still owned Crossair and had a successful airport service business (Gateway). It could have continued as a corporation in these businesses. But the company found it virtually impossible to see going out of business in its core business as the most profitable strategy. Had the CEO tried to sell off the landing slots, he probably would have been fired.

It is the job of the CKO to point out that the system has changed and that old business models no longer work. Exit can be the right answer.

Consider Compaq's reluctant decision to exit the personal computer industry by selling itself to Hewlett-Packard. Compaq sold personal computers through retail dealers, but it knew that Dell's electronic build-to-order model using telephone and Internet sales was a much lower cost model. When new computer models come out, retailers are not left with a lot of the old models to be sold at drastically knocked down prices. Electronic sales channels also let the manufacturer instantly know what is selling and what is not selling. Manufacturers don't have to wait until the inventories pile up at the retailers to change their production plans.

But Compaq also knew its current dealer network would quit selling its products the minute they heard that Compaq was planning to go electronic. Since it takes time to gear up to sell electronically, the shift could cost Compaq six to twelve months of sales. Sales would fall to zero during the transition. Once its customers shifted to different suppliers, they might never come back. Compaq knew where it needed to be, but getting to that profit maximizing point was difficult, expensive, and perhaps impossible. The economic dilemma is simply stated: The present sales strategy leads to extinction, but the firm cannot navigate a shift to the sales channel that leads to survival.

As yet no major company has had the guts to take the short-run hit and shift distribution channels. And perhaps they shouldn't. The losses come early and the gains much later. Using discounted net present values, it is possible, perhaps likely, that the current discounted net present value of the profit stream that leads to extinction (stick with the old sales channel) is greater than the current discounted net present value of the profit stream that leads to long-run survival (move to the new sales channel). The right economic answer to this problem is as simple and straightforward as it is brutal. Choose the old sales channel that leads to economic suicide. Don't waste money looking for magic cures. Slow decline and eventual exit are the right, most profitable strategies. The goal is paying out the most money relative to what was initially paid in, not being the company that stays alive the longest. Had the company sold out earlier, Compaq would have been worth a lot more money to its shareholders.

McDonald's problems are not those of exit. They are those of maturity. The company's success was built on being a fast food hamburger chain catering to families with children in an era where mothers were increasingly going into the paid labor force and more and more meals were being eaten away from home. Given the number of outlets it already has in America, a declining number of families with children, and meals eaten away from home near or at their natural saturation limits, McDonald's is in a mature industry where sales cannot grow at the rate they have in the past. Outside the United States the company can still grow rapidly, but inside the United States it cannot grow rapidly with its existing business model.

One option is to struggle to find a way out of this dilemma with a new business model. But that there is a way out is not obvious. So far all of the options tried by McDonald's have failed. Each of these failures eats up a lot of money, diverts management attention from running the core business, and disconcerts existing customers as McDonald's switches from one menu to another. These failing attempts to find an alternative business model led McDonald's to report its first ever quarterly loss at the end of 2002 and to announce that it would close more than two hundred stores in the United States and Japan.[8]

McDonald's has yet to recognize that it is in a mature industry where it will earn a lot of money but will be given stock market multiples that are appropriate to a mature industry with slower growth, not those accorded rapidly growing companies in rapidly growing industries. The right strategy is to accept this reality and learn to live with it. Resisting this reality makes things worse, not better. McDonald's needs a CKO to remind them of these facts of life. Making their stores attractive to those in their twenties with Internet connections, their latest strategy, is unlikely to work.

In capitalism companies don't remain successful companies very long. Of the twelve largest firms in America in 1900, only one, General Electric, was still on the list a hundred years later in 2000 and many of the other eleven no longer even exist. Big dying companies don't hurt an economy's performance as long as they are replaced by big growing companies. Death is part of life.

"Staying alive" versus "making the most money relative to what has been invested" lies behind the arguments about the virtues of being a conglomerate firm operating in many different industries versus being a single product–focused firm. When it comes to making money, conglomerates have to be a second best option. Investors can always buy a portfolio of companies that gives them the same risk diversification of a conglomerate. Investors don't want money diverted internally from the successful aspects of the conglomerate to keep the less successful parts of the conglomerate going. But if the issue is survival, conglomerates are a first best option. The transistor destroyed General Electric's vacuum tube business, once its most profitable division, but the company survived as one of America's largest companies because of its many other activities. More focused companies on the 1900s list of the twelve largest companies, like International Harvester (farm machinery) and Anaconda (nonferrous metals), did not survive.

The CKO tries to determine when an industry has become mature, when it is smart to retreat, and when the time for exit has arrived. Understanding these realities is even harder than knowing when and where to advance. No one receives praise for timely retreats or quick exits. It is not the job of the CKO to manage an exit strategy—that is the job of the CEO—but it is the CKO's job to point out the realities companies face as products move through their technological and economic life cycles.

Knowing when to exit is the best example of the need for a CKO. For reasons of ego and peer prestige, finding a CEO able and willing to execute an exit strategy is almost impossible, even when it is clearly the most profitable option. Exit may not be possible for social and psychological reasons. But the firm should have good intelligence about where it stands nevertheless. Those in charge of operations may choose to ignore good intelligence, but they should be forced to have it.

Modern technologies are producing what might be called the barbell economy. In a barbell economy all of the companies are at either end of the barbell (small or big) and no one is in the middle. Go to any strategic consulting company for advice, and they will tell your firm, no matter what its industry, that you face two strategic options: become a dominant global player or become a highly specialized, nimble, niche player. The midsized national firm is doomed to extinction.

In the auto industry, for example, it is widely believed that when the current consolidation is over two decades or so from now, there will be only six to eight firms left standing, and four of the survivors—Volkswagen, Toyota, Ford, and General Motors—are already known.[9] The Volvos, Saabs, Jaguars, Rolls Royces, and Rovers are all gone as independent auto companies. To have a chance at remaining viable and being one of these remaining two to four global players, Mercedes bought Chrysler in 1998 and Renault bought a big piece of Nissan in 2000. How can the Fiats and Peugeots survive? They can't. A big part of Fiat was sold to General Motors.

In finance a firm can aim to become a big global player doing everything everywhere (a Goldman Sachs, for instance) or a niche player, fast on its feet, a player who is the world's greatest expert in some small area of finance but not a midsize national bank or midsize national insurance company. As a result, those who would be corporate survivors must merge to get larger or, where it is not possible to be a global player, sell divisions to become a more focused niche player. Which is the right strategy? What should be bought and what should be sold? The CKO provides the information and context in which these decisions can be made intelligently.

How does a firm find a good CKO, given that the category does not yet exist? Pick some technologically savvy, fast track young person between 30 and 40. Tell them they are the firm's new CKO and they should come back in two months to tell you what they are going to do.

A NATIONAL CKO

Put simply, countries, like companies, have to learn the best way to play the new economic game. Countries have, if anything, a harder learning problem since they are used to playing national economic games where they controlled the rules and regulations. Like companies, they now have to play the game where they do not control the rules and regulations and where they have to learn to be players—and not referees.

Like companies, governments face a knowledge-based future and have inherited a historical emphasis on finance. Ministers of finance or secretaries of the treasury come at or near the top of the pecking order in any cabinet because they understand the intricacies of financing government activities. But, like having a better CFO in a company, having a better minister of finance is not going to yield a future competitive advantage. Having a national CKO who understands where the knowledge-based global economy is headed is where the future edge is to be found.

Warfare is to government what music is to the private economy—its oldest activity. The technologies of the third industrial revolution have created what the French call an ultra or hyper power. A hyper power is a superpower with communication systems that let it see everything, hear everything, and talk to everyone while at the same time shutting down the communications systems of its enemies, rendering them deaf, dumb, and blind.

As we saw in Iraq, an ultra power has the ability to use all of the new communication, sensing, and precision weapons to fight a very different war than has been fought in the past.[10] Ground sensors are dropped from planes to locate enemy soldiers and vehicles (some can be seen through one hundred feet of rock), small micro-robotic drones give bird's-eye views of enemy territory, land-based robotic munitions automatically attack enemy vehicles with armor piercing projectiles, and unseeable stealth bombers attack from the air. Miniaturization is key—thirty-pound sensors become three-pound sensors.[11] Just a glimpse of what is to come was seen in the fighting in Iraq. This is a military revolution that is just getting underway. In the future small robots, not human soldiers, will do the house-to-house searches for snipers.

Ultra powers require different military models than those used in the past. Clausewitz, in his military classic *On War*, emphasizes that the main military problem during a war is the "fog of war"— no one knows precisely where their own troops or those of the enemy are located.[12] But with modern technology the fog of war is gone. The ultra power knows exactly where its own troops are (soldiers each carry an electronic chip that locates them using the GPS to within one meter at every moment in time), and as long as the ultra power is fighting a conventional army, sensors and satellites can show the exact location of enemy troops.[13] The enemy can disappear only if they fade into the civilian population. Because of this knowledge-based revolution in military technology, generals have to have entirely new strategic and tactical battle plans.[14] Conversely, those fighting an ultra power have to abandon their conventional armies and become guerrilla groups using terrorism as their weapon.

There is a reason why the United States is the only ultra power. The shift is expensive. The United States spends more money on defense than do all of NATO, Russia, China, Japan, Iraq, and North Korea combined.[15] And since the American defense budget is rapidly going up while defense budgets are going down in most of the rest of the world, the military spending gap between the United States and the rest of the world is widening rapidly. The existing spending gap produces a world where America has nine supercarrier battle groups and a tenth under construction, whereas no one else in the world has even one supercarrier. No one else can move an army half way around the world and fight a war in three months. The United States has five types of stealth aircraft deployed or under development. No one else in the world has even one such plane. Its 9,000 M1 Abrams tanks dwarf any other tank forces, and it has by far the best tank killing aircraft. What it means to be a military power and what must be done to remain or become a military power have simply changed.

New technologies and new global realities are requiring similar changes in behavior in civilian government activities. National governments simply cannot regulate the economic game or control its outcome to the degree that has been possible in the past. Firms now have the option of moving their headquarters and their production elsewhere if they don't like national rules and regulations.

These realities are seen in corporate taxation. Political pressure eventually forced Stanley Works to back down, but when the company's executives got shareholder approval to move their headquarters to Bermuda, they estimated they would lower their income tax payments by 28 percent.[16] In America they were taxed on their earnings in the rest of the world, not just their American earnings. In Bermuda they would still have to pay U.S. taxes on their U.S. earnings, but they would not have to pay U.S. taxes on their earnings elsewhere in the world. Many others had already moved—Nabors Industries (the world's largest operator of land-based drilling rigs), Cooper Industries, Ingersoll-Rand, and Weatherford International. Everything else being equal, why would any firm locate in a place with higher taxes? If they were to be so foolish as not to move, they would have higher costs and lose market share. In a real sense, in the long run they have no choice but to move.

Any government that tries to exert the old controls simply finds its institutions legally and electronically moving offshore and outside its jurisdiction of control. Not surprisingly, wishing to hold onto their present regulatory powers, governments talk about controlling the global flows of capital and the regulation of global financial institutions. A Tobin tax (a small tax on each international financial transaction) to slow capital movements among countries is often suggested, but how would you collect it? Global financial markets would simply move to where the tax wasn't levied. There would always be at least one country that would not participate in the system since they would see nonparticipation as the route to their economic success. And they would be right.

Because countries need corporations more than corporations need countries, the relative bargaining power of governments and multinational corporations is shifting in favor of corporations. High profile multinational companies that bring technology, market linkages, and supplier networks with them no longer pay taxes to governments. In this new balance of power, governments often pay taxes to multinational companies. To get an Intel plant, the state of Israel paid Intel $600 million in grants, the financing of plant infrastructure, and tax rebates.[17] Paying taxes to companies may even make sense economically. Intel, for example, is Israel's largest exporter and largest private employer. Countries can refuse to pay taxes to companies but, if they do so, those companies simply locate elsewhere.

The reversal of traditional positions is not limited to developing countries. Huge sums were paid by the citizens of Alabama and South Carolina to get BMW and Mercedes Benz to locate auto assembly plants in their states. The UK, Norway, Germany, and the Netherlands all recently lowered taxes on shipping companies to keep them from legally reorganizing themselves in low tax countries. In even the biggest and wealthiest countries, national economic power is slowly melting away.

Consider the potential American financial crisis surrounding the financial firm Long Term Capital Management. Because of the Russian financial crisis in 1998, European interest rates started to diverge even though they had to converge by January 1999 with the establishment of the Euro. Long Term Capital Management had placed reasonable but very large bets ($1,000 billion) on convergence. Fearing that the collapse of Long Term Capital Management would trigger a U.S. financial crisis, Alan Greenspan organized a rescue when these bets started to go wrong. He was vigorously criticized in the financial press—why not just shut the firm down? But Long Term Capital Management was technically not an American firm. Like most derivative firms, its legal headquarters was in the Cayman Islands, even though its people were in New York, Tokyo, and London. Legally, the Federal Reserve Board had no jurisdiction over Long Term Capital Management. As a result, Greenspan had to operate indirectly through the American banks, over which he did have jurisdiction, that had lent large sums to Long Term Capital Management. The largest and most powerful government in the world had lost some of its powers of economic control.

Many other examples of the loss of governmental economic powers can be given. With modern transportation systems, countries find it is impossible to stop illegal immigration. Millions see better standards of living elsewhere on their village TV sets and decide to move to get those higher standards of living. In the process, what it means to be a country fades. A country that cannot control its own borders is in a fundamental sense not a real country. Similarly, pornography is produced electronically somewhere in the world where it is not illegal, put up on the Internet, and national governments lose their power to enforce their own standards of decency. Much of the pornography in the Persian Gulf, where women with bare arms are regarded as pornographic, originates in the United States.

Third world countries often feel they have completely lost the ability to control their own destinies. This was clearly seen in the 1997 Asian economic crisis. No one country could by itself stop its crisis. In the East Asian meltdowns, the IMF effectively replaced local governments when it came to economic decision making during the economic crisis.

As firms go global, some firms are certainly going to have dominant national market shares. What should antitrust laws do, if anything, about these dominant positions? The Microsoft and General Electric–Honeywell antitrust cases are two good examples of the issues.

Traditionally, antitrust suits are not brought unless it can be shown that the consumer is being hurt. Yet the Microsoft trial began with the economists for both sides agreeing that no consumer had been hurt by Microsoft's large market share in operating systems. The reasons were simple. In software the costs are all in the development phase and almost none of the costs are incurred in making additional copies of the system. If there were a hundred different operating systems each with an equal 1 percent market share (a competitive market), all would have to cover the same large development costs, and the costs of an operating system to the end user would have to be much higher than what was being charged by Microsoft. And whatever you believe about Microsoft's behavior (did it cross the line from aggressive behavior to illegal practices?), its behavior did not create its monopolistic position. It got its dominant position because of what economists call networking effects. Everyone wants to use the same system, since it is simply more efficient if we all use the same system even if better systems exist. Apple's operating systems were certainly better in the 1980s and probably still are better in the early 21st century. But those better systems are irrelevant. No one wants to go into a hotel business office in Hong Kong and have to learn how to use a different system. Applications software programmers don't want to write different programs for many different operating systems. Buyers want to buy the operating system that has the most applications software written for it. If we all buy the same operating system and same applications software, we all have better and cheaper computer systems. If Microsoft had never existed, or if it were now to be broken up by the anti-trust authorities, some other operating system would quickly come to have Microsoft's dominant market share.

Since it is not harming the end consumer, Microsoft effectively stands accused of running other companies out of business. But that is what capitalism is supposed to be all about. Driving the inefficient out of business is what creates capitalism's efficiency.

The time to bring an antitrust case against Microsoft is when there is evidence that the consumer is being hurt.

The General Electric–Honeywell antitrust suit revolved around the same issue. Should a merger be forbidden because it might drive other companies out of business even though that merger would almost certainly lower costs to buyers? Combining GE's engine division with Honeywell's avionic capabilities would not have changed the structure of the aircraft manufacturing industry. Since the two companies' product offerings did not overlap, there still would have been the same number of engine manufacturers and the same number of avionics producers in the industry. Since just a few airlines buy most of the world's commercial airliners and two companies, Boeing and Airbus, make all of the world's commercial airliners, there is no reason to believe that GE-Honeywell would have been able to raise prices above competitive levels. The fear was not that prices would go up. Just the opposite was likely to happen. GE-Honeywell would probably have lowered prices for those who agreed to a package deal where they bought both sets of products from GE-Honeywell. What the European antitrust authorities were worried about was not higher prices to the consumer but precisely that these package deals might lead to lower prices to buyers and drive European competitors out of business.

Whatever one believes about these two cases, they present three global issues. First, antitrust laws need to be consistent in a global economy. The American antitrust authorities had earlier approved the GE-Honeywell merger. Second, antitrust laws have to take into account the impact of new technologies. What seems like an inefficient monopoly can actually lead to lower-cost computing systems. Third, is the purpose of antitrust laws consumer protection or company protection?

In both cases and on both sides of the Atlantic the antitrust authorities needed the advice of a national CKO to help them understand the new global economy in which they were administering laws that had been little changed for a century.

With globalization the scope, reach, and powers of national governments shrink and, as a consequence, governments become less important. If national governments cannot control their own destiny economically, why should their citizens support them politically? Attachments to what look like ineffectual governments grow weaker.

Small successful city-states such as Singapore demonstrate that no one has to live with a neighbor they don't like. Compromising with other ethnic groups so that both of you can live in a larger country with the economies of scale necessary to produce higher standards of living isn't necessary. National economies of scale aren't all that important in a global economy. One can opt out and still succeed economically because the economies of scale that matter are the global economies of scale, which are available to everyone who participates in the global economy.

Outsiders aren't going to intervene to stop this ethnic splintering. The end of the Cold War means that superpowers have little interest in preventing other countries from disintegrating unless they are right next door and the chaos threatens to spread. Local wars in faraway places such as Sudan and Sri Lanka aren't going to bring the superpowers into military conflict with each other.

As a result, countries like companies are merging to become dominant global players or splitting apart to become smaller more focused players. Those splitting to become more focused players include the USSR, Czechoslovakia, and Yugoslavia. Fifteen less diverse more focused countries emerged where the old USSR used to be. Those merging to become dominant global players include everyone in the European Union and those wanting to join it.

In Africa both are going to happen.[18] Ten thousand different ethnic groups aren't going to live forever in a handful of countries defined by the accidental meetings of British and French armies in the 19th century.

In the 20th century, governments came to think of themselves as economic air traffic controllers controlling the flows of their economies. With globalization this power is disappearing for governments large and small. Governments are still important in the knowledge-based economy, but instead of being air traffic controllers of economic events within their borders, governments are increasingly having to becoming airport builders constructing runways to attract global economic activity (local as well as foreign) to locate within their borders. Can they build a good runway where their citizens and their companies can successfully take off and land as they play in the global economy? Is the local airport good enough to let foreign companies land? That economic airport is built out of educated workers, social infrastructure that includes legal systems and the means of ensuring personal safety, and physical infrastructure dealing with transportation, power, and communications. And if one wishes to play at the highest levels, countries must finance the basic research and development that thrusts technology forward.[19]

Countries need to gain control of knowledge streams to maximize their wealth just as firms seek to control knowledge streams to make themselves profitable. As a result, countries, like companies, need a CKO. Consider one of many strategic choices: where should a country invest their R&D funds? Even a country as big as the United States, with a total private and public R&D budget in excess of $300 billion, a budget bigger than the total GDP of most countries, cannot invest in everything.

For all but the very largest countries, decisions as to where to invest are vital. If small or mid-size countries invest in everything, they will be wasting their money since they won't be investing enough to succeed in anything. But if they focus their R&D investments, they risk investing where there are no technological payoffs. The problem is similar to that of drilling oil wells. If one has only money enough to drill one oil well, the risks are very high. Using the money to drill a lot of wells one hundred meters deep is guaranteed not to find any oil. Nations, like firms, need a technological strategy.

Government departments come into being when something seems important enough to warrant a new cabinet position. The auto and air transportation problems of a geographically dispersed American economy led to the creation of the Department of Transportation in 1966. In response to the first OPEC oil shock, the Department of Energy was created in 1977. The new Department of Homeland Security is the most recent illustration of the pattern. Put bluntly, national crises lead to new cabinet departments.

Over time departments grow large, and once in place they are politically impossible to contract or kill. Positions of influence, such as a congressional committee chair, become dependent on their continuation. As a result, cabinet positions are a living historical record of what were once important national issues. Agriculture is the best example. Agriculture is a relatively small industry today. It employs only 2 to 3 percent of the workforce, most of its employees work part time, and it produces only 5 percent of the GDP. Yet in term of employees the Department of Agriculture is one of America's largest departments. If America were starting over today, no one would create a separate department for an industry so small. Similarly, if the war on terror is won and every terrorist in the world disappears, one can bet that the new Department of Homeland Security will continue to exist.

In the rest of the world most cabinets have a minister of trade. America does not have one because America has never had an international financial crisis. As with anti-terrorism activities, trade functions in the U.S. government are spread across a wide number of agencies (a cabinet-level U.S. trade negotiator, Commerce, Treasury, Defense, State, and Justice); as a result, America's trading policies are highly uncoordinated. Logically it would make sense to merge the existing agencies that deal with trade into a single Department of Industry and Trade. To think this is going to happen, however, would be politically naïve.

The congressionally appointed U.S. Trade Deficit Review Commission privately agreed that such a department would make sense but did not even bother to make this recommendation in its report, since it was so outside the bounds of political reality. Even with a huge crisis, other government departments were reluctant to yield the parts of their departments that needed to be moved into the new Department of Homeland Security. None of them wants to become less important; all want to share the extra funding that will go to the agencies that deal with homeland security—or any other new crisis.

If one were being logical and equally naïve, this new Department of Trade and Industry would be complemented by a Department of Knowledge responsible for creating new knowledge and thinking about how America can organize itself to better succeed in a knowledge-based global economy. It would include many of the technology functions now in the Department of Education, the National Science Foundation, the Department of Agriculture, the National Institutes of Health, the Department of Defense, and the Office of the President's Science Adviser. The Department of Industry and Trade would seek to strengthen today's industries, and the Department of Knowledge would seek to create and strengthen tomorrow's industries with the development of leading edge new technologies and skills.

To get either will require big economic crises. America has not had a foreign trade crisis to mobilize support for a single agency that focuses on international trade. When America does have a big balance-of-payments crisis, you can bet that a Department of Trade will be one of the first considerations in Congress. If America starts to slip behind dramatically in the new knowledge-based economy, America will get a Department of Knowledge. But that is to be behind the technological and economic curve rather than to be ahead of the curve. Catch-up is a much harder game to play than keep-up or stay-ahead.

The bottom line is simple. Having a national agency whose permanent job it is to think about how one uses advances in knowledge to make Americans wealthier is as important for the country as having a secretary of defense. Although the creation of such a department won't happen without a crisis, it is still worth thinking about what such a department might do.

Economic development is a process that doesn't happen automatically in either the developed or the developing world. If it did, the world would not have underdeveloped countries or countries that have gone from rich to poor, such as Argentina. Developed and developing countries alike need technology strategies if they are to remain or become economically successful. Development begins with the understanding that economic growth requires something more than free markets. By themselves they will not generate high levels of economic growth.

New Zealand is the prime illustration. Prior to throwing its socialistic inheritance aside, New Zealand was a rapidly slipping high-income country. It had fallen from the position of third richest country in the world per capita in the 1950s to the twentieth position in the early 1980s. In 1984 it began to liberalize, and in the end it went farther than anyone else in the world. It even went so far as to privatize its post office. No one could have done more or has done more.[20] Among countries New Zealand ranks on top in an economic freedom index created by a right-wing think tank.[21] It has none of the afflictions that hold back underdeveloped countries. It is one of the most honest, best-educated, and socially stable countries in the world.

But since freeing its markets, its growth has been the slowest in the developed world—less than half as fast as the OECD average.[22] Its growth per capita is just half as fast after the reforms as it was before the reforms. As a result, New Zealand has slipped farther down the league tables and is now twenty-third in per capita GDP rankings despite its radical free market reforms. Something besides free markets is obviously required.

Defenders of free markets as stand-alone, silver bullet solutions to slow growth often blame New Zealand's failures on agricultural protection in the rest of the world. This protection prevents New Zealand from taking advantage of its natural comparative advantage—namely, that it is the best place on earth to grow animals. But the advantages of free markets are not supposed to depend upon what others do to free their markets.

Being willing to privatize and deregulate at the right time are important. But as New Zealand illustrates, free markets by themselves do not automatically lead to economic growth. In a knowledge-based economy societies have to create their own comparative advantage. It isn't given to them by Mother Nature as gold mines or oil wells or favorable agricultural conditions. Every area of the world has to develop its sources of man-made comparative advantage. It is the job of the national CKO to chart the paths that exist for creating the technological comparative advantages that will lead to any region's global success. New Zealand needed a CKO and did not have one.

The importance of creating man-made sources of comparative advantage can be seen in South Korea and Taiwan. Neither became successful by creating free markets although both have recently freed up their markets. Both first sought to acquire and exploit technologies that would allow them to compete in global markets. They did not centrally plan their economies, but each had a national technological strategy for economic development that revolved around becoming the masters of some particular technologies. But the strategies were different for historical and cultural reasons. One size does not fit all.

The one thing they have in common is education. Both invested to rapidly turn what were countries with high levels of illiteracy into what today are some of the best-educated countries in the world.

Because South Korea's ruling elite had been educated in what was a Japanese colony until the end of World War II, South Korea emulated the Japanese model. Very large export-focused companies were created in a sheltered home market and foreign investments in Korea were discouraged. South Korea spent a lot on research—in percentage terms almost as much as the United States. No other developing country comes close. Among developing countries it is also the only country that has developed global brand names. With a global brand name, Samsung has been able to make itself into the world's largest consumer electronics company.

If success is measured by per capita GDP, Taiwan has been even

more successful than South Korea. Taiwan developed a very different technological model. Taiwan was also a Japanese colony prior
to World War II, but Taiwan ended up being ruled by outsiders
who came from the mainland in 1949. They had not been educated in Japanese ways. Having acquired a socialist inheritance from
their days on the mainland, they were suspicious of large private
monopolies. Whereas South Korea encouraged large companies
and company groups, Taiwan actively discouraged them. Much
smaller family-owned firms were encouraged. To this day Taiwan's
corporations are very restricted when it comes to horizontal or verti-
cal mergers. Large business groups are simply not allowed to develop.
The largest ten companies account for 67 percent of the Korean
GDP but only 17 percent of the Taiwanese GDP. But the socialist
part of that mainland inheritance also shows. Many of the largest
Taiwanese companies are or were government owned, and the state
sector is twice as big in Taiwan as it is in South Korea.

Today Taiwanese companies completely dominate supply chain
manufacturing in electronics, making all of the world's scanners
and most of the world's laptops. The foreign firms that sell these
products provided much of the technology Taiwan needed for exe-
cuting its strategy. They taught Taiwanese firms to make the components and products these foreign firms wanted. But Taiwan's
government-sponsored science parks were also a big part of the
success. They aimed to create advanced production technologies
that Taiwanese firms could use in their supply chain activities. The
government also made investments to help new corporations, such
as the Taiwan Semiconductor Manufacturing Corporation
(TSMC) get started and still holds some of those investments even
though TSMC is one of the country's biggest success stories. Taiwan also has a complex system of tax incentives for high-tech
companies where they pay few taxes if they invest enough.

Our national CKO also knows that the two city-states that are
often given as illustration of simple market success, Singapore and
Hong Kong, are below the surface much more complex and on
some economic dimensions highly regulated. All of the land in

Hong Kong is owned by the government, and at one time 80 percent of the population lived in government housing. Hong Kong
has also bought company shares during stock market crashes. Our
national CKO knows the history: Hong Kong was not rich before
Mainland China started its economic reforms in the late 1970s. It
got rich by moving activities into Mainland China to take advantage of much lower labor costs. It provided the headquarters management skills the mainland needed to penetrate foreign markets
after thirty years of being isolated from the rest of the world; it also
provided the Chinese connections foreigners needed to operate in
the PRC.

Because of its geographic position of being in but not of
China, Hong Kong did not need a technological strategy. Technologically, it is a backward place in comparison with Singapore, Taiwan, or South Korea. As those who have always lived inside the
PRC become more managerially and financially sophisticated, it
will be interesting to see if Hong Kong can hold its economic
place without a technological base. (Hong Kong recognizes this
defect and is now trying to rectify it.)

Singapore is famous for its social regulations, but it also holds or
held a financial stake in every major Singaporean corporation. In
some ways it is socialism done "right." Singapore Airlines, usually
ranked as the world's best and among the most profitable airlines, is
government owned. The government is a major shareholder in
Charter Semiconductor, Singapore's attempt to get into the semiconductor foundry business. Singapore's governmental Economic
Development Board (EDB) aggressively fights for foreign direct
investment and the technology that goes with it. To persuade foreign firms to put their regional headquarters in Singapore so Singapore could become the headquarters city for Southeast Asia, the
government built what is the best infrastructure in the region—and
perhaps in the world.

Looking at Europe, our national CKO would see Ireland evolving a quite different strategy for acquiring the technology necessary
to go in two decades from being one of the poorest countries in

Western Europe to being a country with a per capita GDP that for the first time in its history is above that of England. This growth did not happen because Ireland's markets were freer than those in the UK.

Rather than attempting to create its own technological base, as was done in Taiwan or South Korea, Ireland explicitly sought to import technology by attracting high-tech foreign direct investment. These foreign investors would bring technologies and skills with them that Ireland did not have. Ireland had the basics, a good education system, but it needed something to attract FDI—it had to offer some reason why foreign firms should go to Ireland rather than to some other location.

To gain a competitive advantage, Ireland decided to offer foreign firms a zero corporate income tax rate. If a firm wanted to produce in the European Union, why not do it in Ireland where corporate income taxes did not exist, rather than producing elsewhere where heavy corporate income taxes were going to be collected? If a firm is building products for Europe, why not build them in the country with the lowest taxes? Eventually the European Union forced the Irish to equalize foreign and domestic corporate income tax rates. A single rate of 12.5 percent came into effect in 2003, but this is still far below what is being collected elsewhere in the European Union.

It is true that Ireland got a lot of money from the European Union to help it make infrastructure investments, but so did Greece. Greece and Ireland used to be classified together as among the poorest countries in the European Union. The Greek prime minister says that he does not want to become an "Irish tax haven." He doesn't have to become an Irish tax haven if he has an alternative strategy for acquiring the technologies necessary to move Greece out of its position as the poorest country in the European Union. But he doesn't, and Greece simply remains the poorest country in the European Union.

The lessons of economic development at all levels are clear.

Whether one is rich or poor, one has to get ahead of the technological curve to succeed. This is clearly seen if one looks at the largest and most-advanced economy in the world. America leads the world economically not because its markets or trade policies are freer than those in the rest of the world. They aren't. It is a leader in the world economically because it is a leader, perhaps the leader, in pushing technology forward. This is especially true when there are disruptive technologies that require large changes. America has neither an explicit strategy of picking industrial winners nor a system of giving special tax breaks to high-tech firms, but it does have mechanisms for placing its bets on the technologies that will be winners. A lot of these bets involve government money. The computer was first used by the Defense Department in World War II. The Internet began as a defense communications system in 1968. The National Institutes of Health led the biotechnology revolution.

When it comes to engineering comparative advantages for nations and firms, technology policies are central to economic success and failure. Those who are just slightly ahead of the wave win; those who are just slightly behind the wave lose. Finding the route for getting up on that economic/technological surf board is what the job of the corporate or national CKO is all about.

{ 10 }

THE STRUCTURE AND
ATTITUDES OF SUCCESS

The economic institutions, policies, and practices for reshaping a better globalization can be built. The more difficult problem is embedding the right attitudes in the right social structures. All social and economic systems require a set of congruent attitudes if they are to be successful.

Ancient Egypt was the world's biggest economy and had the globe's highest standard of living in its time. Technologically, it was the leader. The elite had learned to read and write. They could send messages and keep records. They were the first to organize an irrigation system. To do so, Egypt had to build the social organization required to erect the canals that could direct and allocate the waters of the annual floods on the Nile.

For Egyptians boldness meant being willing to undertake construction projects that soared into the sky (the pyramids) or burrowed deep into the ground (the Valley of the Kings). These were construction projects that had never been undertaken, and nothing similar in scope and scale would be undertaken again for thousands of years.

Egypt was not a democracy. A pharaoh ruled. To do so he had to have followers who believed in continuity and the wisdom of the pharaonic system even when the pharaoh was not wise. Looking back modern humans probably cannot even understand the attitudes that produced Egypt's success. Think of a belief in the afterlife so strong that it led to the building of what were to become the world's largest structures for thousands of years—pyramids designed to last forever, but built for only one man after he died. Think of the expense in terms of hours of work. Modern humans would rise up in riot and revolution if similar economic sacrifices were demanded of them.

Congruent attitudes, social organization, and culture made Egypt's success possible while most in the rest of the world were illiterate hunter-gathers.

Later successes such as those of ancient Greece or Rome tell similar stories. Each in their day was the world's economic leader because they acquired new technologies and because they were able to organize them into new productive systems. Think of the stadiums that were built all across the Roman Empire to host gladiatorial games. Thousands of people and animals were slaughtered in a single day in the Coliseum in Rome. These were not the equivalent of auto races, where modern spectators come to see the thrill of a possible accident. In Rome the route to political and economic success ran through a military career. Rome's military empire required hand-to-hand up close combat with its enemies. It required an individual willingness to die and a population that did not see death as abhorrent. The gladiatorial games were necessary to build the right attitudes.

The British Empire was made possible by the first industrial revolution. As the industrial pioneer, Britain had the wealth to conquer countries and create an empire and the technology to build a navy to defend it. It became a British Empire, not someone else's empire, because of British beliefs and attitudes—its social organization. Nothing about it was similar to the world's previous biggest empire, the Roman Empire. It wasn't constructed in the same way or maintained in the same way. One was contiguous; the other was scattered around the globe. One insisted that everyone participate in Roman culture; the other did not encourage subject peoples to adopt the British culture. The attitudes that lay behind the British Empire were very different from those that lay behind the Roman Empire, but it was a set of attitudes that allowed the British to take advantage of the first industrial revolution. The Romans could not have done so.

Today no one could organize successful societies based on the Egyptian, Roman, or British models. Technologies are different, but it is really radically different human attitudes that make a return to those past glories impossible.

Those who treat capitalism as if it were a religion rather than an economic system like to talk about capitalism's need for risk takers. Individual willingness to take risks is what makes capitalism successful; more important, in their eyes, that willingness justifies the very high incomes made by successful capitalists. They tend to forget that every criminal is a risk taker. By any objective standard there are more individual risk takers in poor countries than in rich countries. Afghanistan and Somalia are full of individuals who are willing to risk their own lives for almost nothing.

As a young man working in underground mining, I met many individuals willing to do the most dangerous jobs with no extra pay. Doing so made them into macho men in their own eyes and the eyes of their friends. Taking risks with one's own life was to be embraced rather than avoided. Their willingness to take risks, however, was not what made those mines productive. It would be more accurate to say that picking up the messes those risk takers created when they took too many risks (put too many sticks of dynamite in a hole), if anything, lowered output (they blew up things that were not supposed to be blown up).

Having individuals willing to take risks is not the secret of capitalism. Organizing an array of productive risks people can choose among and an array of unproductive risks they are not allowed to choose comes far closer to the truth. In productive societies individuals have to be willing to learn, but no one learns to read and write as an isolated risk-taking individual. Individuals have to be taught to read and write. Social organization creates educated individuals. We learn a collective alphabet. Societies where everyone is educated are much more productive than those where just a few are educated. My education pays off more for me if you also are educated. The whole is far more than the sum of the parts. In productive economies no one is allowed to remain uneducated. To remain uneducated is not a permissible individual choice since it leads to collective economic decline.

Individuals need to be bold. But what boldness means differs depending upon time, place, and the array of technologies available to them. The first industrial revolution required technological tinkerers such as Britain's Watt, Bessemer, and Arkwright, who were bold enough to willingly fiddle with new mechanisms for linking mechanical devices with new power sources. But boldness is not just an individual characteristic. Success also required a British society bold enough to willingly invest in the unproven technologies that would generate the textiles, railways, and steel industries that made Britain the industrial pioneer it was.

The second industrial revolution required societies willing to commit to universal education and make social investments in research and development based upon academic science. Universal, compulsory, free education was a bold move.

Similarly, societies, and not individuals, will have to decide whether they are willing to jump into the third industrial revolution and globalization. Voyages of geographic or technological exploration have to be socially organized.

If the pyramids were the Egyptians boldly moving into space and the Valley of the Kings was the Egyptians boldly moving to the center of the earth, what are the 21st century equivalents? What tasks do we need to engage in to prove that we are bold enough to leap into the third industrial revolution and the globalization that flows from it. The first test of our boldness is found in biotechnology. Who is going to be bold enough to take advantage of it? The second test of our boldness revolves around the proper economic roles of men and women. Who is going to be bold enough to redefine the traditional roles?

TO BE, OR NOT TO BE, BIOLOGICALLY BOLD

The 21st century will be the century of biology. The ability to change our own genetic structure will probably come to be seen as the most important technological breakthrough in all of human history. The ability to control genetic diseases and tailor medical treatments to individual genetic makeups has already begun and will accelerate rapidly.

Often the pressures to participate in the biotech revolution are seen as flowing from globalization. Sinister foreign producers are forcing genetically modified products upon those who do not want them. Twenty-first century success, with or without globalization, will require individuals as well as societies bold enough to explore the possibilities of modern biotechnology. Those who don't will fall behind.

In early 2003, eighty-one thousand people sat waiting for organ transplants in America. Of those, sixteen per day died for lack of transplantable organs, and only sixty-three per day received life-saving transplants.[1] It is transgenic pigs that are going to provide the organs for transplantation so no one dies waiting for a human organ that never comes. Biotechnology already produces insulin for diabetics.[2] It is genetic manipulation that is going to find a cure for Alzheimer's.

Genetic engineering will allow us to make spider silk, as strong as Kevlar but significantly more elastic, for much-improved sutures in medicine and for body armor far superior to Kevlar.[3] Tomatoes have already been modified to grow in salty soils ruined by badly managed irrigation systems that would otherwise remain idle.[4] Genetically modified plants resist pests without pesticides, grow without the need for chemical fertilizers, and use much less water. Caffeine-free coffee can be grown, rather than chemically manufactured. Genetic manipulation has a huge potential to help both the environment and the humans who use that environment.

Scientific principles tell us that molecular biological computers can be 260,000 times as powerful as electronic computers.[5] Biotechnology is going to create new activities and products that are today unimaginable.

Already biotechnology is fundamentally redefining what it means to be diseased. People today who are extremely short are by modern definition "diseased" and the proper object of corrective genetic treatments. The process has already begun with genetically manufactured growth hormones to make the short taller.

Similarly there is a strong movement to declare being "too fat" a disease, rather than a lack of self-discipline. Throughout human existence hunger pangs were important to get humans, even if full or fat, to eat more during the summer months to prepare them for the winter months, when they would have little to eat and have to survive the annual famine. For a world of food surpluses, humans should have the opposite biological message—a feeling of perpetual fullness. Mother Nature will make these genetic changes in us in a few million years, slowly killing off those of us who get too fat, but biotechnology might be able to make these changes for us in a just a few years.

Yet like the potential European explorers who failed to follow up quickly on the Viking successes, there are those of us who don't want to follow up on these early successes in biotechnology. In Europe in particular there abound widespread fears that monsters may lurk in genetically modified plants and animals. No genetic monsters have ever been found. Nor is there a scientific reason to believe they exist. Britain's Royal Society can find no evidence that genetically modified plants and animals damage health.[6] People talk about superweeds, but there are no known superweeds. Bad plants don't accidentally make themselves in the wild. Just like the good plants, they have to be made in laboratories. As the Harvard biologist Richard Lewontin says, "Nothing is significantly changed in this situation [humans altering plants] by the introduction of genetic engineering."[7] Biotechnology is not spreading microbes but altering the genes in normal reproduction. The plant or animal is normal even if it is produced by a different process.

But no one can prove there aren't monsters. Science can never prove a negative. Monsters are not logically impossible. If we wait for science to prove conclusively that there are no monsters associated with genetically modified plants and animals, we will wait forever—like those would-be European explorers waiting for proof that sea monsters did not exist.

For the fearful the biotech revolution unfortunately comes as a package. Potential genetic breakthroughs in medicines, agriculture, materials, and computing cannot be separated from genetically modified plants and animals since the processes for producing them often involves growing drugs or manufacturing materials in genetically modified plants and animals. Transplantable organs come from transgenic pigs. Spider silk is grown in genetically modified goats' milk. The Vitamin A that people need to prevent a form of blindness found in the third world is attached to the rice they eat. Drugs for hepatitis B are grown in potatoes. Bioplastics are already competing with high end petroleum-based plastics, but they have to be grown on farms in genetically engineered plants rather than being made in huge centralized industrial plants.[8] To reject genetically modified plants and animals is to reject the entire revolution.

Those fearing biotechnology often claim to be protecting the third world. But the third world has embraced genetically modified crops. The acreage devoted to growing genetically modified crops in the developing world (up 200 percent in China) is growing much faster than that in the developed world (up 18 percent in the United States) precisely because it offers a chance to raise farm incomes in places where farm incomes are now very low.[9] Three-quarters of those who plant genetically modified crops are farmers in the poor world.[10] Such crops may be disruptive, but they are viewed as a positive disruption. The third world's worries are not about monsters but about being excluded from this revolution by the high costs of acquiring the new technologies. They do not want to be protected from genetically modified plants by first world protestors. They want a chance to participate profitably in the revolution.

One can speculate why American and European attitudes are so different on genetically modified plants and animals. The United States has not had the high profile food and drug problems (mad cow disease, hoof and mouth, thalidomide, PCBs in the Coke) that have plagued Europe. Perhaps Americans have been lucky, or perhaps the U.S. Food and Drug Administration is just better than its European counterparts. In European discussions about genetically modified plants and animals, however, there are two big worries, and not one. "There may be monsters" is actually fear number 2. The number 1 fear is "there won't be monsters and those Americans are going to have a fifty-year-year lead in conquering this exciting new territory." Europeans don't want to jump, but they also don't want the Americans to attempt the voyage into the land of biotechnology for fear that Americans will succeed.

The only way to know whether there are or are not monsters is to take an intellectual scientific and economic voyage of exploration. If there are monsters, those who do the exploring will not return. If there are no monsters, those who do the exploring will conquer new lands with incredible potential richness.

Some of the fears flow from our religious inheritance. For those who think of God creating life in all of its forms, the third industrial revolution requires societies willing to play God. In many ways all of science is learning to play God. The development of the hydrogen bomb was playing God—tapping into God's source energy, the fuel that powers the sun. All of medicine is interfering with God's plans for life and death. He, after all, made germs and diseases. But there is something about changing our own genetic structure that makes modern biology seem much closer to playing God. Many religions tell us we were made in the image of God. But human beings are now going to be changing that image.

Even those who are not religious like to believe they are unique. That is why cloning raises so many fears. Another me could be built. Biotechnology threatens that sense of my being unique. I don't want someone to build another me. But if I need an organ transplant, I want modern biology via transgenic pigs to be able to clone another kidney just like my kidney so it won't be rejected by my antibodies. I don't want to die because cloning was not allowed. Schizophrenia rules.

Those against genetically modified foods do not really believe the real issue is the accidental development of superweeds. At a deep subconscious level, even if they are not religious, the protestors believe we are changing things we have no moral right to change. The real issue is not danger to the environment or to ourselves, but playing God. But because the protestors are not religious, they cannot overtly voice their real objections.

There are real ethical problems to be found in modern biology. The answers to the ethical questions posed by modern biology, however, are not found in the Ten Commandments. Finding ethical principles for a new world not imagined in our ancient religious texts requires boldness.

TO BE, OR NOT TO BE, GENDER BOLD

One could tell the story of how men came to dominate women and hold an overwhelming proportion of the powerful decision making jobs in all societies. No Amazon societies have ever existed because men are physically stronger than women, and physical strength has been central in all past economic systems. Hunting was the male role and gathering the female role in hunter-gather societies. Gathering may have added more to family income—economic studies seem to indicate that this is so—but because of the real dangers involved in hunting the prestige went to the hunters.

In settled agricultural societies wars were central to economic success because acquiring more land was the central ingredient in producing more food. Warfare's hand-to-hand combat required physical strength. Those who lost wars became slaves to those who won wars.

Industrial societies were still dominated by jobs that required strength. Coal mining, the energy to fuel the first industrial revolution, employed millions of men. To this day males dominate coal mining, oil and gas production, and electricity generation—the industries that produce energy.

Given that our religions arose in societies where women played a less economically important role than men, it is not surprising that women's lower status was mirrored in most of the world's religions. Women literally sit in less prestigious places (in the back or upstairs) and are not allowed to be rabbis, mullahs, or in many instances Christain clergymen. Usually this exclusionary practice is defended on the grounds that women have, not a lower status, but a different status. But this is sophistry of the worse sort. Those individuals who run religions wield extreme power. They tell others what to do in the name of God. Anyone excluded from this role has less influence in that religion and consequently in that society. It was a role from which women were, and often still are, excluded.

In a knowledge-based economy the jobs that require physical strength above that of a normal women are few. One can set tests of carrying great weights up fire ladders that will stop women from becoming firefighters, but firefighters never actually carry such loads up ladders while fighting fires, and fire departments never require firefighters to pass that test every month to see if they remain fit enough to be firefighters, dismissing those who fail.

Warfare probably does still have a few jobs that require physical strength, but those jobs are not the ones that win wars. Wars are won by the army with the best knowledge workers. In modern armies women will be able to do most of the important jobs. A young Israeli friend tells me that one of the best pilots in his squadron is a woman. And, in any case, in the near future the fighter pilot in a very expensive airplane will easily be beaten by a cheap drone aircraft flown from a computer screen. Conquering land and natural resources is also no longer central to economic success.

Since there are no longer real areas where male strength is important, societies have invented athletic games where male strength becomes important. But the male who scores the winning goal is not equivalent to the male who brings home the bison that will keep the family alive for the winter. One is an artificial hero, and the other is a real hero.

Half of potential human knowledge resides in female heads. To make these potential ideas into real ideas requires equal education and equal economic opportunities for women. Those societies willing to tap into that potential knowledge are going to economically pull ahead of those unwilling to tap into that potential knowledge. Even the success of male children seems to depend more upon the education of the mother than upon the education of the father. Any country that does not take advantage of educated females is going to fall behind the leaders.

America is not a perfect model of the full utilization of female talent, but a country that does not use its female talent at least as well is not going to have the American standard of living. Women provide 47 percent of the American workforce and earn one-third of total American earnings. More than half of the students in America's medical schools are female, and soon more than half of its doctors will be female.

America is not insistent upon equal treatment for women in other countries, since major parts of America's religious establishment—the Roman Catholic Church and the Southern Baptists, for instance—still do not allow women equal roles as clergymen. That is why America has not signed the UN Treaty on Women. It is why America does not protest against countries that discriminate against women the way it protested against countries that discriminated against blacks.

Part of the reason the Japanese have never been willing to apologize for their horrendous behavior in places like China during World War II is that the emperor was not punished after the war. If he was guilty of nothing, the average Japanese could be guilty of nothing. He was their ultimate leader, religious as well as secular. Religion plays the same emperor role vis-à-vis women today. If organized religions can put women in subordinate roles, then every other human institution may put women in subordinate roles. Religions are, after all, the moral role model.

I believe that countries that don't give women the opportunity to play equal roles should be treated the way Americans treated South Africa when it was practicing apartheid. That these countries base their discrimination on religious beliefs is completely irrelevant. There were also some churches that assigned blacks subordinate roles in their religious beliefs. We cannot force others to change their beliefs, but we can officially object to those beliefs.

SELF-CONFIDENCE

Self-confidence is probably the central attitude in successful globalization. The bold think of today's globalization as an opportunity: My culture will be enriched, the range of my experiences will be widened, and my economic circumstances will be made better. The timid see globalization as a threat: My culture will fade, I won't like the new experiences, and I clearly see the economic losses globalization will bring. The gains may be far bigger than the losses, but I focus only on the losses.

Globalization requires individuals bold enough to be participants in environments that are not those in which they grew up and naturally feel comfortable. But it also require societies bold enough to believe they can take individuals from different cultures and integrate them into a new, as yet unspecified, culture. The new immigrant is not a threat—he or she is an opportunity. The individuals and societies self-confident enough to accept the changes demanded by the third industrial revolution, yet able to remain unique individuals and societies true to their basic values even if those values themselves change, will ultimately win. For in the end the third industrial revolution and the globalization that flows from it cannot be stopped.

But there will be those who stand aside from the revolution and do not participate in it. They will be on the globe but not in the global economy. They will remain in a national industrial world while others move into a global knowledge-based economy. Historically, they will join those who did not leap into the steam revolution or into the electrification revolution and fall behind.

All societies that have been successful over long periods of time know when to change. We think of ancient Rome or Egypt as consistently successful. They weren't. Their history was, in fact, full of ups and downs. Downturns occurred, but they did not lead to disintegration. In Egypt the gap between the Old Kingdom and the New Kingdom was marked by a period of occupation and foreign rule. Rome lost many a battle. Both empires lasted for hundreds and, in the case of Egypt, thousands of years because they could go down without going out and because they could change without collapsing. And no matter how much they changed, they continued to believe they were mighty Egypt and Imperial Rome. Both Egypt and Rome disappeared when they lost their self-confidence and the ability to adapt to changing circumstances.

Winners get ahead of the technological wave so they can catch it and ride their economic surf boards to success. The winners are not always first movers, since first movers often move too soon. But they watch those first movers very closely to see what can be learned about the arrival of a wave worth catching.

Today's perfect wave is being generated by the global knowledge-based economy that is emerging to replace the national industrial economies of the previous two centuries. It is there for those bold enough to catch it. Everything there is to be found geographically has been found. But who knows what exciting new continents there are to find in the technologies of the third industrial revolution. Like the geographic explorers who had the compasses and the ships, we today have all of the tools necessary to start exploring some brand-new, never-known areas.

Those who leap sometimes lose, but those who do not leap always lose.

Fortune favors the bold.

Notes

CHAPTER 1

1. Brian Knowlton, "A Rising Anti-American Tide," *International Herald Tribune,* Dec. 5, 2002, page 1.

2. Robert Kagan, *Of Paradise and Power* (New York: Alfred A. Knopf, 2003).

3. Guy de Jonquieres, "Companies 'Bigger' than Many Nations," *Financial Times,* Aug. 13, 2002, page 3.

4. Bureau of Economic Analysis, "Operations of US Multinational Companies," *Survey of Current Business,* Mar. 2002, page 24, and Dec. 2002, page 115.

5. "Measuring Globalization," *Foreign Policy,* Jan./Feb. 2003, page 69.

6. *Atlas of the 20th Century* (London: Hammond, 1996), pages 18–19; World Maps," *Atlas of the World* (New York: Oxford University Press), pages 4–5.

7. *The Economist,* "A Survey of Japan," Apr. 20, 2002, Special section, page 1.

8. "Health and Living Standards—Japan," *Euromonitor,* <http://www.euromonitor.com>.

9. Bureau of Economic Analysis, "Table 1.1, Gross Domestic Product," July 31, 2002; FDIC, "Managing the Crisis: FDIC and RTIC Experience," 1997 FDIC, "History of the Eighties: Lesson for the Future," 1997, page 39.

10. George Gray and David Ropeik, "What, Me Worry?" *Boston Globe,* Nov. 11, 2001, page E8.

11. U.S. Census Bureau, "No. 1092. Motor Vehicle Accidents—Number and Deaths: 1980 to 1999," *Statistical Abstract of the United States: 2001,* page 684.

12. Ibid.

13. James Glanz, "In Collapsing Towers, a Cascade of Failure?" *New York Times,* Nov. 11, 2001, pages B1, B11; "Wounded Buildings Offer Survival Lessons," *New York Times,* Dec. 4, 2001; James Glanz and Michael Moss, "Poor Fireproofing Played Role in Collapse of Towers," *International Herald Tribune,* Dec. 14, 2001, page 3; Jim Dwyer, "Firefighters Piece Together What Went Wrong Sept. 11," *International Herald Tribune,* Feb. 1, 2002, page 2; James Glanz and Eric Lipton,

"Towers Withstood Impact but Fell to Fire, Report Says," *New York Times,* Mar. 29, 2002, page 1; James Glanz, "Study of Sept 11 Collapse Ends Mostly in Questions," *New York Times,* May 1, 2002, page C18.

14. David Leonhardt, "The Long Boom's Ugly Side," *New York Times,* May 12, 2002, page 1.

15. Natalie Angier, "The Urge to Punish Cheats: It Isn't Merely Vengeance," *New York Times,* Jan. 22, 2002, page F1.

CHAPTER 2

1. Angus Maddison, *Dynamic Forces in Capitalist Development: A Long-Run Comparative View* (Oxford and New York: Oxford University Press, 1991).

2. Rudi Dornbush, *Keys to Prosperity* (Cambridge, Mass.: MIT Press, 2000), page 4. Taken from Angus Maddison.

3. Federal Reserve Bank of Kansas City, *"Global Economic Integration: Opportunities and Challenges," Aug. 2000.*

4. David S. Landis, *The Wealth and Poverty of Nations: Why Some Are So Rich and Some So Poor* (New York: W.W. Norton, 1998).

5. Nicholas Crafts, "Forging Ahead and Falling Behind," *Journal of Economic Perspectives,* Spring 1998, page 200.

6. International Monetary Fund, *International Financial Statistics Yearbook 2001* (Washington, D.C., 2001).

7. For a more extensive discussion of the implications of a knowledge-based economy, see Lester C. Thurow, *Building Wealth: New Rules for Individuals, Companies, and Nations in a Knowledge-based Economy* (New York: HarperCollins, 1999).

8. *The Economist,* "A New Kind of Solidarity," Nov. 16, 2002, page 10.

9. John Schmid, "Recession Looms in Germany," *International Herald Tribune,* Nov. 22, 2001, pages 1, 4.

10. Thomas Paul D'Aquino and David Stewart-Patterson, *Northern Edge* (Toronto: Stoddart, 2001), page 179.

11. John Vinocur, "Fortuyn Dared to Touch Hot Topic," *International Herald Tribune,* May 10, 2002, page 1.

12. "Globalism and the World's Poor," *The American Prospect,* Winter 2002, page A15.

13. A.T. Kearney, "Measuring Globalization," *Foreign Policy,* Jan./Feb. 2001, page 56.

14. *The Economist,* Dec. 8, 2001, page 87.

15. A.T. Kearney, "Measuring Globalization," *Foreign Policy,* Jan./Feb. 2003, page 60.

CHAPTER 3

1. Doug Henton, Kim Walesh, Liz Brown et al., "2002 Index of Silicon Valley," *Joint Venture: Silicon Valley Network,* 2002, page 4.

2. "Comparing Three Markets—Nasdaq, NYSE, and Amex," *Nasdaq Stock Market,* <http://www.marketdata.nasdaq.com/asp/Sec1Summary.asp>.

3. Charles P. Kindleberger, *Manias, Panics, and Crashes: A History of Financial Crises,* 3rd edition (New York: John Wiley & Sons, 1996) Appendix B.

4. Mark Hulbert, "Is It Free Fall, or Just a Blip?" *New York Times,* Apr. 21, 2002, page BU7.

5. *The Economist,* "Do You Sincerely Want to Go Crazy," Jan. 19, 2002, page 75.

6. Saul Hansell, "Online Sales Fall Short of Hopes," *New York Times,* Jan. 17, 2001, page 3.

7. Bob Tedeschi, "E-tail Welcomes Ho-Hum Season," *International Herald Tribune,* Nov. 26, 2001, page 11.

8. Martha McNeil Hamilton, "Some Online Yuletide Cheer for Traditional Stores," *International Herald Tribune,* Dec. 5, 2000, page 19.

9. Geraldine Fabrikant, "A Dwindling Few in Search of Value," *New York Times,* June 18, 2000, page 7.

10. Financial Times, <http://news.ft.com>, Aug. 14, 2002, page 1.

11. Danny Hakim, "Now That the Thrill Is Gone, Investors Turn Back to Basics," *New York Times,* Oct. 30, 2000, page 1.

12. William Hanley, "Hot Stock," *Financial Post,* Dec. 11, 1999.

13. *(Manchester) Guardian,* Mar. 13, 2000.

14. *Time Magazine,* Oct. 25, 1999.

15. *(London) Sunday Times*, Jan. 9, 2000.

16. *(London) Independent,* Feb. 19, 2000.

17. Warren Buffet, "To the Shareholders of Berkshire Hathaway," Mar. 1, 2000.

18. "Fortune Global Five Hundred," *Fortune Magazine,* July 22, 2002, pages 144–47 and F1–F13.

19. Stephen L. Slavin, *Macroeconomics,* 5th edition (Boston: Irwin McGraw-Hill, 1999), page 13.

20. Commodore International, <http://www.thocp.net/companies/commodore.htm>.

21. Alan Beattie, "How the Reputation of the 'Maestro' Crumbled," *Financial Times,* Sept. 26, 2002, page 11.

22. Ibid.

23. Derek DeCloet, "Enron's Reports Contained Signs of Rot Early Last Year: Ontario Pension Manager Sold in First Half of 2001," *Financial Post,* Mar. 26, 2002, page IN3.

24. Daniel Altman, "How Citigroup Hedged Bets on Enron," *New York Times,* Feb. 8, 2002, page C1.

25. Patrick McGeehan, "2 Early Enron Lenders Didn't See the End Coming," *New York Times,* Jan. 22, 2002, page C1.

26. Scott Nelson, "As Price Fell, Funds Bought Enron Stock," *Boston Globe,* Feb. 2, 2002, page C1.

27. Peter J. Howe, "Fiber Optic Cost $70 b More than Necessary," *Boston Globe,* Mar. 11, 2002, page C1.

28. Barnaby J. Feder, "New Math Turns Fiber Glut into Strategic Inventory," *International Herald Tribune,* Nov. 26, 2001, page 10.

29. "3G License Winners Revealed," *Communications World,* May 5, 2000.

30. Dianne See Morrison, "Germany Gets Greedy with 3Gs," *Red Herring,* Aug. 21, 2000, <http://www.redherring.com/insider/2000/0821/tech-%20madness082100.html>.

31. *The Economist,* "Dicing with Debt," Jan. 29, 2002, page 22.

32. *The Economist,* "Cramming Them In," May 11, 2002, page 34.

33. *The Economist,* "Will There Be a Double Dip?' Aug. 10, 2002, page 58.

34. Alan Beattie, "After the Binge," *Financial Times,* Oct. 31, 2002, page 11.

35. *The Economist,* "Going through the Roof," Mar. 30, 2002, page 59.

36. David Barboza, "Ex-executives Say Sham Deal Helped Enron," *New York Times,* Aug. 8, 2002, pages A1, C12.

37. John Cassidy, *Dot.Con* (New York: HarperCollins, 2002), foreword.

38. Richard Waters, "Pressure Forces Ebbers to Leave WorldCom," *Financial Times,* May 1, 2002, page 1.

39. *Associated Press Newswires,* Sept. 6, 2002, Internet Web Site.

40. *The Economist,* "Face Value a Helluva Problem," Sept. 21, 2002, page 66.

41. Ian Cheng, "Survivors Who Laughed All the Way to the Bank," *Financial Times,* July 31, 2002, page 8.

42. Gretchen Morgenson, "In a Wall St. Hierarchy, Short Shrift to Little Guy," *New York Times,* Apr. 29, 2003, page C1.

43. David Leonhardt, "Hiring in Nation Hits Worst Slump in Nearly 20 Years," *New York Times,* Feb. 6, 2003, page 1.

44. Francis X. Clines, "Painful Choices for States Facing Wider Budget Cuts," *New York Times,* Feb. 8, 2002, page A17.

45. Yumiko Suzuki, "Real Estate Market," *Nikkei Weekly,* Apr. 22, 2002, page 3.

46. *The Economist,* "A Survey of Japan," Apr. 20, 2002, Special section, page 5.

47. Ken Belson, "Record Loss Is Foreseen by Japanese Bank," *New York Times,* Jan. 22, 2003, page W1.

48. *Nikkei Weekly,* "Economic Forecasts Still Gloomy," Feb. 24, 2003, page 2.

49. *The Economist,* "Capitalism and Its Troubles," May 18, 2002, Special section.

50. "Fortune Global Five Hundred," *Fortune Magazine,* July 22, 2002, pages 144–47 and F1–F13; *The Economist,* "An Uncertain Giant," Dec. 7, 2002, page 9.

51. Howard French, "Japan Anxiously Looks Ahead," *New York Times,* Aug. 11, 2002, page 5.

52. *The Economist,* "Economist Intelligence Unit Country Report," June 2002; "Japan Report," April 20, 2002.

53. Bureau of Economic Analysis, "Table 1.1, Gross Domestic Product," July 31, 2002, <http://www.bea.gov/bea/dn/nipaweb/index.asp>; FDIC, "Managing the Crisis: FDIC and RTIC Experience," 1997; FDIC, "History of the Eighties: Lesson for the Future," 1997, page 39.

54. Gavin Buckley, "A Banking Crisis: Reformers Do Not Reform. Blame Is Difficult," *Milken Review,* Third Quarter, page 29.

55. David E. Rosenbaum, "The Savings Debacle: A Special Report: A Financial Disaster with Many Culprits," *New York Times,* June 6, 1990, page 1.

56. Keith Bradsher, "Hong Kong Reducing Benefits and Wages," *New York Times,* Feb. 26, 2003, page A7.

57. Ken Belson, "Japan's Production Falls to 14 Year Low," *New York Times,* Dec. 28, 2001, page W1.

58. "European Growth Forecast Slashed," *International Herald Tribune,* Dec. 14, 2001, page 13.

59. Tony Major, "ECB Slashes Prediction for 2002 Growth in Eurozone," *Financial Times,* Dec. 14, 2001, page 9.

60. *The Economist,* "Stockmarkets in America and Europe: Stop This Dream," July 20, 2002, pages 63–64.

61. Floyd Norris, "A Bad Quarter for US Markets Was Worse in Other Countries," *New York Times,* Oct. 1, 2002, page C1.

62. *The Economist,* "Long Term Unemployment," Aug. 3, 2002, page 80.

63. *The Economist,* "Government Budget Balances," Oct. 12, 2002, page 97.

64. *German Council of Economic Experts,* "For Steadiness—Against Actionism," Annual Report 2001/2002.

65. *Germany Council of Economic Experts,* "Twenty Proposals for Employment and Growth," Annual Report 2002/2003, chapter 1.

66. Paul Krugman, "For Richer," *New York Times Magazine,* Oct. 20, 2002, page 64.

67. Barbara Hagenbaugh, "Nation's Wealth Disparity Widens," *USA Today,* Jan. 23, 2003, page 1.

68. "Forbes World's Richest People, 2002," Forbes.com, <http://www.forbes.com/>.

69. Lawrence Mishel, Jared Bernstein, and Heather Boushey, *The State of Working America* (Ithaca: Cornell University Press, 2003), page 167.

70. Daniel Altman, "Blunt Portrait Drawn of the US Work Force in 2020," *New York Times,* Aug. 30, 2002, page C4.

71. Thomas Piketty and Emmanuel Saez, "Income Inequality in the United States, 1913–1998," *Quarterly Journal of Economics,* Feb. 2003, page 1.

72. Council of Economic Advisers, *Economic Report of the President* (Washington, D.C., Feb. 1999), page 357.

73. U.S. Department of Commerce, Economics and Statistics Administration, U.S. Census Bureau, "The Big Payoff: Educational Attainment and Synthetic Estimates of Work-Life Earnings," July 2002, page 3.

74. Lawrence Mishel, Jared Bernstein, Heather Boushey, *The State of Working America.* Economic Policy Institute. 2003. pages 151—153. World Bank, "2001

World Development Indicators CD-ROM"; CIA, "The World Factbook 2001," <http://www.cia.gov/cia/publications/factbook>.

75. U.S. Department of Commerce, Economics and Statistics Administration, U.S. Census Bureau, *Statistical Abstract of the United States: 1980* (Washington, D.C., 1980), page 421; U.S. Department of Commerce, Economics and Statistics Administration, U.S. Census Bureau, *Statistical Abstract of the United States: 1974* (Washington, D.C., 1974), page 347; Bank of Japan, Statistics Department, *Economic Statistics of Japan: 1980,* pages 285, 287; Euromonitor Publications, *European Marketing Data and Statistics, 1972* (London), page 144; International Labor Organization, Bureau of Statistics, <http://www.ilo.org/stat/>.

76. Bureau of Labor Statistics, "Job Creation."

77. Richard Lewontin, "Genes in the Food!" *New York Review of Books,* June 21, 2001, page 84.

78. *The Economist,* "Employment Costs," Nov. 16, 2002, page 102.

79. Dani Rodrik, *Has Globalizatoin Gone Too Far?* (Washington, D.C.: Institute for International Economics, 1997).

80. Peter Kilborn, "Global Economy Taking Toll on Small Towns," *New York Times,* Feb. 16, 2002, page 1.

CHAPTER 4

1. *The Economist,* "Meanwhile in Another World," Feb. 9, 2002, page 32.

2. George Gray and David Ropeik, "What, Me Worry?" *Boston Globe,* Nov. 11, 2001, page E8.

3. *The Economist,* "Living with a Superpower," Jan. 4, 2003, page 19.

4. "The Wasps Did It," *Foreign Policy,* Jan./Feb. 2002, page 14.

5. Council of Economic Advisers, *Economic Report of the President,* (Washington, D.C., Feb. 1999), page 366.

6. Brian Knowlton, "A Rising Anti-American Tide," *International Herald Tribune,* Dec. 5, 2002, page 1.

7. Carlotta Gall, "Long in Dark, Afghan Women Say to Read Is Finally to See," *New York Times,* Sept. 22, 2002, page 1.

8. Susan Dominus, "Shabana Is Late for School," *New York Times Magazine,* Sept. 29, 2002, page 40.

9. Edward Rothstein, "Damning (yet Desiring) Mickey and the Big Mac," *New York Times,* Mar. 2, 2002, page A17.

10. Donald McNeil, Jr., "Not Only in America: Gun Killings Shake the Europeans," *New York Times,* May 11, 2002, page A3.

11. Alexander Stille, "Globalization and Cinema," *Correspondence: An International Review of Culture and Society,* Fall/summer 2001, page 1.

12. Burrin, Philippe, *France under the Germans: Collaboration and Compromise* (New York: W.W. Norton, 1996). (Translated from the French original: Janet Lloyd, *La Frace a' l'Heure Allemande: 1940–1944.*)

13. Philip H. Gordon, "Liberté! Fraternité! Anxiety!" *Financial Times,* Jan. 19, 2002, page 10.

14. Adam Pasick, "Philips Shuns New Anti-piracy CDs," *International Hearld Tribune,* Jan. 19, 2002, page 11.

15. Tyler Cown and Eric Crampton, "Uncommon Culture," *Foreign Policy,* July/Aug., page 28.

16. A.T. Kearney, "Measuring Globalization," *Foreign Policy,* Jan./Feb. 2001, page 56.

17. "Sudan War Zone Leaves Its Print; Aid Worker Sees Grace amid Death," *Washington Times,* March 21, 2002.

18. "Would Jesus Join the EU?" *Foreign Policy,* Spring 2003, page 18.

19. Nicholas D. Kristof, "What Does and Doesn't Fuel Terrorism?" *International Herald Tribune,* May 8, 2002, page 8.

20. Tony Judt, "America's Restive Partners," *New York Times,* Apr. 28, 2002, page wk15.

21. Niall Ferguson, "2011," *New York Times Magazine,* Dec. 2, 2001, page 76.

22. Karl Marx, *Das Kapital, kritik der politischen okonomie* (Stuttgart: Cotta, 1962–1964).

23. "Globalism and the World's Poor," *The American Prospect,* Winter 2002.

24. Steven Erlanger, "European Right Taps into Fears of an EU 'Invisible Invasion,'" *International Herald Tribune,* May 6, 2002, page 5; Tony Judt, "America's Restive Partners," *New York Times,* Apr. 28, 2002, page wk15.

25. Jane Perlez, "Australians Fear Their Idyll Will Be Upset by the Boatload," *International Herald Tribune,* May 10, 2002, page 2.

26. *The Economist,* "Outward Bound," Sept. 28, 2002, page 24.

27. U.S. INS (Immigration and Naturalization Services), "Report on H1-B Petitions Annual Report Fiscal Year 2000," 2000, page 3. <http://www.bcis.gov>.

28. Gregory Rodriguez, "The Overwhelming Allure of English," *New York Times,* Apr. 7, 2002, page 3.

29. *The Economist,* "Outward Bound," Sept. 28, 2002, page 24.

30. Amy Chua, *World on Fire: How Exporting Free Market Democracy Breeds Ethnic Hatred and Global Instability* (New York: Doubleday, 2003).

31. Stanley Hoffmann, "Why Don't They Like Us?" *The American Prospect,* Nov. 19, 2001, page 18.

CHAPTER 5

1. David E. Brown, *Inventing Modern America* (Cambridge, Mass.: MIT Press 2002), page 58.

2. Samuel Brittan, "The Best Path to Prosperity," *Financial Times,* Feb. 14, 2002, page 11.

3. James Glans and Eric Lipton, "Burning Diesel Is Cited in Fall of 3rd Tower," *New York Times,* Mar. 2, 2002, page 1.

4. Serge Schmemann, "Annan Cautions Business as Forum Ends," *New York Times,* Feb. 5, 2002, page A14.

5. These data all come from the National Income and Production Accounts table 5.1.

6. Samuel Brittan, "Why World Deflation Is Remote," *Financial Times,* Nov. 22, 2001, page 15.

7. *The Economist,* "Counterfeiting in Asia," Nov. 10, 2001, page 58.

8. Robert Norton, "Economic Hypochondria," *Fortune,* May 27, 2002, page 42.

9. In 2002 current account inflows were $1217 billion and outflows were $1681 billion.

10. U.S. Trade Deficit, Review Commission, *The U.S. Trade Deficit,* Government Printing Office, 2000, page 50.

11. C. Smith, S. Hall, and N. Mabey, "Econometric Modeling of International Carbon Tax Regimes," *Energy Economics* (London Business School, April 1995), pages 133–46.

12. Ibid. page 55.

13. Robert Norton, "Economic Hypochondria," *Fortune,* May 27, 2002, page 42.

14. "On Intellectual Property," *Daedalus,* Spring 2002.

15. Ibid.

16. Frances Williams, "Demand for Patents up Almost 25%," *Financial Times,* Feb. 14, 2001, page 6.

17. Amy Harmon, "In the 'Idea Wars,' a Fight to Control a New Currency," *New York Times,* Nov. 11, 2001, page 2; <http://web.lexis-nexis.com/universe/> (accessed June 5, 2002)

18. *The Economist.* "The Right to Good Ideas," June 23, 2001, page 21.

19. World Trade Organization, "The Doha Declaration Explained." <http://www.wto.org/>.

20. Bob Sherwood, "From Fake Handbags to Car Parts, Piracy Is Booming," *Financial Times,* Apr. 30, 2003, Special Report, Intellectual Property, page III.

21. "Vietnam Trade Pact Already Boosting Trade- US Official," *Wall Street Journal Online,* May 7, 2002; <http://online.wsj.com/article/0,,BT_CO_20020507_002502.djm,00.html.> (accessed June 5, 2002).

22. *The Economist,* "The Right to Good Ideas," June 23, 2001, page 21.

23. *The Economist,* "Counterfeiting in Asia," Nov. 10, 2001, page 58.

24. Devin Lenonard, "This Is War," *Fortune,* May 27, 2002, page 83.

25. A.R. Lakshmanan, "China Losing Its Campaign against Piracy," *Boston Globe,* May 26, 2002, page E1; Devin Lenonard, "This Is War," *Fortune,* May 27, 2002, page 83.

26. *The Economist,* "AIDS' Unhappy Anniversary," Dec. 1, 2001, page 76; John Donnelly, "World's Aids Crisis Worsening Report Says," *Boston Globe,* June 16, 2002, page 1.

27. Henri E. Cauvin, "HIV Survey in South Africa Suggest Plateau in Infections," June 11, 2002, page A11.

28. *The Economist,* "The Spectre Stalking the Sub-Sahara," Dec. 2, 2000, page 52.

29. *The Economist,* "How to Live with It, Not Die of It," May 11, 2002, page 12.

30. UNAIDS and World Health Organization, "Global Summary of the HIV/AIDS Epidemic," Dec. 2001, page 6.

31. Anthony J. Sinskey, "Economic Perspective on Drug Discovery and the New Biology," MIT Program on the Pharmaceutical Industry.

32. Geoff Dyer, "The Book of Life Has yet to Transfer to the Bottom Line," Financial Times, Nov. 27, 2001, page I; Robert Pear, "Research Cost for New Drugs Said to Soar," New York Times, Dec. 1, 2001, page C1.

33. W. Lesser, "The Effects of Trips-Mandated Intellectual Property Rights on Economic Activities in Developing Countries" (New York: Cornell University, April 17, 2001).

CHAPTER 6

1. Asian Development Bank, "Key Indicators 2001 of Developing Asian and Pacific Countries," <http://www.adb.org/Documents/Books/Key_Indicators/2001/tap.pdf>; World Bank, "2001 World Development Indicators CD-ROM."

2. Bureau of Economic Analysis, "Table 2.6, Personal Consumption Expenditures by Type of Product," Aug. 2, 2002, <http://www.bea.gov/bea/dn/nipaweb/index.asp>.

3. James E. Rauch and Vitor Trindade, "Ethnic Chinese Networks in International Trade," *The Review of Economics and Statistics,* Feb. 2002, page 116.

4. Joel Sobel, "Can We Trust Social Capital," *Journal of Economic Literature,* Mar. 2002, page 139.

5. *The Economist,* "Adult Illiteracy," Nov. 24, 2001, page 106.

6. James E. Anderson and Douglas Marcouiller, "Insecurity and the Pattern of Trade: An Empirical Investigation," *The Review of Economics and Statistics,* May 2002, page 342; Wei, Shang-Jin and Andrei Schleifer, "Local Corruption and Global Capital Flows," *Brookings Papers on Economic Activity* No. 2, Jan. 1, 2000, pages 321–26.

7. Transparency International Corruption Perception Index 2002.

8. "Hostage, Inc.," *Foreign Policy,* (July, Aug. 2002): pages 27–30.

9. Raymond Bonner, "US Links Indonesian Troops to Deaths of Two Americans," *New York Times,* Jan. 30, 2003, page A3.

10. Lester C. Thurow, *Head to Head: The Coming Economic Battle among Japan, Europe, and America* (New York: William Morrow, 1992), page 204, as taken from J. Bradford De Long, "Productivity Growth, Convergence, and Welfare," *American Economic Review,* Dec. 1988, pages 140–41, and Robert Summers and Alan Heston, "The Penn World Table (Mark 5): An Expanded Set of International Comparisons, 1950–1988," *Quarterly Journal of Economics,* May 1991, pages 351–54. There are, of

course, some small lightly populated nonindustrial countries that have become rich because of oil.

11. Edwin O. Reischauer, *Japan: The Story of a Nation* (New York: Knopf, 1989). In 1830 men in Japan were as literate as those in the United Kingdom and women were more literate.

12. International Monetary Fund, *International Financial Statistics Yearbook 2001* (Washington, D.C., 2001), page 360.

13. U.S. Department of Commerce, Long Term Economic Growth (Washington, D.C., 1973), page 212. Working farmers spend many hours per day on the job, but in cold climates they work relatively few hours per year. Little is done in the winter or in the summer when crop are growing. In warm weather countries farmers work many more hours per year, since crops are grow year-round and different crops have different planting and harvesting times. As a result, the same gains in hours of work when moving from agriculture to industry do not occur.

14. Nicholas Crafts, "Forging Ahead and Falling Behind," *Journal of EconomicPerspectives,* Spring 1998, page 200.

15. Raymond Vernon, *Exploring the Global Economy* (Cambridge, Mass.: University Press, 1985).

16. Ezra Vogel, *Japan as Number One* (Cambridge, Mass.: Harvard University Press, 1979).

17. Ronald Dore, *Taking Japan Seriously* (Stanford, Calif.: Stanford University Press, 1987).

18. Lester C. Thurow, *Head to Head* (New York: Warner Books, 1992), chapter 4, page 113.

19. Edoardo Amaldi, "The First 17 Solvay Conferences in Physics (1911–1978)" (Rome: "Istituto di Fisica "Guglielmo Marconi," Universita delgi Studi), <http://solvayins.ulb.ac.be/fixed/Reference2.html>.

20. National Science Board, *Science & Engineering Indicators, 1996* (Washington, D.C., 1996), page 3.25.

21. Michael L. Dertouzos, ed. *Made in America* (Cambridge, Mass.: MIT Press, 1989).

22. International Monetary Fund, *International Financial Statistics Yearbook 2001* (Washington, D.C., 2001), pages 602 & 1028.

23. National Science Board, *Science & Engineering Indicators, 1996* (Washington, D.C., 1996), page 3.25.

24. *The Economist,* "Still Reluctant," May 18, 2002, page 25.

25. *The Economist,* "FDI Inflows," Aug. 17, 2002, page 24.

26. World Bank, "FDI and Indicators of Financial Market Development, Selected Countries," *World Developments Indicators,* 2001.

27. *The Economist,* "Globalization and Its Critics," Sept. 29, 2001, Special section, pages 3 & 6.

28. The Economist Intelligence Unit, *Indonesia Country Report,* Dec. 2002, page 37.

29. Jacques Morisset and Olivier Lumenga Neso, "Administrative Barriers to Foreign Investment in Developing Countries," May 2002, page 11.

30. Ibid., page 13.

31. Thomas Crampton, "As China Rises, Some Ask: Will It Stumble?" *International Herald Tribune,* Dec. 18, 2001, page 1.

32. *The Economist,* "Adult Illiteracy," Nov, 24, 2001, page 106; Bureau of Labor Statistics, "Job Creation."

33. World Bank, "2001 World Development Indicators" CD-ROM; CIA, "The World Factbook 2001," <www.cia.gov/cia/publications/factbook>.

34. Richard McGregor and Sumathi Bala, "Asian Tigers Fear Last Supper Thanks to Ravenous China," *Financial Times,* June 12, 2002, page 22.

35. James Brooke, "Seoul Feels the March of Chinese Capitalism," *International Hearld Tribune,* Jan. 9, 2003, page 10.

36. China Statistics Press, *China Statistical Yearbook* (Beijing), 2001, page 59.

37. Ning Zhou, Yunshi Want, and Lester Thurow, "The PRC's Real Economic Rate of Growth," MIT Working Paper.

38. Ian Cheng, "Survivors Who Laughed All the Way to the Bank," *Financial Times,* 31 July 2002, page 8.

39. U.S. Department of Commerce, Economics and Statistics Administration, U.S. Census Bureau, *Statistical Abstract of the United States: 2001* (Washington, D.C., 2002), page 802–5.

40. Jeffrey G. Williamson and Kevin H. O'Rourke, *Globalization and History* (Cambridge, Mass., MIT Press, 2000), page 17; "Employment in SOE—Urban Percentage," *China Statistical Yearbook* (Beijing, China Statistics Press, 2001), page 107.

41. Chi-Chu Tschang, "China Production Rises as Spending Takes Hold," *International Herald Tribune,* Jan. 16, 2003, page B1.

42. *The Economist,* "Economy," Nov. 30, 2002, page 98.

43. Add in Taiwan ($160 billion), and the three together have almost a quarter of the world's total reserves. Perhaps it has something to do with old Chinese habits of burying gold in the ground.

44. Chi-Chu Tschang, "China Production Rises as Spending Takes Hold," *International Herald Tribune,* Jan. 16, 2003, page B1.

45. Thomas Crampton, "As China Rises, Some Ask: Will It Stumble?" *International Herald Tribune,* Dec. 18, 2001, page.

46. "Income Gap Wider as China Reforms," *New York Times,* July 22, 2002, section B6.

47. *The Economist,* "FDI Flows among Emerging Countries 2000," May 18, 2002, page 25; A-241 UNCTAD Division on Investment Technology and Enterprise Development.

48. *The Economist,* "Emerging-Market Indicators," July 13, 2002, page 90.

49. Carlos Lozada, "Economic Growth Is Reducing Global Poverty," *The NBER Digest,* Oct. 2002, page 5.

50. Andy Kamarck, "Why Africa Has Lagged" (as published in an e-mail from Andy Kamarck, <Rdg118pine@aol.com>, to students on June 1, 2002).

CHAPTER 7

1. Laura D'Andrea Tyson, "Its Time to Step Up the Global War on Poverty," *Business Week,* Dec. 3, 2001, page 14.

2. Daniel Altman, "Diagnosis of the World's Health Focuses on Economic Benefit," *New York Times,* Dec. 21, 2001, page W1.

3. *The Economist,* "The Health of Nations," Dec. 22, 2001, page 83.

4. William Easterly, "The Cartel of Good Intentions: The Aid Cartel's Golden Oldies," *Foreign Policy,* July–Aug. 2002, page 42.

5. Michael Peel, "Nigeria Struggles to Shake Off Economic Legacy of Years of Military Misrule," *Financial Times,* Jan. 31, 2003, page 4.

6. Warwich J. McKibbin and Dominick Salvatore, "The Global Economic Consequences of the Uruguay Round," *Brookings Discussion Papers No. 110,* Feb. 1995, page 3; David Buchan, "GATT Deal May Enrich World by $270 Billion," *Financial Times,* Nov. 10, 1993, page 7.

7. Oxfam Policy Papers, "A Genuine Development Agenda for the Doha Round of the WTO Negotiations," January 2002. <Oxfam.org.uk/policy/papers/papers.html>.

8. Clifford Krauss, "Argentina's New Chapter in an Epic of Frustration," *New York Times,* Dec. 22, 2001, page A8.

9. J. Nef, "The Argentinean Crisis of 2001–2002: Analysis and Implications," University of Guelph, Ontario, Mar. 2002, page 12.

10. Lapper, Richard, "Private Forecasts over Argentina Grow Gloomier," *Financial Times,* July 19, 2002, page 3.

11. Benjamin M. Friedman, "Globalization: Stiglitz's Case," *New York Review,* Aug. 15, 2002, pages 48–53.

12. *The Economist,* "Doubts inside the Barricades," Sept. 28, 2002.

13. Michael Massing, "Challenging the Growth Gurus," *New York Times,* Oct. 19, 2002, page A19.

14. Joseph E. Stiglitz, *Globalization and Its Discontents* (New York: W.W. Norton, 2002).

15. Anne O. Krueger, *A New Approach to Sovereign Debt Restructuring* (Washington, D.C., International Monetary Fund, Apr. 2002.

16. World Bank, "2001 World Development Indicators: Current Account Balance (BoP, current US$)."

17. World Bank, "World Development Indicators" (1990–1999); *The Economist* Intelligence Unit, "Economist Intelligence Unit Country Report," 2000–2001.

18. "Per Capita GDP Change in Asian Tigers," *Milken Institute Review,* Third Quarter 2002, page 91.

19. *World Bank,* "Global Development Finance 2002" (Country Table).

CHAPTER 8

1. David Leonhard, "A Sinking Feeling at the Register," *New York Times,* Jan. 19, 2003, section 3, page 10.

2. David Leonhard, "As Companies Reduce Costs, Pay Is Falling Top to Bottom," *New York Times,* Apr. 26, 2003, page B15.

3. *The Economist,* "Remember Fiscal Policy," Jan. 19, 2002, page 64.

CHAPTER 9

1. Ashling O'Connor, "Online Piracy Plagues Music Industry," *Financial Times,* June 13, 2001, page 8.

2. Matt Richtel, "Music Services Aren't Napster but the Industry Still Cries Foul," *New York Times,* Apr. 14, 2002, page C1; Steve Morse, "Burned," *Boston Globe,* Apr. 21, 2002, page L1; *The Economist,* "World Music Sales," May 4, 2002, page 106.

3. Brent Schlender, "All You Need Is Love, $50 Billion, and Killer Software Code-named Longhorn," *Fortune Magazine,* July 8, 2002, pages 56–68.

4. Cisco Systems, "The Number of Companies Acquired by Cisco," <http://www.cisco.com/warp/public/750/acquisition/summarylist.html>.

5. Datastream International, "Value of Apple Computer and Microsoft," Datastream Advance 3.5.

6. Simon Romero and Riva D. Atlas, "Worldcom Files for Bankruptcy; Largest U.S. Case," *New York Times,* July 22, 2002, page A1.

7. "Companies with over $1 Billion in Assets" (2000, 2001, and 2002 filings), <http://www.bankruptcydata.com>.

8. Vanessa Valkin, "McDonald's to Post Its First Ever Loss," *Financial Times,* Dec. 17, 2002, page 15.

9. "KPMG Auto Industry Research: Summary of Research Findings," *Applied* Research & Consulting LLC, Jan. 2000, page 6, <http://www.kpmg.co.uk/kpmg/uk/image/industry%20_research.pdf>.

10. James Dao and Andrew C. Revkin, "A Revolution in Warfare," *New York Times,* Apr. 16, 2002, page D1.

11. Eric Schmitt and James Dao, "Use of Precise Airstrikes Comes of Age in Afghanistan Missions," *New York Times,* Dec. 24, 2001, page B3.

12. "A New Breed of Soldier," *Newsweek,* Dec. 10, 2001, page 16.

13. Andrew C Revkin, "High-Tech U.S. Sensors Can Find al Queda Hideouts," *International Herald Tribune,* Nov. 22, 2001, page 4.

14. Stephen Filder, "A Superpower Displays Its Fighting Caliber," *Financial Times,* Dec. 9, 2001, page 6.

15. Gregg Easterbrook, "American Power Moves beyond the Mere Super," *New York Times,* Apr. 27, 2003, section 4, page 1.

16. David Johnston, "US Toolmaker's shareholders approve 'move' to Bermuda," *International Herald Tribune,* May 10, 2002, page 14.

17. As reported in the local Brazilian and Israeli presses while the author was visiting in these countries.

18. Ian Fisher and Norimitsu Onishi, "Congo's Struggle May Unleash Broad Strife to Redraw Africa," *New York Times,* Jan. 12, 1999, page 1.

19. In the developed world R&D spending ranges from almost 4 percent of GDP in Sweden to just over 1 percent in Spain. *The Economist,* "Research and Development Spending," Aug. 28, 1999, page 85.

20. G. Bruce Knect, "New Zealand Pays for Policies," *Asia Wall Street Journal,* Mar. 18, 2002, page A4.

21. Two city-states, Singapore and Hong Kong, rank above it, but city-states are not countries with rural areas and heavily protected agricultural production.

22. *The Economist,* "New Zealand's Economy," Dec. 2, 2000, page 93.

CHAPTER 10

1. *USA Today,* "Waiting for Organ Transplants," Jan. 22, 2003, page 1.

2. Richard Lewontin, "Genes in the Food!" *New York Review of Books,* June 21, 2001, page 81.

3. *The Economist,* "Soft as Silk, Strong as Steel," Mar. 16, 2002, page 10.

4. Anahad O'Connor, "Altered Tomote Thrives in Salty Soil," *New York Times,* Aug. 14, 2001, page D3.

5. Kenneth Chang, "Scientists Shrink Computing to Molecular Level," *New York Times,* Oct. 25, 2002, page PA18.

6. *The Economist,* "Seeds of Uncertainty," Feb. 9, 2002, page 70.

7. Ibid., page 83.

8. *The Economist,* "Biotechnolgy: Saving the World in Comfort," Mar. 29, 2003, page 14.

9. *The Economist,* "Genetically Modified Crops," Jan. 19, 2002, page 98.

10. *The Economist,* "Climbing the Helical Staircase," Mar. 29, 2003, page 12.

Index